Glass
Toothpick
Holders

Identification
& Values

Second Edition

Neila & Tom Bredehoft
and Jo & Bob Sanford

COLLECTOR BOOKS
A Division of Schroeder Publishing Co., Inc.

Front Cover~Clockwise from upper left: Quezal, Polka Dot, Holly, Hobnail, Double Dahlia with Lens

Back Cover~Clockwise from upper left: Eureka, Bulging Loops, Reverse Swirl, Empress, Amberina

Cover design ▸ Beth Summers   Book design ▸ Erica Weise

COLLECTOR BOOKS

P.O. Box 3009
Paducah, Kentucky 42002-3009
www.collectorbooks.com

Copyright © 2005 Neila & Tom Bredehoft and Jo & Bob Sanford

The current values in this book should be used only as a guide. They are not intended to set prices, which vary from one section of the country to another. Auction prices as well as dealer prices vary greatly and are affected by condition as well as demand. Neither the authors nor the publisher assumes responsibility for any losses that might be incurred as a result of consulting this guide.

Searching For A Publisher?

We are always looking for people knowledgeable within their fields. If you feel that there is a real need for a book on your collectible subject and have a large comprehensive collection, contact Collector Books.

CONTENTS

PREFACE

Many devotees of Early American pattern glass collect examples of patterns made in the late 1800s to the early 1900s. Literally hundreds of patterns are available, making it almost impossible to collect a piece in each pattern. As a result, many people specialize in specific pieces, including toothpick holders. Toothpicks are particularly inviting to people because they come in a variety of patterns and colors and take a minimal amount of room to display. However, even a display of these small beauties can soon require a large space due to the great variety available.

Many popular pressed glass patterns included toothpick holders. There were also many novelty toothpicks made that had no matching pieces. Others were made to match a limited number of pieces, often salts and peppers and syrups. There is a thriving national club devoted to toothpick holder collecting and disseminating information on these interesting small Victorian items. For information about this club, contact:

CHRISTINE GROVES
National Toothpick Holder Collectors Society
P.O. Box 852
Archer City, TX 76351

Toothpick holders were a fad. They first made their appearance in the 1880s and for the most part were out of vogue by the 1910s. Manners changed so that it was considered impolite to pick one's teeth in the company of others. Toothpick holders were made in almost every type of material, such as china, wood, metal, and others. The holders in this book are primarily pressed glass, but we have also included a sampling of art glass toothpicks, mostly blown.

There has been considerable debate about whether the true name of the item is a *toothpick* or a *toothpick holder*. While it is certain that all are holders of toothpicks, most old company catalogs simply called the pieces "toothpicks," and so will we. Another area of discussion is whether a piece is a true toothpick or had another original use. Most toothpick collectors choose to add other small items to their collections to create interest and fill in patterns that do not have toothpicks. While this book primarily shows toothpicks, it also includes a few other items such as mustard bottoms, bar glasses (often sold wholesale as toothpicks), open salts, match holders, and other, miscellaneous, pieces.

For years there have been many stories circulated about the buying, selling, and trading of molds. Some stories tell of the glassworker going to another factory and taking his molds with him. The molds were a huge investment for each factory and were protected, not sold. The physical size and weight of the molds made it highly improbable that they were freely moved from site to site. Below is an article that sheds considerable light upon the subject. This does not mean that molds did not change hands, however. When a company was sold or went through bankruptcy proceedings, the molds were a valuable asset to be dealt with and were often acquired by another company.

There will be a good many new sets of ware out this fall, and the manufacturers are expending quite a sum of money in their preparation. Molds for a line of ware cost all the way from $600.00 to $1,000.00, and as high as $1,500.00, so that frequent changes come very expensive. Sometimes a set fails to achieve popularity with the trade, and then the molds are of no more value than so much old iron. On the other hand, a pattern that meets the popular demand oftentimes works injury to the originator, for he can sell none of his old wares, of which he may have quite a stock on hand, and they become valueless. So a great deal of judgment and discrimination are required in catering for the wants of customers in this regard. –August 1883, CGJ.

Collections composed of toothpicks can be as limited or as varied as the collector wishes. We encourage you to enjoy your own unique collection, and we hope this book will be of help in identifying your glass toothpicks.

Neila & Tom Bredehoft
Jo & Bob Sanford

We wish to give heartfelt thanks to the following people for their help with this book. All have contributed important information and help in making this project more complete.

C. Ron Baker, Jackson Douglas, David Fairchild, Eileen Flaks, Leighton Fossey, Ted Friesner, Sarah Jenkins, Judy Knauer, Mary Ann and Dick Krauss, Dori Miles, Mel Murray, Dave Peterson, Jacqueline Sanders, Davis Schepps, Jerry Volkmer, Nancy and Harry Ware, the staff of the Rakow Library, Corning Museum of Glass, and the staff of the Delaware County District Library, Delaware, OH.

HOW TO USE THIS BOOK

This chapter will answer many questions about this book, its scope, and its organization. Please take time to read it in its entirety.

ORGANIZATION

This book is organized by manufacturer. While we strongly believe some toothpicks were made by earlier companies (in the cases of National Glass and U.S. Glass especially), we have listed the toothpick under the factory for which we found the earliest documentation rather than guessing which company originated the pattern. Each toothpick within a manufacturer's category is placed in alphabetical order by name of the pattern. The chapter on unattributed toothpicks is likewise arranged alphabetically. Each company has a short history to help clarify its relationship to other contemporary companies.

OMN (Original Manufacturer's Name): If we found the correct original name of a pattern in an original catalog or an old ad, we have used this as the original name. This may cause some confusion among current collectors familiar with old names, but the return to the original name will be a great service to those in the future. These more familiar old names have been listed in the index to assist you in locating your toothpick. This entry also includes the company's original pattern number, if known.

AKA (Also Known As): This entry contains the popular name used for each toothpick or pattern before finding the original name. Often these have been used for many years. In cases where we have been unable to find any specific name or only a line number, we endorse the use of the popular name/names.

DATE: This entry is perhaps the most difficult to verify. We have examined many, many original catalogs, but often these are undated. For firm dates, we have relied on trade journals or contemporary ads. Trade journals reported on most new lines, and often companies illustrated patterns when they first appeared on the market. The dates shown are introduction dates. Occasionally if we cannot prove a date, we use *ca.* (circa) to indicate it is likely that the toothpick was produced about this time, but we have limited the use of this as much as possible.

COLORS: We have listed all colors we know for each toothpick. On many we have listed various stains, enamels, or other decorations. While we are sure the list is not complete, it should be helpful to know the possibilities for each toothpick. Again, if the company used a specific term for its color, we have used that name in the descriptions. We have tried to standardize the names of colors by using the names describing them when they were made. These names include *canary* for vaseline, *opal* for milk glass, and *ivory* for custard. Also, we have usually used the word *plated* for cased glass. We have found that in Victorian times, *plated* was the more common term for this glass.

Also included in this category are current values for each toothpick. Many decorations are available, especially on art glass toothpicks. We feel that all decorations, unless very worn or detracting to the item, should have at least a modest increase in value over a plain toothpick. In the case of art glass such as Burmese, C. F. Monroe, or Smith Bros. decorated pieces, the value of the toothpick is based as much on its decoration as the glass from which it is made. The more elaborate the decoration, the more the toothpick increases in value. Be aware that these art glass pieces are limited in this book to the examples shown; prices listed are for the specific decoration shown. Different decorations or different glass bodies may be valued at higher or lower prices than those shown. Additions of metal holders, cages, or other fittings add to the value of toothpicks.

SIZE: The measurements in this book were made with much difficulty. Sometimes toothpick holders of the same pattern do not have exactly the same measurements. Measurements listed here were made without including handles, flared tops, or bases when considering the width, unless noted otherwise. Usually the measurement was taken of the widest portion. Heights will vary on many because of hand finishing, such as flaring, crimping, or cupping rims. Keep these things in mind while measuring and comparing. Occasionally, measurements are of the tops, but this is indicated in each entry. Do not worry if your toothpick is slightly different in size. For the most part, we have measured pieces to the nearest ⅛."

NOTES: Included in this category are pertinent facts regarding the toothpick. We have included patent information, reproductions, trade quotations, and other incidental information of interest. Trade quotations are taken mainly from two periodicals of the time, *Crockery & Glass Journal* (CGJ), and *China, Glass and Lamps* (CGL). Quotations from these are shown in italics.

IDENTIFICATION

The illustrations included in this book are mostly photographs. If a line drawing accompanies the photo, it was taken from an original catalog or an original ad to verify that the piece was correctly identified and attributed. In some cases we used entire ads, and sometimes we used pieces other than toothpicks.

As you read this book, you will find some familiar words missing, such as *looks like*, *could have been made by*, *appears to be*, *the shape of _____ factory*, *probably*, and other guessing phrases. We feel if the knowledge is not available, we should not speculate, because guesses have very little value except to the person making the guess. All attributions are verified by original material except for a few patterns that have long been attributed to various companies by earlier researchers. In these instances, we have said "attributed by" to help the collector realize we have seen no concrete proof of the correct manufacturer. Glass company catalogs are remarkably scarce, so many patterns remain unidentified as to original maker.

If we have been unsuccessful in identifying manufacturers, we have listed those toothpicks in the chapter for unattributed toothpicks. Some authors have previously speculated on the makers of these items, but we feel it is much safer to wait until positive proof is found. However, realistically, many toothpicks will never be properly identified as to manufacturer. Almost every Victorian-era company made toothpicks, the large well-known companies as well as the small, obscure ones. Often the smaller companies did not have catalogs printed (or at least none seem to have survived). We know many of these companies made toothpicks, because they are specifically listed in old ads or trade journal reports. Research continues on many.

A comment should be made about attribution by shards at factory sites. While this may sometimes be helpful, it should not be considered proof that pieces were made at the site. Many companies bought cullet. Pieces of this cullet could easily be mixed with true shards of patterns made by the company. We think that shards are interesting, but there should be added documentation if they are used in the primary attribution of patterns.

COLOR PRODUCTION

Occasionally we use *ca.* (circa) to list a date that we think is appropriate for a toothpick. Sometimes, but rarely, this is based on the known colors for the toothpick. In the mid-to-late 1880s, almost every pressed glass manufacturer was making colored glass, a new departure in glass at the time. The easily made colors (made by almost all) were clear, amber, blue, and sometimes canary (vaseline). By the time the U.S. Glass Co. and the National Glass Co. were founded in the 1890s and 1900s, these colors had been discontinued by most companies. New colors such as emerald green and Dewey Blue (near cobalt) had been introduced. In the mid-1890s, several firms that specialized in applied stains were decorating glass, mostly clear and emerald pieces.

The following is a list of known colors used for toothpicks by each company. Many companies, especially those that remained in business for many years, made many other colors besides these.

Adams & Co.
   Amber, apple green, aqua, blue, canary
Aetna Glass & Manufacturing Co.
   Amber, blue, clear opalescent
A. J. Beatty & Sons
   Amber, blue, canary, clear opalescent, blue opalescent, canary opalescent
Beaumont Glass Co.
   Canary, emerald, rose, clear opalescent, canary opalescent, green opalescent
Bellaire Goblet Co.
   Amber, blue
Belmont Glass Co.
   Amber, blue
Bryce Bros. Glass Co.
   Amber, amethyst, blue, canary, opal
Cambridge Glass Co.
   Emerald
Canton Glass Co.
   Amber, blue, canary, opal

Central Glass Co.
   Amber, blue, canary
Challinor, Taylor & Co.
   Black, mosaic (purple and amber slag), olive (opaque green), opal, Roseblush (opaque pink to opal), turquoise (opaque blue)
Columbia Glass Co.
   Amber, blue
Consolidated Lamp & Glass Co.
   Blue opaque, clear opalescent, green opaque, mauve, opal, pigeon blood, pink opaque, rubina, ruby opalescent, yellow
Co-operative Flint Glass Co., Ltd.
   Amber, aquamarine, dark blue, green, opal
Dalzell, Gilmore & Leighton
   Floradine (ruby with opalescent white), onyx (cream with platinum flowers), emerald (as part of National Glass Co.)
Dithridge & Co.
   Blue, green, ivory, opal, pink

Doyle & Co.
Amber, blue
Dugan Glass Co.
Amethyst, blue, blue opalescent, clear opalescent, green, green opalescent, ivory, pink slag
Geo. Duncan & Sons
Amber, blue, canary, old gold (pale amber)
Eagle Glass & Mfg. Co.
Opal, blue
Enterprise Manufacturing Co.
Amber, blue, green, opal
Fenton Art Glass Co.
Blue, canary, green
Findlay Flint Glass Co.
Amber, blue, clear opalescent
Fostoria Glass Co.
Emerald, opal
Gillinder & Co.
Opal
Greensburg Glass Co.
Emerald
A. H. Heisey & Co.
Canary, emerald, opal, Ivorina Verde (custard)
Hobbs, Brockunier & Co.
Amber, canary, clear opalescent, marine green (apple green), peachblow, rubina, ruby, ruby opalescent, sapphire (blue), sapphire opalescent
Imperial Glass Co.
Imperial green, Rose Marie
Indiana Tumbler & Goblet Co.
Amber, blue, canary, chocolate (as part of National Glass), green, Nile Green (opaque)
Jefferson Glass Co.
Apple green, blue, blue opalescent, canary opalescent, clear opalescent, dark green, electric blue, green, green opalescent, ivory, wine
King, Son & Co.
Amber, blue, canary, green, light blue opaque
LaBelle Glass Co.
Amber, blue, canary, clear opalescent, ruby opalescent
Libbey Glass Co.
Amberina, ivory, opal
McKee & Bros.
Amber, blue, emerald, opal, rose pink

McKee-Jeannette Glass Co.
Amber, blue
Model Flint Glass Co.
Amber, blue, blue opalescent, canary opalescent, clear opalescent, emerald
Mosaic Glass Co.
Amber
Mt. Washington Glass Co.
Burmese, canary, ivory, Lusterless white (opal satin), Rose Amber (amberina)
New England Glass Co.
Amberina, green opaque, peachblow
New Martinsville Glass Co.
Emerald
Nickel Plate Glass Co.
Blue opalescent, clear opalescent, green opaque, ruby, ruby opalescent
Northwood
Blue, blue opalescent, blue opaque, canary, canary opalescent, clear opalescent, ivory, mauve, opal, rainbow, rubina, ruby, ruby opalescent
O'Hara Glass Co.
Amber, blue, canary. Emerald and Dewey blue when part of U.S. Glass Co.
Ohio Flint Glass Co.
Opal
Richards & Hartley Glass Co.
Amber, apple green, blue, canary
Riverside Glass Co.
Canary, emerald, royal purple, opaque, ivory, rose pink
Robinson Glass Co.
Chocolate (while part of National)
Royal Glass Co.
Chocolate (while part of National)
West Virginia Glass Co.
Amethyst, blue, blue opalescent, clear opalescent, green, opal, rubina, ruby opalescent
Westmoreland Glass Co.
Blue, green, opal
Windsor Glass Co.
Amber, blue

TRADEMARKS

Most pressed glass companies did not mark their wares with a trademark, but a few did. Not all pieces the companies made were marked.

Cambridge Glass Co.
"Nearcut." Later a *C* in a triangle.
Central Glass Co.
"Krys-Tol."
Dugan Glass Co.
D in a diamond.

A. H. Heisey & Co.
H in a vertical diamond.
John Higbee & Co.
A bee with "H I G" on wings and body.
Imperial Glass Co.
"Nu-Cut" or an iron cross with "IM PE RI AL" in the

four sections. Later trademarks include a *G* super-imposed with an *I*.

Jefferson Glass Co.
"Krys-Tol."

McKee Bros.
"Prescut." Later, "McK" in a circle.

Northwood & Co.
"Northwood" in block letters or script. Also an *N* in a circle.

Ohio Flint Glass Co.
"Krys-Tol."

U.S. Glass Co.
Intertwined "U. S. G. Co."

Westmoreland Glass Co.
A keystone surrounding a *W*. Also, a *W* superimposed on a *G*.

Art glass companies and decorators also used trademarks. Some included the manufacturer and also the type of glass. These are usually ink stamps on the bottoms of toothpicks.

DECORATING COMPANIES

There were at least three major decorating companies in the Pittsburgh area that decorated much pattern glass in the late 1890s.

Mueller Glass Staining Co.
1811 Sidney Street

...report plenty of orders coming in for all their new lines and for some of their old ones as well. The demand covers the lines of McKee & Bros., Riverside Glass Works, and the United States Glass Co., and is larger than can be filled with desirable promptness. –February 1895

C. W. E. Mueller was the originator of ruby work in America. This company manufactures ruby, amber, crystal and gold, green and gold glassware, engraved and plain, also ivory and gold, opal and gold and decorated ware. –February 1903

J. Rodgers
1714 Sidney Street

...is running his factory and furnaces up to their limit, and getting out what he considers about the finest line of ware he ever made ready for the market, including a number of new patterns from George Duncan's Sons & Co., the Thompson Glass Co., the United States Glass Co., and others. –February 1895

Rodgers decorated many patterns with ruby and amber stains.

Oriental Glass Co.
Eighth and Sarah

The Oriental Glass Co., Pittsburgh, who were the first to originate, perfect, and systematically engage in the manufacture of ruby stained glassware in the United States, and have maintained themselves among the foremost manufacturers and decorators of fancy glassware ever since, have favored us with illustrated color leaflets of their leading patterns. –June 1897.

Oriental Glass decorated many A. H. Heisey & Co. patterns, both in ruby stain and amber stain and in various enamel decorations. It also decorated many patterns from other companies. In 1899, it listed itself as "decorators of glass in all styles. Ivory and Gold, Blue and Gold, Green and Gold, Crystal and Gold, Opal Decorated, Ruby, Gold and Engraved, Ruby, Plain, etc., etc."

In addition to the Pittsburgh decorating companies, Beaumont Glass Co. of Martins Ferry, Ohio, and later of Grafton, West Virginia, began as a decorating company before turning to glass manufacture. Its decorations consisted of ruby stain, applied gold, and various enamels. Riverside's patterns were primarily decorated by this company.

The mold makers in the U.S. are very busy at present. It may not be generally known that glass presses and molds are made here for use in British factories, but such is the case. There are two large mold shops in Pittsburgh, and two or three small ones. Nearly all the tableware factories have mold shops of their own, but the bottle houses invariably get their molds made outside. This business does not include the making of blowing tubes and other glass making utensils, but is confined to molds and glass pressing machinery.
–December 1882, *CGJ*

Decorations on art glass are complicated, as they are often hand done in great detail, in contrast to decorations on pressed glass, which are usually simple applications of gold, colors, or stains. Companies such as Mt. Washington, New England Glass Co., and others made many exotic glass colors and decorated them with equally exotic decorations. Often names are used exclusively for the type of decoration, such as Pomona or Royal Flemish. L. C. Tiffany and Steuben used several iridescent finishes on their glasses, resulting in Favrile and Aurene, among others. C. F. Monroe was a decorating company only; it made no glass, but bought blanks and marketed the resulting decorated product as its own. It often marked its pieces, and it also used the name Wavecrest for a line of its wares.

Top Row (L to R): G. Davis, Challinor, Taylor & Co.; A. C. Brown, Canton Glass Co.; P. E. Brady, A. & J. Beatty; S. C. Dunlevy, La Belle Glass Co.; W. J. Patterson, Columbia Glass Co.; John Walsh, Bacon Glass Co.; A. C. Snively, Belmont Glass Co.
Middle Row (L to R): Chas. Mustin, Dithridge & Co.; W. B. Ranney, Co-operative Flint Glass Co.; H. M. Felker, Cumberland Glass Co.
Bottom Row (L to R): F. Gottschalk, Buckeye Glass Works; J. D. Robinson, Libbey Glass Co.; A. C. Boggs, Bellaire Goblet Works; Eugene Ellis, Ripley & Co.; Ed Gilmore, Dalzell, Gilmour & Leighton; W. Mulloy, Pittsburgh Glass Co.

...An old photograph which we came across not long ago since...shows what is confidently supposed to be the first group picture ever taken of glass salesmen who gathered in the Monongahela House in Pittsburgh in days gone by....The glass salesman, like every other representative that carries the visiting card and the grip, must be possessed of certain requisites.... When we mention the names of Adams, Heisey, Bryce, Gillinder, Ripley, Northwood, Dugan, and others who have plodded the weary way, encountered the second-rate hotels, met the sometimes grouchy and unpleasable buyer, and been heir to the thousand ills that encounter the man on the road and then rose to responsible and honorable positions as producers, we know that the glass salesman of today has a tradition of which he need not be ashamed.

...It has always been popularly supposed that W. B. Ranney was the first salesman to display glass samples at the Monongahela House. Many of those in the glass trade at the present day credit him with being the real founder of the present "Glass Exhibit." But investigation shows that Mr. Ranney's title is not entirely clear, and it is a question in the mind of the writer whether the real founder was not S. C. Dunlevy, and that he laid the foundation in January, 1883...

The picture which is reproduced was taken in 1886.

P. E. Brady, at that time with the A. & J. Beatty Co., of Steubenville, O., is now one of the veteran glass salesmen, and is representing the Rochester Tumbler Works, with whom he has been for some time.

S. C. Dunlevy, with the La Belle, Bridgeport, now occupies a responsible position on the office force of the United States Glass Co.

W. J. Patterson, who represented the Columbia Glass Co. of Findlay, O., in 1886, may now be found with the W. H. Hamilton & Co., bottle manufacturers, of Pittsburgh.

H. M. Felker, who was one of the younger generation at the time the picture was taken, represented the Cumberland Glass Co., Cumberland, Md., is now the New York representative of the United States Glass Co.

J. D. Robinson is the only one in the group who is at present connected with the same concern that he was at that time. He represented the Libbey Glass Co., and now he is secretary and treasurer of the same institution.

A. C. Boggs, who carried the samples of the Bellaire Goblet Co., first of Bellaire and then of Findlay, O., has until recently been with the Evansville Glass Co., of Evansville, Ind., but will after Jan. 1 have charge of the Chicago sample rooms of the Cambridge Glass Co.

Eugene Ellis, who represented Ripley & Co., of Pittsburgh, did not have a sample room at the Monongahela House at the time the picture was taken, but happened to be present and was included. He is at present with Plume and Atwood, traveling out of their Chicago branch.

Ed Gilmour [sic, but Gilmore is correct] represented the Dalzell, Gilmour & Leighton Co., of Findlay, O. Mr. Gilmour has forsaken the ties and occupies a lucrative position with the Pittsburgh Trust Co.

Five of those whose faces we gaze upon are no more. Without comment, but with all reverence, we set down who they are:

A. C. Brown, who represented the Canton Glass Co., Canton, O.; A. C. Snively, who represented the Belmont, of Bellaire, O.; W. B. Ranney, who represented Co-operative Glass Co., of Beaver Falls, Pa.; G. Davis, who represented the Challinor-Taylor Co., of Pittsburgh; Ferdinand Gottschalk, who represented the Buckeye Glass Works, of Martins Ferry, O.

–December 1906, CGL

PATTERNS BY COMPANY

ADAMS & CO.
PITTSBURGH, PENNSYLVANIA
1861 – 1891

John Adams, Augustus A. Adams, William Adams, James Dalzell, George Easton, and Godfreid Miller organized Adams & Co. in 1861 in Pittsburgh's South Side at 10th and William Streets. In 1884 they took over the former Challinor, Taylor & Co. property on Eighth Street and built their new factory on that location.

The name and management of this firm remained the same until 1891, when the factory became one of the original members of the new United States Glass Co. The designation for Adams & Co. became Factory A.

Adams & Co. made primarily tableware, including the well-known XLCR (King's Crown or Ruby Thumbprint), Palace (Moon and Star), Art, and Crystal Wedding patterns.

See also United States Glass Co., Factory A.

Blue

OMN: BOOK, No. 9

DATE: ca. late 1880s based on colors known

COLORS: clear, $70.00; amber, $95.00; blue, $105.00; opaque blue, $135.00; white slag, $85.00.

SIZE: 3" tall x 1⅜" wide x 2¼" long

NOTES: The original Adams catalog suggests this book is for "matches or picks." Shown in the composite U.S. Glass Company catalog circa 1891. See U.S. Glass for more discussion about this catalog. Known with an allover metal cage.

No. 9 Book Matches or Picks

OMN: KETTLE, No. 2, No. 3

DATE: ca. late 1880s based on colors known

COLORS: clear, $40.00; amber, $65.00; blue, $65.00; canary, $85.00.

SIZE: No. 2: 2½" tall without lid x 3" wide.

NOTES: Shown in the composite U.S. Glass Company catalog circa 1891. See U.S. Glass for more discussion about this catalog.

No. 2 Kettle Mustard.

No. 3 Kettle.

No. 2 Mustard and cover, amber

Blue and canary

OMN: No. 4

AKA: OVAL BASKET

DATE: 1892

COLORS: clear, $45.00; amber, $55.00; blue, $60.00; canary, $80.00; opal, $58.00.

SIZE: 2¾" tall x 2¼" wide

NOTES: Listed in catalogs as No. 4 Novelty "for toothpick or matches." This basket is really round, not oval! Shown in the composite U.S. Glass Company catalog circa 1891. See U.S. Glass for more discussion about this catalog.

No. 4 Toothpick or Matches.

OMN: SAXON

DATE: 1888

COLORS: clear, $18.00; clear with engraving, $25.00; clear with ruby stain, $70.00; clear with blue stain, $75.00.

SIZE: 2⅜" tall x 2⅛" wide

NOTES: This pattern originated with Adams & Co., and was included in catalogs assembled from member companies and compiled by U.S. Glass in 1891. The toothpick was also sold as a match holder.

TOOTH PICK or MATCH.

Clear with ruby stain

Clear

OMN: SKUTTLE, No. 1

AKA: SKUTTLE, DAISY & BUTTON

DATE: ca. late 1880s based on colors known

COLORS: clear, $48.00; apple green, $120.00; aqua, $60.00; blue, $60.00; canary, $125.00.

SIZE: 2½" tall x 2" wide

NOTES: Shown in the composite U.S. Glass Company catalog circa 1891. See U.S. Glass for more discussion about this catalog.

Apple green, blue, and canary

No. 1 Skuttle Matches or Picks.

Clear with ruby stain

OMN: XLCR

AKA: KING'S CROWN, RUBY THUMBPRINT

DATE: 1891

COLORS: clear, $22.00; clear with ruby stain, $35.00; clear with ruby stain & engraving, $42.00; clear with amber stain, $70.00; clear with amber stain & engraving, $80.00.

SIZE: 2½" tall x 2½" wide

NOTES: *Adams & Co. have an exceedingly pretty pattern in their new table line. This ware is massive and solid in appearance. This line they have both plain and engraved.* –December 1890. Also sometimes called Excelsior. Illustrated in a 1892 Butler Bros. catalog as "Handsome 5 cent Toothpick. Price, 43 cents a dozen." This popular pattern was reissued in the 1950s by Tiffin Glass of Tiffin, Ohio, in modern shapes. The toothpick was not reproduced at this time.

MUSTARD and COVER.
ENGRAVED.

TOOTH PICK ENGRAVED.

Clear with amber stain

AETNA GLASS & MANUFACTURING CO.
BELLAIRE, OHIO
1880 – 1889

This June 1880 report tells of the beginning of this company: *The new Aetna Glass and Manufacturing Company is about ready to initiate proceedings, and, before this will appear in print, will have lighted their fires in their new 13-pot Gill furnace, which has just been completed and said to be one of the most successful yet erected. The circulars of this company have just made their appearance, announcing the opening and the styles of ware they will manufacture, which will consist of stemware, plain and blown ware, as lemonade glasses, gas shades, champagnes, punch tumblers, stem, barware, clarets, beer mugs, wines, etc. We were yesterday shown some of their new designs which, for uniqueness and beauty, we have never seen excelled.*

One of their new ideas is a steamboat and hotel goblet, or a goblet with boats and hotels blown in it; so when contracts are made the name of boats or hotels will be engraved thereon. Birds will be the chief ornaments on the blown ware, and these in new and beautiful designs. The main building of these works is 300 feet long by 60 wide, and three stories high, and includes mold shops, cutting shop, engraving and packing rooms. In this building is a steam elevator, the machinery, a forty-horsepower engine to run the machinery, besides a small engine running the elevator at night. There is a store house and packing room (100 ft. by 60 ft.) and other smaller buildings. There is a switch in the Bellaire and Southwestern road for their purposes, and the Baltimore *and Ohio and Cleveland and Pittsburgh roads are only a few rods off, while they have a wharf on the Ohio River for their Southern and Western trade. The stack of the furnace is 74 feet, and the factory is 68 ft. clear on the inside. The workmen in these works are the best that all the other works could turn out, many of them having served years with Hobbs, Brockunier & Co. and in the Central, and who have come to this and taken stock in it, as $10,000 of the stock was reserved for such of the workmen as desired to subscribe. Their aim, they say, will be to make good and fresh goods. Captain R. T. Devries, general agent of the B. & O. R. R. Co., is president, and W. H. Brinton secretary of the company. Their traveler is Capt. Seymour Dunlevy, a very pleasant gentleman, who will soon recommend himself to the trade. H. J. Leosult, for many years at the Central Glass works, will be the manager of these works. – CGJ.*

Aetna Glass was organized and began production of glass in 1880. The years 1889 and 1890 were full of turmoil and reorganization, and another reorganization followed in November of 1890 in which the company became the Aetna Glass Manufacturing Co. Most production was during 1883 to 1888.

Some of the patterns and pieces made by the company include Adonis, the Jumbo fruit bowl, Butterfly butter pats, the Flanged Horseshoe butter dish, the No. 300 White House set, the Octagon set, the No. 270 Cabbage egg dish, the Snowflake set, the Rebecca jug, the No. 304 Hobnail and Pillar set, the No. 269 epergne, the Goddess of Liberty, and the Auld Lang Syne set. These wares are listed in reports of the company in trade journals, but many of the items are unidentified today.

Blue top, satin body

OMN: ADONIS

AKA: GONTERMAN SWIRL

DATE: ca. 1888

COLORS: clear with amber top, $240.00; clear with amber top, opalescent, $350.00; clear with amber top, satin, $300.00; clear with blue top, $240.00; clear with blue top, opalescent, $350.00; clear with blue top, satin, $300.00.

SIZE: 2½" tall x 1⅞" wide

NOTES: Both color variations are also found with allover satin finish. This pattern was made in many tableware pieces. Pieces also sometimes bear a patent date. The colored rims are of applied colored glass, not stains applied to clear glass.

Amber top, opalescent body

OMN: EGYPTIAN

AKA: CHERUBS

DATE: 1887

COLORS: clear, $95.00; blue, $185.00; amber, $175.00.

SIZE: 2¾" tall x 2¼" wide

NOTES: This unusual toothpick holder has open squares between the figures and pillars. All three figures are in different positions. *The Aetna Glass Co. have just presented a new Egyptian match or toothpick holder that is as novel and pretty a design as in the market. It is the product of the enterprising secretary, Mr. E. B. Bowls, and will no doubt have a splendid run. Three human figures adorn the "Egyptian pillars" and as one of the novelties of this company it will be a leader. –1887.*

Amber

Detail of figure

Detail of figure

Detail of figure

A. J. BEATTY & SONS
STEUBENVILLE, OHIO — 1863 – CA. 1889
TIFFIN, OHIO — 1888 – 1891

The A. J. Beatty & Sons Co. evolved from the old Steubenville Flint Glass Works in Steubenville, Ohio, in 1863. A. J. Beatty died shortly thereafter, leaving the running of the company to his two sons. In the early years tumblers were a specialty of this company, and it made no tableware. In 1888, the company contracted for a new factory at Tiffin, Ohio, and continued to operate both factories for a time. In 1891, both factories joined the United States Glass Co. and became part of the combine, Tiffin being designated as Factory R and Steubenville as Factory S. By this time, Factory S was not operating and did not reopen.

Well-known tableware patterns made by Beatty include Beatty Rib, Beatty Waffle, Orinoco, and Van Dyke.

OMN: No. 87

AKA: BEATTY RIB

DATE: 1888

COLORS: clear opalescent, $40.00; blue opalescent, $52.00; clear opalescent, tall, $150.00; blue opalescent, tall, $195.00.

SIZE: 1⅞" tall x 2" wide, short type; 2⅜" tall x 2¼" wide, tall type

NOTES: This was the first of the well-known Beatty opalescent patterns and was first made at the Steubenville plant. This and Beatty Waffle were both covered by patents issued to the company. Beatty Rib was made in a full tableware line. The catalog shows two different toothpicks, but the illustrations are deceiving. One of the toothpicks shown appears to have a rounder bottom than the other. However, the catalog illustrations are rather crudely drawn, so it is unknown if this is a true rendition. There is a known taller second toothpick, much harder to find than the shorter version. Beatty blues can vary widely in shade, from quite pale to almost cobalt. Blue opalescent comes in shades from pale to almost cobalt.

Blue opalescent

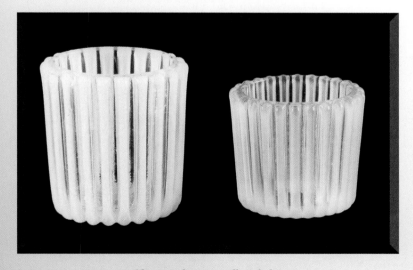

Clear opalescent, tall and short

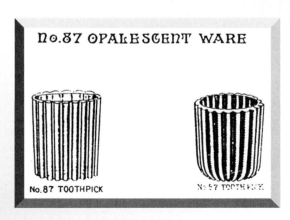

NO.87 OPALESCENT WARE

No.87 TOOTHPICK   No.57 TOOTHPICK

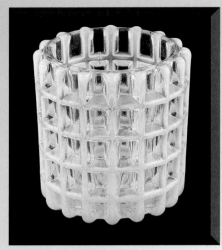

Clear opalescent

OMN: No. 88

AKA: BEATTY WAFFLE, BEATTY HONEYCOMB

DATE: 1888

COLORS: clear opalescent, $42.00; blue opalescent, $52.00.

SIZE: 2⅜" tall x 2½" wide

NOTES: This pattern was made first at Steubenville and then at Tiffin, Ohio. A full table service was available. Company catalogs call this only "opalescent ware."

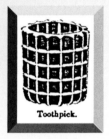

Toothpick.

Blue opalescent

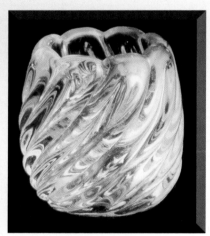

Clear

OMN: ORINOCO

DATE: 1891

COLORS: clear, $65.00.

SIZE: 2⅛" tall x 2" wide

NOTES: *A. J. Beatty & Sons, Tiffin, O., have a nice display...their new line "Orinoco," will be a leader this season. It is a twisted pattern, clear and bright as crystal and the pieces are solid and heavy. –January 1891.* This rather extensive tableware line was introduced in early January 1891 as Beatty's new pattern for the annual Pittsburgh show.

Tooth Pick

OMN: No. 100

AKA: OVERALL HOBNAIL

DATE: 1889

COLORS: clear, $35.00; amber, $42.00; blue, $48.00; canary, $55.00; opalescent clear, $48.00; opalescent blue, $85.00; opalescent canary, $110.00.

SIZE: 2⅜" tall x 2¼" wide

NOTES: This pattern was made in a full tableware line including a table set, water set, several styles of salts, and other items. It is an interesting pattern because of all the color variations. There are two sizes. On the base of the larger one is a circle of nine hobs around a row of five. On the smaller, the base has nine hobs around nine smaller hobs.

TOOTH PICK

Clear

Amber

Blue

Clear opalescent

Canary opalescent

Blue

OMN: VANDYKE, No. 555

AKA: DAISY & BUTTON WITH V ORNAMENT

DATE: ca. 1885

COLORS: clear, $35.00; amber, $48.00; blue, $50.00; canary, $65.00.

SIZE: 2⅛" tall x 2⅛" wide

NOTES: This pattern was introduced while the company was in Steubenville, but production continued at Tiffin. Vandyke was made in a full tableware line. Vandyke was given patent No. 16371 on November 10, 1885.

Clear

BEATTY-BRADY GLASS CO.
STEUBENVILLE, OHIO — 1895 – 1896
DUNKIRK, INDIANA — 1896 – 1899

The sons of A. J. Beatty, George Beatty, and James C. Brady purchased the abandoned factory of the former A. J. Beatty & Sons at Steubenville, Ohio, from the U.S. Glass Co. in 1895. The new company was called the Beatty-Brady Glass Co. In 1896 the company moved to Dunkirk, Indiana, following the new natural gas fields that had been found in the area. A 1898 reorganization listed George Beatty as president, J. Paxton as treasurer, and J. Wey as secretary. In 1899 Beatty-Brady became a member of National Glass Co., designated Factory No. 1, Beatty-Brady Glass Works.

Well-known patterns made by the company include Shrine, Bethlehem Star, Nogi, Gibson Girl, and Star Band.

See also: National Glass Co., Factory No. 1.

OMN: ORIENT

AKA: SHRINE

DATE: ca. 1896

COLORS: clear, $65.00.

SIZE: 2⅜" tall x 2¼" wide

Clear

NOTES: Following the dissolution of the National Glass Co., the molds for this pattern were bought by Jenkins. It was continued by Indiana Glass Co. and shown in its 1904 catalog. We also found the following quote from a trade journal, which appears to describe Orient or at least a pattern quite similar to it: *...show their new "Crescent" tableware set, a bright star surrounded by the Oriental crescent, which cannot be strictly classed as an imitation cut pattern, but has the roundness and wearing quality of the best pressed shape, with the light diffracting effect of cut glassware.* –January 1896. This description listed the pattern as being made by Bryce, Higbee & Co. Hopefully, continued research will lend more information about these two quite different attributions.

BEAUMONT GLASS CO.
MARTINS FERRY, OHIO — 1895 – 1902
GRAFTON, WEST VIRGINIA — 1902 – 1906

The Beaumont Glass Co. was organized in 1895 by Percy Beaumont and others from the former Northwood factory in Martins Ferry, Ohio. At the outset it was known primarily as a decorating firm, and it is known that the company decorated the Esther and X-Ray patterns of the Riverside Glass Co. of nearby Wellsburg.

By 1899, it was manufacturing its own glass tableware, including patterns such as Flora, Columbia, Ellipses, and Inside Ribbing. In 1902 the factory was moved to a new plant at Grafton, West Virginia. In 1906 Percy Beaumont sold his interest in the firm, and it became Tygart Valley Glass Co. which continued many of the Beaumont patterns. Tygart Valley also acquired some of the Riverside Glass Co. molds.

Radical changes in the management and ownership of the Beaumont Glass Co., Grafton, W. Va., have recently taken place… Percy Beaumont has sold his stock to other parties… George McCaskey, of Washington, Pa., has charge of the office and sales department, and John Bryson, who has been with the company for some time, is manager of the manufacturing department and has general oversight of the plant. Frank Watts, of Baltimore, succeeds B. M. Hildreth, of Wheeling, in the directorate, and George McCaskey replaces Mr. Beaumont.

We now desire to announce the fact that the above concern is now in the hands of new management, composed of men of extended experience in the glass business. The president, Wm. Morgan, is cashier of the foremost bank in Grafton… We are now producing a very large line of stationer's glassware, consisting of cut and pressed inks of every description, sponge cups, and in fact, everything which goes to make a complete line of glass for stationer's use. We also have a line of tableware molds which we have been working constantly and are producing cut glass novelties of very attractive designs, besides many other articles of glassware. –June 1906.

Clear

OMN: No. 108

AKA: CADMUS

DATE: 1902

COLORS: clear, $52.00.

SIZE: 2⅜" tall x 2" wide

NOTES: This tableware pattern originated with Beaumont and was continued by Tygart Valley. The catalog illustration is of the sugar. This pattern was also made by Dugan of Lonaconing, Maryland, according to a 1915 ad.

108—Covered Sugar

Canary with gold decoration

OMN: No. 100

AKA: COLUMBIA

DATE: 1900

COLORS: clear, $30.00; clear with engraving, $36.00; clear with gold decor, $36.00; canary, $58.00; canary with gold decor, $68.00.

SIZE: 2½" tall x 1⅞" wide

NOTES: *One of the new patterns displayed is the Columbia, No. 100 (alike to the Co-operative Flint Glass Co.'s pattern only in name). This they have in crystal and canary, gold decorated and engraved, and the line numbers about 35 pieces. –January 1900.*

Tooth Pick.

Tooth Pick.

Emerald with gold decoration

OMN: No. 103

AKA: DUCHESS

DATE: ca. 1901

COLORS: clear, $65.00; clear with rose stain, $165.00; clear with gold decor, $70.00; emerald green, $175.00; emerald green with gold, $225.00.

SIZE: 2¾" tall x 2⅛" wide

NOTES: This pattern can finally be credited to Beaumont, due to the numbering system and inclusion in the Tygart Valley catalog with many other Beaumont patterns.

Clear with rose stain and enamel decoration

OMN: No. 106

AKA: ELLIPSES

DATE: 1902

COLORS: clear, $65.00; clear with rose stain, $228.00; rose, $385.00; rose with gold decor, $395.00.

SIZE: 2⅜" tall x 2" wide

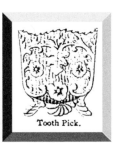

106—Covered Sugar

NOTES: *The shape is larger at the top and bottom than in center, or of a concave design. It is an imitation cut punty figure running up and down, and the rim is scalloped. The line is an exceptionally pretty one and is made in crystal, emerald, and gold, and crystal and gold. The design has a particularly rich effect when decorated in gold, but decorated or plain, it is as pretty as can be.* –November, 1901. *Their new line, No. "106," is a figured punty pattern, graceful shapes, rich, brilliant metal, highly fire polished and about as perfect in every way as can be. It is made in crystal, and crystal and gold, rose color, and rose and gold.* –January 1902. Note that the first quote mentions emerald green. While we have seen pieces of the pattern in this color, we have not seen the toothpick, but be aware that this is a possibility. The catalog illustration is of the sugar as shown by Tygart Valley.

Rose stain and gold in ellipses

Canary opalescent

OMN: No. 99

AKA: FLORA

DATE: 1900

COLORS: clear, $48.00; clear opalescent, $138.00; clear, gold decor, $52.00; canary opalescent, $325.00; green, $145.00; green with gold decor, $155.00; green opalescent, $310.00; blue opalescent, $560.00.

SIZE: 2⅞" tall x 2⅞" wide

NOTES: No. 99 was Beaumont's new pattern for 1900, introduced in January at the Pittsburgh show.

Tooth Pick.

Spoon holder

OMN: No. 109

AKA: INTERLOCKING HEARTS

DATE: ca. 1901

COLORS: clear, $60.00.

SIZE: unknown

NOTES: This tableware pattern was an old Beaumont pattern continued by Tygart Valley. The illustration shown is the spoon, but the toothpick was listed in the accompanying price list.

OMN: No. 105

AKA: JOHANNA

DATE: 1902

COLORS: clear, $32.00; clear with gold decor, $38.00; clear with "color figure decorations," $40.00; clear with rose stain and enameling, $125.00.

SIZE: unknown

Clear with rose stain and enameling

105—Tall Celery

NOTES: *'No. 105' is a perfect pattern of graceful design, scalloped rim and will be made in crystal only.* –November 1901. *The plain pattern is a dandy. They are showing this line in gold band and delicate color figured decorations, that are about the neatest things we have seen for a long time.* –December 1901. This pattern was brought out for the 1902 season. The catalog illustration is of the celery, but a toothpick was listed in the price list, although not shown in the Tygart Valley catalog. This is a pattern that has previously been unlisted.

OMN: No. 101

AKA: PRESSED OPTIC

DATE: 1900

COLORS: clear, $35.00; clear with engraving, $42.00; clear with gold decor, $45.00; clear with ruby stain, $110.00; canary, $145.00; canary with floral decor, $165.00; canary with gold band, $158.00.

SIZE: 2¼" tall x 2½" wide

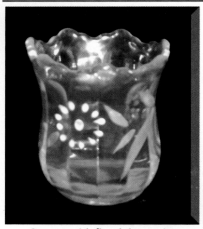

Canary with floral decoration

No. 74 decoration

NOTES: This pattern was introduced new for fall in September, 1900. *The Beaumont Glass Co., of Martin's Ferry, have out illustrations, in color, of their new No. 101 pattern and everybody in the trade who desires to see really elegant goods should have them. The line comprises sets; berries, large and small; pitcher, water bottle, finger bowl, syrup, custard, tumblers, pickle tray, toothpick, tall celery, condiment set, oil, jelly or olive tray, salts and peppers. They have these in canary with floral decorations; canary in gold band; crystal with decorations, crystal engraved; crystal in gold and crystal plain. The shapes are pretty and adapted to practical uses and the line will undoubtedly prove a seller of the first magnitude.* –September 1900.

102—Tooth Pick

OMN: No. 102

AKA: WIDMER

DATE: ca. 1902

COLORS: clear, $58.00; clear with ruby stain, $165.00.

SIZE: 2¾" tall x 2⅜" wide at top

NOTES: Originally a Beaumont tableware pattern, but continued after Tygart Valley took over the factory.

Clear

BELLAIRE GOBLET CO.
BELLAIRE, OHIO — 1876 – 1888
FINDLAY, OHIO — 1888 – 1892

The Bellaire Goblet Co. was organized in 1876 by E. G. Morgan, W. A. Gorby, Henry Blackburn, John Robinson, and C. H. Over. In 1879, they purchased the former Ohio Glass Works and sold their original plant to the Lantern Globe Co. The main production at this plant was goblets and stemware.

In 1888 the company moved to Findlay, Ohio. Shortly before the move, the company began to branch out by manufacturing its first known line of tableware, now known as Stars and Bars. After successfully operating in Findlay for several years, in 1891 the firm joined U.S. Glass Co., becoming known as Factory M.

Patterns made by the company include Stars and Bars, Log and Star, Milton, Queen's Neckace, and Bellaire Basketweave. The company also made many interesting novelties, one of the first being the Plymouth Rock paperweight introduced in 1882. Other figurals include the various railroad cars in the Stars and Bars pattern, the turtle salts, and the Pig on a Flat Car.

No. 91. Caster.

No. 91. Cologne Set, 8-oz. bottles.

No. 91. Toothpick.

Clear

OMN: No. 91

AKA: BELLAIRE

DATE: 1891

COLORS: clear, $48.00; caster set, $210.00; cologne set, $210.00.

SIZE: 2⅝" tall x 2⅜" wide

NOTES: Made in a moderate line of tableware. Note the two styles of caster sets, which each use a toothpick as the top of the handle. Do not confuse this pattern with another made at Findlay called Giant Bullseye, which does not have a toothpick. Most items in Bellaire have a "belt" of small circles about the main portion of the body.

Clear

OMN: CLOCK, No. 435

DATE: 1889

COLORS: clear, $325.00; amber, $425.00; blue, $450.00.

SIZE: 3¾" tall in front, 2⅞" tall in rear, 1⅞" wide x 1½" deep

NOTES: According to an original catalog, this is a match holder. Indeed, it has a striking surface on the back for lighting matches.

Blue

OMN: CORSET, No. 417

DATE: 1899

COLORS: clear, $145.00; amber, $225.00; blue, $250.00.

SIZE: 2⅞" tall x 2½" wide

NOTES: A single item novelty. "Patent Appl'd For" is found on the base. In an 1886 jobber's catalog, the toothpick is shown as a perfume holder and described as a "corset shaped, assorted color toothpick holder filled with a bottle of perfume."

Amber

OMN: unknown

AKA: PIG ON A FLAT CAR

DATE: unknown

COLORS: clear, $250.00; amber, $425.00; blue, $465.00.

SIZE: 3⅛" tall x 2½" wide x 5½" long

NOTES: The true function of this item is not known, as it does not appear in catalogs, but is documented by shards found at the factory site. It may have been a toothpick, but it also may have been only a novelty. The barrel receptacle is quite small to hold anything significant.

Blue

Amber

Clear

OMN: No. 101

AKA: QUEEN'S NECKLACE

DATE: late 1890

COLORS: clear, $68.00; caster set, toothpick handle, complete, $285.00.

SIZE: 4½" tall x 2⅛" wide

NOTES: A full tableware line made only in clear glass. The toothpick is one of the few tall footed toothpicks and for many years was misidentified as a wine, but original catalogs clearly refer to it as a toothpick. A caster set that held three condiments was also made with a toothpick top.

OMN: SHOE, No. 437

DATE: 1889

COLORS: clear, $300.00+.

SIZE: unknown

NOTES: We have seen this item only in a catalog illustration; thus, we have no dimensions. The catalog also does not give a function for this piece, but we include it here, as it fits well in a toothpick collection.

OMN: No. 600

AKA: STARS & BARS

DATE: 1886

COLORS: clear, $110.00; amber, $150.00; blue, $238.00.

SIZE: 2½" tall x 2" wide

NOTES: The first tableware pattern made by this firm in numerous pieces, including the elusive covered railroad car and the celery, master salt, and individual salt, all in the railroad car design. The pattern was designed by Melvin L. Blackburn, partner in the firm and mold maker. A toothpick holder with a similar pattern is Stars and Bars with Leaf.

Clear

Amber

Blue

BELMONT GLASS CO.
BELLAIRE, OHIO
CA. 1866 – 1890

Little specific information is known about this company. It introduced colors in its products in 1885. Following many difficulties in management, the company ceased making glass in 1890. It never again operated as a glass factory.

Products were primarily some pressed tableware and novelties.

OMN: unknown

AKA: DOG & HAT

DATE: 1885

COLORS: clear, $58.00; amber, $95.00; blue, $110.00; canary, $135.00.

SIZE: 2¾" tall x 1¼" wide

NOTES: Many reproductions have been made in several colors. The reproductions have a much smaller hole in the hat portion.

Blue and clear

BOSTON & SANDWICH GLASS CO.
SANDWICH, MASSACHUSETTS
1825 – 1887

SANDWICH COOPERATIVE GLASS CO.
SANDWICH, MASSACHUSETTS
1888 – 1891

This factory was founded in 1825 by Deming Jarves and called the Sandwich Mfg. Co. It became Boston & Sandwich Glass Co. in 1826. The factory closed in 1887 during a workers' strike. It was reorganized as the Sandwich Cooperative Glass Co. in 1888, but it quickly failed. Other attempts to reorganize the factory and reopen it for production met with similar fates.

OMN: unknown

AKA: BASKET

DATE: ca. late 1800s

COLORS: blue opaline, $65.00.

SIZE: 2" tall x 2¼" wide

NOTES: Attributed to Boston & Sandwich. Most likely, other colors were made.

OMN: unknown

AKA: TORTOISE SHELL

DATE: ca. 1890

COLORS: clear, dark ruby spatter, $500.00+.

SIZE: 2" tall x 2" wide

NOTES: Tortoise shell or spatter glass was made by several American glass companies and was also imported from Europe.

BRYCE BROS.
PITTSBURGH, PENNSYLVANIA
1882 – 1891

Bryce Bros. was one of the many names of this factory during its history. It was founded in 1850 by James, Fred, and Robert Bryce and Fred McKee and known then as Bryce, McKee & Co. In 1854 McKee withdrew, and two new partners, William Hartley and J. Richards, joined the firm, which then changed its name to Bryce, Richards & Co. In 1865, Richards and Hartley both withdrew to start their own company, Richards & Hartley. W. Walker joined the original company as a partner, and the firm became known as Bryce, Walker & Co. In 1882, when the remaining members of the firm were only the Bryces, the company became Bryce Bros. It continued with this name until 1891, when it joined U.S. Glass and became Factory B.

Patterns made by Bryce Bros. or one of its incarnations include Pittsburgh, Old Oaken Bucket, Coral, Magic, Princess, Regal, Monarch, Orion, and others.

OMN: ATLAS

DATE: 1889

COLORS: clear, $28.00; clear with ruby stain, $95.00; opal, $68.00; opal, enamel decor, $70.00; opal satin, $75.00.

SIZE: 2⅛" tall x 1¾" wide

NOTES: Patented on November 12, 1889, as No. 19,427. This toothpick was advertised in an 1892 Butler Bros. catalog as a "Crystal Drop Tooth-Pick Stand, A Bright, Fast Moving 5-Center."

Clear

Clear with ruby stain

Opal with enamel decoration, satin

OMN: BUCKET, TOY, No. 1 and No. 2

DATE: ca. late 1880s

COLORS: clear, $28.00; clear with rose stain, $48.00; amber, $38.00; blue, $48.00; canary, $60.00.

SIZE: No. 1 small: 1⅞" tall x 2⅛" wide. No. 2 large: 2" tall x 2½" wide.

Blue, clear with rose stain

NOTES: These buckets were not part of the Old Oaken Bucket pattern, but are a series of at least four sizes of "toy buckets," the manufacturer's name for them. Larger buckets were made in four sizes as jelly containers.

Clear

OMN: COAL HOD

DATE: ca. late 1880s

COLORS: clear, $48.00; amber, $75.00; blue, $75.00; canary, $95.00.

SIZE: 2⅜" tall x 2" wide

NOTES: Ascribed to Bryce Bros. by Ruth Webb Lee. We have not found this in any Bryce catalog we have examined, but it is shown in a jobber's catalog.

Blue

OMN: FASHION

AKA: DAISY & BUTTON

DATE: ca. late 1880s

COLORS: Regular: clear, $32.00; amber, $48.00; amethyst, $95.00; blue, $85.00; canary, $85.00. Turned-down rim: clear, $40.00; amber, $55.00; amethyst, $100.00; blue, $90.00; blue with ruby stain, $125.00; canary, $90.00. Pineapple shape: clear, $65.00; clear with ruby stain, $145.00; amber, $125.00.

SIZE: Regular: 2¾" tall x 2¼" wide. Turned-down rim: 2¼" tall x 2⅜" wide. Pineapple: 2½" tall x 2½" wide.

No. 2 Fashion Toothpick

Clear

NOTES: This toothpick has several variations in the hand finishing; it can be found in different shapes. Occasionally it is found with an allover ornate metal cage. A variation is also know with a turned down rim that is sometimes ruby stained. This has been called Daisy & Button with Turned-Down Rim. Another variation is the Daisy & Button Pineapple.

Amber

Blue with metal cage, No. 2

Canary

Ruby stain

OMN: No. 720

AKA: FINECUT WITH SAUCER

DATE: prior to 1891

COLORS: clear, $45.00; canary, $75.00; amber, $50.00.

SIZE: 2½" tall x 2¼" wide

NOTES: This was sold originally as a covered mustard, but the base is often included in toothpick collections today. It is likely that blue was also made, but this is not verified at this time.

720. MUSTARD.

Mustard base, canary

Amber

OMN: HAPPY THOUGHT

AKA: BASKET, FINGER-GRIP

DATE: unknown

COLORS: clear, $58.00; amber, $78.00; blue, $145.00.

SIZE: 2½" tall x 2⅛" wide

Clear

Amber

OMN: LIBERTY TORCH

AKA: HAND WITH TORCH

DATE: 1888

COLORS: clear, $65.00; amber, $75.00; blue, $105.00.

SIZE: 3¾" tall x 1⅝" wide

NOTES: A wholesaler's catalog calls this a candlestick.

OMN: OLD OAKEN BUCKET

AKA: WOODEN PAIL

DATE: 1885

COLORS: clear, $30.00; amber, $38.00; amethyst, $65.00; blue, $48.00; canary, $65.00.

SIZE: unknown

NOTES: This is a full tableware pattern. The small Toy Buckets without feet shown on page 26 technically are not part of this pattern, although they go well with it. Notice that this toothpick has a bail molded in the glass; the No. 4 Covered Toy Bucket has a metal bail. There is also a toy spoon that goes to a child's table set.

Clear

Blue

OMN: WALL POCKET

AKA: WALL BASKET

DATE: 1888

COLORS: clear, $45.00; amber, $65.00; blue, $85.00; canary, $85.00.

SIZE: 2½" tall x 2¼" wide

NOTES: This wall pocket sometimes has a mirror mounted in the circle on the front. Its sale was continued by U.S. Glass Co. after Bryce Bros. joined the combine.

Wall Pocket

BRYCE, HIGBEE & CO.
PITTSBURGH, PENNSYLVANIA (OFFICES)
HOMESTEAD, PENNSYLVANIA (FACTORY)
1879 – 1907

Bryce, Higbee & Co. was organized in 1879 by John Bryce, Charles Bryce, and John B. Higbee. Their factory site was called the Homestead Glass Works, located in Homestead, Pennsylvania. In 1907 the factory was destroyed by flood, and it was never rebuilt.

Patterns of tableware made include Charm, Vici, Crescent, Fleur de Lis, Admiral, Oregon, Bowknot, No. 1900 Paris, Tiffany, Estoria, Mirror, Waldorf, Oxford, Monarch, and Highland.

OMN: unknown

AKA: BANDED BARREL, BEAUTY (Butler Bros.)

DATE: 1890s or 1900s

COLORS: clear, $25.00; amber, $40.00; blue, $45.00; canary, $45.00; green, $40.00.

SIZE: unknown

NOTES: Also made later (ca. 1919) by New Martinsville Glass. There are two variations, one with small dots and one with distinct teeth.

Clear

OMN: unknown
AKA: BUTTON & STAR PANEL
COLORS: clear, $38.00.
SIZE: 2⅜" tall x 2⅛" wide

OMN: DELTA
AKA: PANELED THISTLE
DATE: 1910
COLORS: clear, $38.00.
SIZE: 2¼" tall x 2¼" wide
NOTES: Marked with the Higbee trademark, a bee with "HIG" on wings and body.

Clear

OMN: FLEUR DE LIS
AKA: ARCHED FLEUR DE LIS
DATE: 1898
COLORS: clear, $45.00; clear with amber stain, $110.00; clear with ruby stain, $375.00.
SIZE: 1⅜" tall x 1½" wide
NOTES: *Bryce, Higbee & Co. have named their leading new pattern the Fleur de Lis, which name it takes from the most prominent figure in the design. –December 1897.*

Clear

AKA: GATLING GUN
DATE: unknown
COLORS: clear, $38.00; amber, $68.00; blue, $70.00.
SIZE: 2⅞" tall x 1⅝" wide
NOTES: Actually a mortar, but since there is another known as Mortar, we will endorse the collector name. Originally this had a matching round lid. The original purpose is not known. Possibly it was sold with or without the lid.

Blue and amber

Clear

OMN: unknown
AKA: MEDALLION SUNBURST
DATE: 1905
COLORS: clear, $42.00.
SIZE: 2⅛" tall x 2⅛" wide

OMN: MENAGERIE

DATE: ca. 1886

COLORS: clear, $95.00; amber, $115.00; blue, $145.00.

SIZE: 3½" tall x 2¼" wide at top

NOTES: This is a spoon to a child's toy table set that includes a turtle covered butter, a bear covered sugar, and an owl cream.

Blue

Amber

OMN: MORTAR

DATE: unknown

COLORS: clear, $42.00; amber, $52.00; blue, $52.00.

SIZE: 2½" tall without lid x 2½" wide

NOTES: This is the bottom of a covered mustard, but is also found in many toothpick collections.

Amber

Clear

OMN: unknown

AKA: SWIRL & PANEL

DATE: unknown

COLORS: clear, $38.00.

SIZE: 2¼" tall x 2⅛" wide

AKA: UTILITY BOOT

DATE: ca. 1889

COLORS: clear, $42.00; amber, $60.00; blue, $65.00.

SIZE: 2⅝" tall without lid x 2¼" wide at top x 3" wide across base

NOTES: This was sold with a lid as an inkwell. It is not known if it was originally sold as a toothpick. It appears in an 1889 Butler Bros. catalog.

Blue

BUCKEYE GLASS CO.
MARTINS FERRY, OH
1878-1896

The Buckeye Glass Company was founded by Henry Helling at Martins Ferry, Ohio. It was housed in the old Excelsior Glass Works. Mr. Helling was president of the company until Andrew Seaman succeeded him in 1884. Mr. Seaman served as president until the company closed. The factory was destroyed by fire in 1896 and was never rebuilt.

The company's patterns include No. 522 Syrian (in 1883), Columbian (in 1892), No. 527 (in 1887), and Venetian (in 1888). The latter two were opalescent patterns. Buckeye also made novelties, including the butterfly toothpick holder illustrated here. One of the many patterns made in lamps is the desirable Pickett, made in several colors.

OMN: BUCKEYE BUTTERFLY

DATE: ca. 1880s – 1890s

COLORS: clear $120.00; amber, $145.00

SIZE: 2¾" tall at highest point, 2" tall at lowest point.

CAMBRIDGE GLASS CO.
CAMBRIDGE, OHIO
1902 – 1958

The new plant of the National Glass Co. here (Cambridge, Ohio) is making progress slowly. They have been delayed a great deal by the structural iron manufacturers, and it does not look as though they will get ready to make glass for three or four months yet, and probably longer, and it will require a much longer time to finish the whole factory. It will certainly be a mammoth concern when completed... There are to be two large buildings covering an area 300 x 700 feet. In one of these is located the furnaces, 3 in all. The furnaces are now topped out and are 115 feet high from top of base, and the latter is 20 feet high... Sheeting is on the biggest portion of the roof, and slating has begun. Both buildings will be roofed with slate. The walls of the other building are finished. –October 1901.

The Cambridge Glass Co. was organized and built by the National Glass Co. but was incorporated as completely independent of the parent company. Many early patterns were successful patterns of member factories of the National Glass Co. that had closed.

Some molds were sent from their original factories to the Canton Glass Co. or the Ohio Flint Works before being sent to Cambridge. Examples of these are some of the molds from Dalzell, Gilmore & Leighton, and Robinson Works. Molds were kept under the control of National management.

Glass production began in 1902, with Arthur Bennett serving as president. The factory closed in 1958. Patterns include Marjorie, Star of Bethlehem, Cambridge Ribbon, and Stratford. Trademarks used by this company are "Nearcut" (early pressed, imitation cut) and a *C* in a triangle (later tableware).

OMN: BUZZ SAW, No. 2697

DATE: 1909

COLORS: clear, $30.00.

SIZE: unknown

NOTES: This is a toy spoon, not a true toothpick.

No. 2697 Toy Tea Set
Extra Heavy Near Cut

"Colonial" No. 2630 Toy Tea Set

OMN: COLONIAL, No. 2630

DATE: unknown

COLORS: clear, $30.00; green, $55.00.

SIZE: unknown

NOTES: This is a toy spoon, not a true toothpick. Known in at least three shades of green.

Clear

OMN: No. 2750

AKA: COLONIAL

DATE: 1905

COLORS: clear, $38.00.

SIZE: unknown

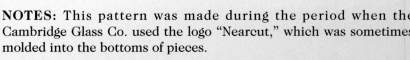

Toothpick.

NOTES: This pattern was made during the period when the Cambridge Glass Co. used the logo "Nearcut," which was sometimes molded into the bottoms of pieces.

Clear

OMN: No. 2651
AKA: FEATHER
DATE: 1910
COLORS: clear, $38.00.
SIZE: 2¼" tall x 1¾" wide

Toothpick.

Toothpick.

Clear

OMN: FERNLAND, No. 2635
DATE: 1907
COLORS: clear, $45.00.
SIZE: Toothpick: 2¼" tall x 2¼" wide
NOTES: This was also made as a toy spoon to a child's tea set.

"Fernland" No. 2635 Toy Tea Set

Clear

OMN: MARJORIE, No. 2631
AKA: BUTTON STAR
DATE: ca. 1905
COLORS: clear, $38.00.
SIZE: 2" tall x 2" wide

Toothpick.

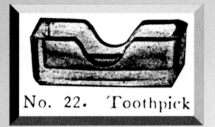

No. 22. Toothpick

OMN: No. 22
DATE: ca. teens to 1920s
COLORS: clear, $38.00.
SIZE: unknown

OMN: No. 157
DATE: ca. teens or 1920s
COLORS: clear, $28.00.
SIZE: unknown

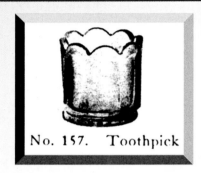

No. 157. Toothpick

OMN: No. 1031
DATE: ca. 1900s
COLORS: clear, $32.00.
SIZE: 2¼" tall x 1⅝" wide

OMN: No. 1035
AKA: INTAGLIO
DATE: ca. 1900s
COLORS: clear, $38.00.
SIZE: 2¼" tall x 1¾" wide
NOTES: This example is cut all over.

OMN: No. 2351
DATE: 1908
COLORS: clear, $38.00.
SIZE: unknown

OMN: No. 2590½

DATE: Probably late teens to early 1920s

COLORS: clear, $28.00.

SIZE: unknown

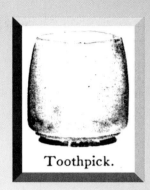

Toothpick.

Shape C

OMN: RADIUM, No. 2635

DATE: 1906

COLORS: clear (any shape), $42.00.

SIZE: 2⅜" tall x 2" wide at top

NOTES: Made in shapes A, B, and C according to catalog. A is straight sided, while B is cupped in at the top.

OMN: No. 120

AKA: WHEELING BLOCK

DATE: 1903

COLORS: clear, $60.00.

SIZE: 4⅛" tall x 1⅞" wide

Clear

CANTON GLASS CO.
CANTON, OHIO — 1882 – 1890
MARION, INDIANA — 1890 – 1899

The Canton Glass Co. was incorporated in 1882 by Joseph K. Brown and A. M. Bacon in Canton, Ohio. Following a disastrous fire in 1885, the company was reorganized with new officers. Production during the repairs to the factory was done at the Massillon glass factory owned by a Pittsburgh glass man well acquainted with the Canton owners, Lorenz Stoehr. In 1890 the Canton factory was completely destroyed by fire, and this time the owners leased a glass works in Beaver Falls, Pennsylvania, in order to continue to fill orders. The company moved to Marion, Indiana, as soon as their new factory was built. It became part of National Glass Co. in 1899. When the National Glass Co. closed the works, this factory never reopened.

Patterns made by Canton include Dew Drop, Stardrop, Primrose, and Barred Forget-Me-Not. Their most famous designs were Jumbo, Barnum, and Swan, all designed by David Barker.

OMN: UNKNOWN

AKA: CHAIR, DAISY & BUTTON

DATE: ca. late 1880s based on color availability

COLORS: clear, $125.00; amber, $225.00; blue, $225.00; opal, $250.00.

SIZE: 4½" tall x 2" wide x 2½" long

NOTES: This attractive novelty had several uses. It has been seen with a pincushion insert in the well. Toothpick collectors add it to their collections. With the kitten lid, it is an inkwell. The attribution of this is taken from J. Stanley Brothers, who researched the Canton Glass Co. in depth in the 1930s. Known in two shades of blue.

With kitten lid, amber

D. D. Toothpick.
Packs 120 doz. to bbl.

OMN: DEW DROP

DATE: uncertain

COLORS: clear, $48.00; opal, $65.00.

SIZE: 1⅞" tall x 1½" wide

NOTES: This toothpick mold ended up at the Cambridge Glass Co. and was shown in one of its early catalogs. However, it originated at the Canton Glass Co.

CANTON GLASS CO. (SEPERATE COMPANY)
MARION, INDIANA — CA. 1902

Everything at the new Canton Glass Works, Marion, Ind., is running along smoothly, with 12 shops employed. The new pressed handle soda is selling well and four shops are kept busy on lemon extractors. Many new samples are being made for the spring trade... –April 1903.

This was a co-operative factory, with F. W. Willson as president, M. L. Lewis as vice president, and Leo Nussbaum as secretary and treasurer. The new Canton Glass Co. was operated by different people and opened in a different location than the original Canton Glass Co., but was also in Marion.

Tableware, drug sundries, novelties, vault lights and bar goods constitute the bulk of the output of this plant. They also give especial attention to making and working private molds. The factory is equipped with a large dynamo-electric light plant with two 50 horsepower engines. They have a roomy mold shop, a cooper shop, a new warehouse, 30 x 120, a packing room, and an engraving department. –November 1903.

New

Old

AKA: KINGFISHER

DATE: ca. 1920

COLORS: clear, $58.00; chocolate, $450.00+.

SIZE: 3⅜" tall x 2¼" wide

NOTES: Reproductions exist in several colors and carnival finishes. On the old, the Kingfisher is almost humpbacked and has a pointed crest. The new Kingfisher is slender and has a rounded head. On the old, the fish tails about the base are right over left. On the newer ones, one set of fish has a left tail over a right.

Clear

No 410—Toothpick.
Packed 48 doz. in barrel.

OMN: No. 410

AKA: CANTON

DATE: 1904

COLORS: clear, $58.00.

SIZE: 2⅜" tall, 2¼" wide

NOTES: The example shown is engraved "Fernville, Mich. World's Fair St. Louis 1904."

OMN: No. 212

AKA: SHAMROCK FIELD

DATE: 1904

COLORS: clear, $55.00.

SIZE: unknown

NOTES: This toothpick has not been shown in previous literature. Named by authors.

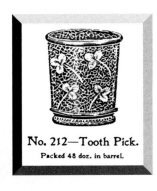

No. 212—Tooth Pick.
Packed 48 doz. in barrel.

OESTERLING & CO.
WHEELING, WEST VIRGINIA
1863 – 1867

CENTRAL GLASS CO.
WHEELING, WEST VIRGINIA
1867 – 1891

CENTRAL GLASS WORKS
WHEELING, WEST VIRGINIA
1895 – 1939

The business of the Central Glass Company was started on the co-operative plan in the spring of 1863, with a capital of $5,000. After the expiration of three years, the company bought the grounds and buildings of the East Wheeling distillery and pork packing house, for the purpose of converting them into a glass manufacturing establishment, which, in point of magnitude and completeness, was destined to stand on a par with anything of the kind in the United States.

In 1867 they obtained a charter to conduct business on a joint stock plan under the firm name of the Central Glass Company, with a capital of $80,000, which also represented the original capital of $5,000. The new company, however, reserved the right of buying in and canceling all the shares which might be offered for sale by its individual members, and the result has been that the original 434 shares have thus been reduced to less than one-half of the original number.

The capital of the company for several past years has been $260,000, the average sales per annum about $400,000, and they employ about 500 hands. Until the introduction of natural gas, they have been operating their own coal fields, comprising fifty acres in the vicinity of the works. Their manufactures are among the most popular in the United States, and are extensively shipped to the Canadian, West Indies, South American, and the German markets.

The production of these works is confined to tableware, bar and lamp goods, the variety, quality, and beauty of which find ready sale. Up to the year 1872, they operated only two furnaces, but during that year added a third, with the necessary out buildings. They also erected on the west side of McCulloch Street their new two story warehouse with excellent offices and selecting and packing rooms attached. The main packing room is

65x85 feet, and the warehouse 287x70 feet. Both are acknowledged to be the most extensive as well as the most practically arranged buildings in this country. Both buildings are connected with the factory by means of an elevated bridge with narrow gauge track. A steam elevator hoists the glass in open hand boxes from the factory floor to the floor of the bridge, which is on a level with the selecting and packing rooms. In addition to the factory on the east side of the street are the following departments: the mould and machine shops, cutting shop, pot making rooms, blacksmith shop, coke ovens, two buildings with eight lears or annealing ovens, and the largest and best arranged engraving shop in the country.

Mr. John Oesterling, the first manufacturer of the works, was a man of wide practical experience and shrewd executive ability. To the fact that he was at the head of the enterprise from its inception in 1863, until his death three years ago, is mainly attributable the great success it has achieved. At the time of his death in 1883 the works had attained a high reputation. Previous to his engaging in the Central works, Mr. Oesterling was employed in the mould room of Hobbs, Barnes & Co., at a salary of about $7 per week. As indicative of his ambition, it may be stated that, while still in the employ of Hobbs, Barnes & Co., he made the first pair of moulds for the Central Company at his home on the kitchen table, his wife holding a candle while he performed the work. Mr. Oesterling was one of the eleven original Republicans in Ritchietown, when it was almost worth a man's life to stand by that party in this locality. He suffered persecution in many ways, among other complimentary attentions being stoned in the street. His copies of the New York Tribune were seized and burned.

Upon the death of Mr. Oesterling, the Directors chose as the head of the great hive of industry Mr. N. B. Scott, long *his trusted right hand man. Mr. Scott's management has more than justified the confidence and the expectation of his associates. He is not only thoroughly versed in the business, but he is very popular with the trade.*

The present officers of the company are N. B. Scott, President and General Manager, succeeding Mr. Oesterling; H. E. Waddell, Secretary; W. E. Goering, Treasurer. Directors, Peter Cassell, August Rolf, N. Crawley, W. E. Goering and N. B. Scott.

A year ago the Central Company purchased the Brilliant Glass Works, sixteen miles from the city to be operated as an annex. The principal output from the Brilliant Annex consists of fancy colored shades, globes, and a line of specialties. About 350 men are employed, and the outlook is very promising for a further enlargement. –Wheeling Intelligencer, 1886.

Oesterling & Co. was organized in 1863 by John Oesterling, Andrew Baggs, William Elson, Peter Cassell, Henry Leasure, John Henderson, and Roy Combs. All were former employees of Barnes, Hobbs & Co. (the forerunner of Hobbs, Brockunier & Co.).

After an 1867 reorganization, the name was changed to Central Glass Co. In 1891, Central joined the U.S. Glass Co. and was designated Factory O. Shortly, in 1895, the plant was purchased by Nathan Scott and reopened as the Central Glass Works; it made entirely different products than did the preceding company.

Specialties include stemware, novelties, lamps, and tableware. Some of the more well-known patterns include Log Cabin, Silver Age (U.S. Coin), Cabbage Rose, Wheat in Shield, Picture Window, Pressed Diamond, Medallion, Polka Dot, Daisy and Button, and Pilgrim.

Clear

OMN: UNKNOWN

AKA: HELENE, WARD'S NEW ERA, ZIPPERED SPEARPOINT

DATE: 1899

COLORS: clear, $58.00.

SIZE: 2½" tall x 2" wide

NOTES: For similar toothpicks, see Co-operative's Twentieth Century and Thompson's Summit. Helene has a top-heavy diamond when compared to Twentieth Century, which has a diamond with equal sides.

Amber

OMN: No. 1396

AKA: HORSE WITH CART

DATE: mid-1880s because of color availability

COLORS: clear, $42.00; amber, $65.00; blue, $75.00; canary, $95.00.

SIZE: 2½" tall x 2" wide

NOTES: 2⅞" tall x 3" long at base x 1½" wide at container

Central Glass Co.

Amber

OMN: MATCH

DATE: prior to 1891 and the merger with U.S. Glass Co.

COLORS: clear, $32.00; amber, $42.00; blue, $50.00; canary, $55.00.

SIZE: 3" tall x 2⅛" wide

NOTES: This item is labeled as a match box in company catalogs, although the designation is written in, not printed. The sides of the match are Daisy and Button.

Canary and blue

OMN: No. T790

DATE: ca. 1915

COLORS: crystal, $38.00.

SIZE: unknown

NOTES: This pattern was made by Central Glass Works, not the early Central Glass Co.

No. T790 Toothpick

OMN: No. T791

DATE: ca. 1915

No. T791 Sanitare Toothpick

COLORS: crystal, $30.00; clear with ruby stain, $70.00; opal, $55.00.

SIZE: 1⅛" tall x 3½" long x 1⅝" wide

NOTES: This pattern was made by Central Glass Works, not the early Central Glass Co. It is marked "Krys-Tol." Reportedly this was known as Chippendale, but without catalog proof we cannot be sure about this, as several colonial-inspired patterns were made. Since the Krys-Tol trademark was used by both Ohio Flint and Jefferson before being used by Central, it is possible this toothpick was made before at one or both of these factories.

Clear

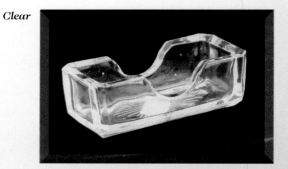

Base

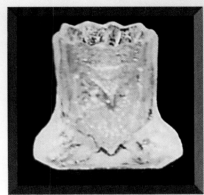

OMN: No. 1397

AKA: OWL IN STUMP

DATE: Prior to 1891 and the merger with U.S. Glass Co.

COLORS: clear, $53.00; blue, $68.00.

SIZE: 2½" tall x 2¾" wide

NOTES: Has been reproduced by Summit Art Glass Co., with some marked with a *V* in a circle.

Clear

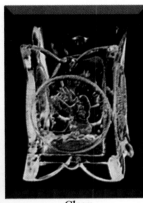

OMN: SILVER AGE (Central), No. 15005 (U.S. Glass)

AKA: U.S. COIN

DATE: 1891

COLORS: clear, $75.00; clear with satin coins, $85.00; clear with amber stain, $185.00; clear with ruby stain, $225.00.

SIZE: 2⅞" tall x 2" wide

NOTES: According to the *Wheeling Intelligencer*, the majority of the pattern was made at the Central Glass Co. for approximately six months before the merger with U.S. Glass. Only lamps were made at Hobbs Glass Co. After the federal marshalls declared that the molds would have to be destroyed because they were accurate dies for U.S. money, the molds were reworked into the Columbian Coin pattern, made by U.S. Glass at Nickel Plate in Fostoria, Ohio. There are many recent and not-so-recent reproductions of this toothpick, varying from the original in placement of the stars.

Clear

Clear, opposite side

CHALLINOR, TAYLOR & CO.
TARENTUM, PENNSYLVANIA
1885 – 1891

Challinor, Taylor & Co. was organized in 1885 by David Challinor, David Taylor, and James Challinor. The firm was well known for tableware, novelties, opal ware, and opaque and mosaic glassware. David Challinor held a patent (1886) for mosaic (marble or slag) glass. In 1891, the company joined the U.S. Glass Co. and was designated Factory C. Some products made by Challinor, Taylor were continued by U.S. Glass.

Some patterns of tableware include Blockade, Oval Panel, Hobnail with Bars, Double Fan, Flower and Panel, Opaque Scroll, and Tree of Life.

Olive, Roseblush, and turquoise are the color names originally used by the company.

See also U.S. Glass Co., Factory C.

OMN: ACORN

COLORS: black opaque, $135.00; opal, $135.00; Roseblush, $135.00.

SIZE: 2¼" tall x 2⅛" wide

NOTES: The salt shaker is pictured in a Challinor catalog. Other items are also shown in a Tygart Valley catalog. These toothpicks are sometimes decorated with enameled flowers and leaves.

Black decorated, opal decorated, Roseblush

Challinor, Taylor & Co.

OMN: ANTIQUE MATCH SAFE

AKA: RING HANDLED SLAG

DATE: ca. 1886

COLORS: mosaic (slag), purple, $128.00.

SIZE: 2⅜" tall x 1⅞" wide

NOTES: Found with other Challinor mosaic pieces in an old wholesale catalog. This catalog listed this as an "Antique Match Safe." The Sowerby, England, version is the company's No. 1264 and is found in various colors.

Mosaic

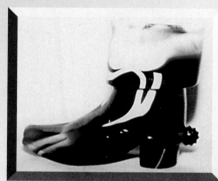

Purple mosaic

OMN: unknown

AKA: BOOT & SPUR

DATE: ca. 1886

COLORS: black, $125.00; mosaic (slag) purple, $145.00.

SIZE: 3¼" tall x 4" long

NOTES: Sometimes referred to as British Boot, but it is an American product, so we endorse the above name. This was described in an 1886 jobber's catalog as a "mosaic boot, a fast selling novelty, filled with a bottle of fine perfume." A very similar boot is being made by Mosser Glass Co. of Cambridge, Ohio, in many colors.

OMN: No. 27

AKA: BUTTERFLY MATCH

DATE: unknown

COLORS: opal, $115.00; decorated opal, $135.00.

SIZE: 2¼" tall x 4¼" wide x 1¾" deep

NOTES: Note the various decorations available in this hang-on-the-wall match safe. Please see Eagle Glass for another type of Butterfly match holder, and the chapter on unattributed toothpicks for another.

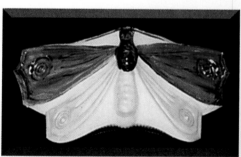

Decorated opal

Roseblush

OMN: No. 20

AKA: FORGET ME NOT

DATE: 1885

COLORS: opaque colors in the following: opal, $90.00; olive, $90.00; Roseblush, $90.00; turquoise, $90.00.

SIZE: 1⅞" tall x 2⅜" wide

Turquoise and olive

1292 Salt, Pepper & Toothpick.
Decorated N⁰ 3½.

OMN: No. 1292

DATE: ca. late 1880s

COLORS: opal, $128.00; decorated opal, $175.00.

SIZE: unknown

NOTES: Note that items in the "set" have no matching decorations! It is most likely that the toothpick was available in these three decorations and probably others done by Challinor.

OMN: No. 21

AKA: ONE-O-ONE

DATE: ca. 1891

COLORS: opaque colors in the following: opal, $95.00; Roseblush, $125.00; olive, $105.00; turquoise, $125.00.

SIZE: 2¼" tall x 2" wide

Roseblush

OMN: unknown

AKA: TUSCAN SQUARE MATCH HOLDER

DATE: ca. 1886

COLORS: mosaic (slag), purple, $48.00; mosaic (slag), amber, $48.00.

SIZE: 3¾" tall

NOTES: Either a match holder or a small novelty vase. It is shown with other Challinor toothpicks in a distributor's catalog. There are at least three versions of this item, possibly indicating three different manfacturers. One version is marked with the Sowerby (England) mark.

OMN: No. 10

AKA: VASE

DATE: ca. late 1880s

COLORS: opal, $125.00; opal, decorated, $170.00.

SIZE: unknown

NOTES: Since the original Challinor catalog indicates "assorted decorations," expect to find several different hand-painted enamel decorations on this item. Also be aware that nearly the same shape was made by Mt. Washington Glass Co.

N⁰ 10 Novelty
Assorted Decorations.

COLUMBIA GLASS CO.
FINDLAY, OHIO
1886 – 1892

The Columbia Glass Co. was organized in 1886 with David C. Jenkins as president and William J. Patterson as secretary-treasurer. This factory was the first to be built at Findlay. In 1891 it joined the U.S. Glass Co. and was designated Factory J. The company closed in 1892, when the natural gas was shut off in a particularly cold winter, and was never reopened.

Some notable patterns include Dew Drop, Henrietta, Radiant, Bamboo Beauty, Columbia, Banquet, and Climax. Novelties made include the Early Bird, the Dog Vase, and the Kitten in Slipper. Patterns made at U.S. Glass Factory J include Heavy Gothic, Pointed Jewel, and Broken Column.

See also United States Glass Co., Factory J.

OMN: COLUMBIA

DATE: 1891

COLORS: clear, $145.00; clear with engraving, $185.00.

SIZE: 2³⁄₁₆" tall x 2" wide

NOTES: This is part of an entire tableware pattern. The toothpick is difficult to find today.

OMN: DEW DROP

AKA: DOUBLE EYE HOBNAIL

DATE: 1887

COLORS: clear, $42.00; amber, $55.00; blue, $68.00.

SIZE: 2³⁄₈" tall x 1³⁄₄" wide

NOTES: This pattern differs from other hobnail patterns in that it has one small hobnail on top of a larger hobnail. Dew Drop was made in a full tableware line that included a toy set.

Blue

Toothpick.

Amber   *Clear*

Blue and amber

OMN: unknown

AKA: EARLY BIRD

DATE: unknown

COLORS: clear, $110.00; amber, $165.00; blue, $195.00.

SIZE: 2⁷⁄₈" tall x 1⁵⁄₈" wide at beak

NOTES: This attractive novelty was made only in a toothpick and a salt shaker.

FOSTORIA SHADE & LAMP CO.
FOSTORIA, OHIO
1890 – 1893

CONSOLIDATED LAMP & GLASS CO.
FOSTORIA, OHIO — 1894 – 1896
CORAOPOLIS, PENNSYLVANIA — 1896 – 1964

The Fostoria Lamp and Shade Co. was organized in 1890 by W. S. Brady, James B. Brown, and Charles Foster at Fostoria, Ohio. In 1893 the firm was purchased by the Consolidated Lamp & Glass Co. Nicholas Kopp, Jr., became the metal maker (chemist), designer, and plant manager. Kopp was renowned for the new and unusual colors he developed.

The Consolidated Glass & Lamp Co., with headquarters in this city, (Pittsburgh) has been chartered with a paid up capital stock of $200,000, with the privilege of increasing it to $250,000. The incorporators and the Board of Directors are: F. G. Wallace, Chas. H. Dean, J. B. Graham, secretary, Jos. G. Walter, treasurer, and Nicholas Kopp, manager. The new company will commence business in their corporate capacity by January 1. Their general offices will be in this city where they will also maintain a large warehouse for the stocking of goods as well as sample rooms. They have secured the extensive factory of the Fostoria Shade & Lamp Co. at Fostoria, Ohio, and will double its capacity at once, besides which they are figuring on obtaining some other plants. The business of the Wallace & McAfee Co., glass and lamp jobbers of this city, and the Fostoria Shade & Lamp Co. will be combined under the new arrangement, and the showing made by both during the last year was very satisfactory. They intend to enlarge the variety of goods made by the present Fostoria Shade & Lamp Co., but will still continue to make a specialty of the fine decorated lamps, founts, and shades which have given the latter concern such a high reputation in recent years. Everything is being pushed so that a complete line will be ready for the trade at the opening of the spring season in January. New and beautiful effects in azure blue, turquoise, and rose colors are being got out and entirely new designs in decorated lamps will be ready for the inspection of the trade. The people managing this concern are not tyros in the business; they are all men of approved competence and large experience and their character as such is certain to assure for the enterprise an unequivocal success. –November 1893.

This is the only concern doing "casing" that is covering the crystal, and the effect is beautiful... The assortment of salts, peppers, toothpicks, etc., is very extensive, the variety of colors covering turquoise, canary, blue, rose, and others. –1894.

The Fostoria factory was destroyed by fire in 1896 and was never rebuilt. The company moved to a new factory in Coraopolis, Pennsylvania. Consolidated Lamp & Glass Co. closed in 1964.

While much of the company's products were in various styles of lamps, tableware patterns also were made, including Quilt, Florette, Iris, Guttate, Criss Cross, Cosmos, Pansy, Bulging Loops, and Argus. Consolidated was known for its plated (cased) glass. Fostoria Shade & Lamp developed a pattern it called Arctic, now referred to as Half Cone. This became the inspiration for later Cone pieces made by Consolidated.

OMN: unknown

AKA: BULGING LOOPS

DATE: 1894

COLORS: Colors may be found with glossy or satin finish. Also, some colors are plated (cased). Blue, $230.00; green, $190.00; opal, $190.00; opal to pink, $225.00; pigeon blood, $235.00; pink, $185.00; yellow, $260.00.

SIZE: 2⅜" tall x 2⅜" wide

Pigeon blood

Consolidated Lamp & Glass Co.

Green opaque

OMN: CONE

DATE: 1894

COLORS: blue opaque, $85.00; green opaque, $80.00; opal, $75.00; pink opaque, $85.00.

SIZE: 2⅜" tall x 2⅜" wide

NOTES: This pattern was inspired by the old pattern, Arctic, made by the Fostoria Shade & Lamp Co. Consolidated adapted the design later in new forms and new colors. Toothpicks are found only in the later pattern by Consolidated. Also known in opal satin, value $85.00.

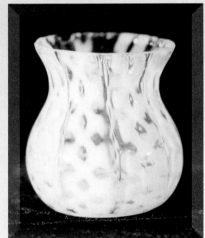

Clear opalescent

OMN: unknown

AKA: CRISS CROSS

DATE: 1894

COLORS: Colors are opalescent with either glossy or satin finish. Clear opalescent, $285.00; ruby opalescent, $800.00+; rubina satin, $750.00+.

SIZE: 2⅜" tall x 2¼" wide

NOTES: Shards found at the factory site include the colors of blue and yellow in Criss Cross. A pale blue, satin finish gas light shade is also known.

Rubina opalescent

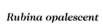

Rubina opalescent, satin finish

Pink, satin finish

OMN: unknown

AKA: GUTTATE

DATE: 1894

COLORS: Sometimes pieces are found in plated (cased) glass. Blue opaque, $170.00; green opaque, $170.00; opal, $165.00; pink plated, $195.00; ruby, $310.00; pink plated satin finish, $225.00.

SIZE: 2¼" tall x 2¼" wide

Green opaque

OMN: PANSY

DATE: 1894

COLORS: blue plated, $95.00; green opaque, $70.00; opal, $65.00; pigeon blood plated, $210.00; pink opaque, $75.00; yellow opaque, $85.00.

SIZE: 2" tall x 2¾" wide

NOTES: Plated refers to cased glass.

Green opaque

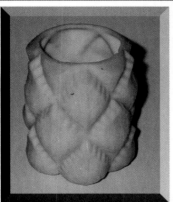

Blue opaque

OMN: PINE APPLE

DATE: 1894

COLORS: blue opaque, $95.00; green opaque, $70.00; opal, $65.00; pink opaque, $100.00.

SIZE: 2⅜" tall x 2" wide

NOTES: Note that the original pattern name is two words, not one. Colors may also come in cased glass.

Crystal iridized finish

OMN: QUILT; FLORETTE

DATE: 1894

COLORS: Colors are opaque, but available in glossy finish or satin finish. Also some were plated (cased). Clear, $50.00; clear, iridized finish, $200.00; blue, $140.00; mauve, $165.00; opal, $85.00; opal to pink, $150.00; yellow, $155.00.

SIZE: 2" tall x 2½" wide

NOTES: The company advertised the pattern both as Quilt and Florette. In April of 1895, trade reports said that Consolidated's new color was mauve and Florette was selling very well in this color, available in satin finish and plated in crystal. Ads after 1894 call the pattern Florette.

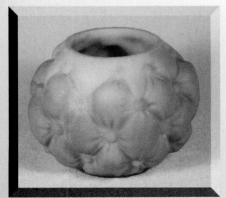

Opal to pink opaque

Pink plated glossy finish

Blue opaque glossy finish

Opal, enamel decorated

OMN: unknown

AKA: SHELL & SEAWEED

DATE: 1894

COLORS: blue opaque, $168.00; green opaque, $145.00; opal, $95.00; blue plated, $195.00; pink plated, $195.00; yellow plated, $200.00.

SIZE: 2¼" tall x 2⅛" wide

NOTES: Plated refers to cased colors. Any of the listed colors may be found in glossy or satin finish.

Opal, enamel decorated

Green opaque, glossy finish

Blue opaque, satin finish

CO-OPERATIVE FLINT GLASS CO., LTD.
BEAVER FALLS, PENNSYLVANIA
1879 – 1930s

The Co-operative Flint Glass Co. was organized in 1879 at Beaver Falls, Pennsylvania. The men involved in the organization included William and Phillip Scharff, E. T. Dunn, Josef Brown, and Charles W. Klein. Charles W. Klein and E. T. Dunn resigned and organized the Findlay Flint Glass Co. at Findlay, Ohio. After fire destroyed Findlay Flint in 1891, Charles Klein returned to Co-operative Flint.

The Co-op made tableware in the following patterns: Columbia, Daisy, Madoline, Royal, Forest, Imperial, Colonial, Unique, Magna, Famous, Twentieth Century, Regina, Lily, Douglas, Ray, No. 130 Currier & Ives, Rex, Radiant, Art Navo, La France, Martha Washington, and Swan. Their novelties and sundries include the Frog toothpick, Anvil salt, and ornate flytraps.

This company manufactures all kinds of tableware, bar and bitter bottles, beer mugs, battery jars, bull's eye lenses, cake covers, champagnes, clarets, wines, claret jugs, ales, cordials, colognes, fount and lamps, fly traps, fish globes, inverted sample bottles, inks, paperweights, sponge cups, jelly tumblers, tin top jars, French jars, ring jars, urn jars, specie jars, glass caps, street and lantern globes, oils, oil and wine sets, druggist's shop furniture, funnels, percolators, graduates, desiccators, seed cups, bird baths, breeding cups, and candlesticks in crystal and opal, and their make is not surpassed anywhere in quality, style, and finish. –November 1893, CGL.

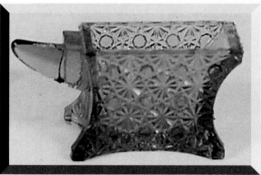

Amber

OMN: ANVIL, DAISY & BUTTON

DATE: ca. mid-1880s

COLORS: clear, $38.00; amber, $42.00; aquamarine blue, $48.00; dark blue, $58.00; green, $52.00.

SIZE: 2" tall x 2⅛" wide x 4⅛" long

NOTES: Shown in a Co-op catalog as an Anvil salt. U.S. Glass also made an Anvil toothpick/salt.

Clear with gold

OMN: ART NAVO

DATE: 1905

COLORS: clear, $70.00; clear with gold decor, $125.00; clear with ruby stain, $275.00; green with gold, $265.00.

SIZE: 2½" tall x 2" wide

NOTES: *Art Navo... The design is a dog-wood blossom decorated in natural colors. The line comes also in ruby and gold and green and gold.* –January 1905. Note that the shapes of the actual toothpick and the catalog illustration are different. Whether or not the shape shown in the catalog was ever made is not known at this time.

Toothpick.

OMN: COLUMBIA

DATE: 1900

COLORS: clear, $38.00; clear with gold decor, $48.00; clear with ruby stain, $285.00; opal, $75.00.

SIZE: 2½" tall x 1⅞" wide

NOTES: This toothpick has been reproduced in two sizes. L. G. Wright offered this reproduction in clear, green, ruby, blue, amethyst, amber, and dark carnival.

Clear with gold

Opal decorated

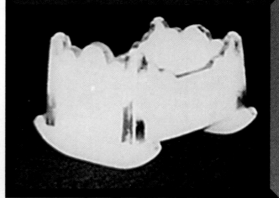

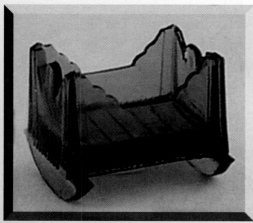

New, amber

AKA: CRADLE

DATE: ca. 1897

COLORS: clear, $45.00; amber, $85.00; opal, $225.00.

SIZE: 1⅜" tall x 1⅝" wide x 2½" long

NOTES: According to old catalog listings, this is a salt. It was reproduced by A. A. Importing. Old examples have wood grain on underside of cradle. May have been made in both styles originally.

Co-operative Flint Glass Co., Ltd.

Clear

OMN: DAISY

AKA: SUNK DAISY

DATE: 1897

COLORS: clear, $35.00; clear with enamel flower, $62.00; clear with gold decor, $48.00.

SIZE: 2⅜" tall x 2" wide

NOTES: *Their new line is called the Daisy and certainly does not belie its name in either quality of metal design or finish. The Daisy has strong oblong border lines, which enclose cross hatched diamond and central daisies alternately, while the bottoms of the bowls are radiated with strong reflecting incut lines... –January, 1897. The Daisy line is made in colored enamels, the flower being brought out strikingly in colors. It is also put on the market in gold decorations, and makes an attractive line in both enamel and gold. –February 1897.*

Toothpick
75 dozen in barrel
Gross weight of barrel 200 lbs.

Clear with cutting

Toothpick
60 dozen in barrel
Gross weight of barrel 170 lbs.

OMN: DOUGLASS

DATE: 1903

COLORS: clear, $38.00; clear with ruby stain, $80.00; clear with engraving, $58.00; clear with ruby (cranberry) interior, $138.00; clear with silver overlay, $60.00.

SIZE: 2⅜" tall x 1⅝" wide

Ruby stain on interior

Ruby stain and engraving

Clear

OMN: FAMOUS, No. 317

DATE: 1899

COLORS: clear, $40.00; clear, orange iridized, $45.00; clear with sterling silver rim, $48.00.

SIZE: 2½" tall x 2" wide

NOTES: Green is a possibility for this toothpick since other pieces of the pattern are known in green. This toothpick has been reproduced.

Opal decorated

Frog Toothpick
18 dozen in barrel
Gross weight of barrel 170 lbs.

OMN: FROG

AKA: FROG ON LILY PAD

DATE: ca. mid-1880s

COLORS: clear, $32.00; amber, $38.00; blue, $45.00; black, $35.00; opal decorated, $125.00+.

SIZE: 3½" tall x 2" wide

Clear

OMN: No. 323

AKA: LATTICE LEAF

DATE: 1906

COLORS: clear, $48.00; clear with gold decor, $52.00.

SIZE: 2¼" tall x 2" wide

NOTES: This pattern is illustrated in a Co-op catalog, but the toothpick is not shown.

Clear with gold decoration

Clear with ruby stain shield

OMN: MADOLINE

DATE: 1893

COLORS: clear, $18.00; clear with enamel, $28.00; clear with engraving, $28.00; clear with gold, $25.00; clear with ruby stain, $42.00.

SIZE: 2⅜" tall x 2⅛" wide

NOTES: *...a new table pattern, "Madoline," named for the little daughter of Mr. Chas. W. Klein, secretary and treasurer of the company... There are 60 pieces of this pattern and they have it in plain and engraved.* –July, 1893. *This is a perfectly plain pattern, the pieces are large and massive, and use as well as beauty was considered when it was designed. They have it in showy engravings, large and prominent... They have the "Madoline" in three different styles of decoration – enameled ferns, apple blossoms and daisies – and four different styles of gold decorations.* –January 1894. A January 1895 report stated: *The Madoline line has been rejuvenated and brought out in four new and catchy decorations, in floral, landscape, marine, and scroll designs.*

Toothpick
80 dozen in barrel
Gross weight of barrel 200 lbs.

Salt
75 dozen in barrel
Gross weight of barrel 195 lbs.

OMN: RADIANT

DATE: 1908

COLORS: clear, $45.00; clear with ruby stain, $148.00.

SIZE: unknown

NOTES: The original catalog illustration labels this a salt, an example of the uncommon mistakes in original catalogs.

Clear with cutting

OMN: RAY

DATE: 1921

COLORS: clear, $32.00; clear with cutting, $45.00.

SIZE: 2¼" tall x 1⅞" wide

NOTES: Shown in the Co-operative Flint Glass Co. catalog of 1921.

Toothpick.

Clear with enamel decoration

OMN: REGINA

AKA: REEDING

DATE: 1902

COLORS: clear, $45.00; clear with enamel decor, $55.00; clear with gold, $52.00.

SIZE: 2½" tall x 2" wide

NOTES: *...has two new lines for this year that will require very little coaching... The "Regina" is a semi or almost plain pattern with prisms at bottom. It is a pretty line and is highly commended by every one. The "Regina" is decorated in four different styles of crystal and gold and enameled and gold. The enamel is something new, being transparent, and produces a fine effect.* –January 1902.

Toothpick.

Toothpick
65 dozen in barrel
Gross weight of
barrel 195 lbs.

OMN: REX

DATE: unknown

COLORS: clear toothpick, $75.00; clear toy spoon, $38.00.

SIZE: unknown

NOTES: This pattern contains both a toothpick and a toy spoon, which are different in form.

Toy Spoon
90 dozen in barrel
Gross weight of barrel 190 lbs.

Opal with enamel decoration

OMN: ROYAL

DATE: unknown

COLORS: clear, $30.00; clear with ruby stain, $65.00; opal, $48.00; opal with enamel decor, $65.00.

SIZE: 2⅛" tall x 1⅞" wide at top

121—Toy Opal Pot
85 dozen in barrel
Gross weight of barrel 210 lbs.

OMN: TOY POT

DATE: unknown

COLORS: opal, $28.00.

SIZE: unknown

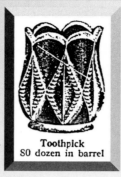

Toothpick
80 dozen in barrel

OMN: TWENTIETH CENTURY

DATE: unknown

COLORS: clear, $52.00; blue, $110.00.

SIZE: 2½" tall x 2" wide

NOTES: For similar patterns, see Helene by Central and Summit by Thompson.

Clear

Blue

DALZELL BROS. & GILMORE GLASS CO.
WELLSBURG, WEST VIRGINIA
1883 – 1888

DALZELL, GILMORE & LEIGHTON GLASS CO.
FINDLAY, OHIO
1888 – 1899

Dalzell Bros. & Gilmore was organized in 1883 by brothers Andrew C. Dalzell, James B. Dalzell, and W. A. B. Dalzell, along with E. D. Gilmore. Before the factory was completed in Wellsburg, West Virginia, they leased and operated the old Brilliant Glass Works at Brilliant, Ohio. The construction of the factory was plagued by problems, including a flood, and operation began in 1885. Andrew Dalzell died in 1887 within weeks of the announcement of the planned move of the factory to Findlay, Ohio. The Findlay factory opened and started to make glass in 1888.

The new Findlay concern, called Dalzell, Gilmore & Leighton, was organized by James Dalzell, W. A. B. Dalzell, E. D. Gilmore, William Leighton, Jr., and George Leighton (William's son). William Russell became plant manager. The Leightons were renowned for their knowledge of glass chemistry and design.

With the death of James Dalzell in 1893, W. A. B. Dalzell became the company president. In 1899 Dalzell, Gilmore & Leighton joined the National Glass Co. as Factory No. 6.

Tableware patterns made by Dalzell, Gilmore & Leighton include Reverse Torpedo, Genoese (Eyewinker), Columbia, Paragon, Alexis (Priscilla), Amazon, Ivanhoe, Quaker Lady, and Magnolia. The company was famous at the time for kerosene lamps and the clinch-on collar patented by W. A. B. Dalzell. The most famous ware made by this factory is its highly desirable Oriental Ware (Findlay Onyx) and Floradine.

See also National Glass Co., Factory No. 6.

OMN: ALEXIS, No. 61D

AKA: PRISCILLA

DATE: 1895

COLORS: clear, $55.00; clear with ruby stain, $285.00.

SIZE: 2⅜" tall x 2¼" wide

NOTES: Alexis was made in a full tableware assortment. Lamps in this pattern were made in green. According to a report of January 1895, the Oriental Glass Co. decorated the Alexis pattern. *In the forefront is the new "Alexis" pattern, consisting of three score and ten pieces of ware, each one of which is literally as pretty as a picture. The design is an original one, and it works out in the most brilliant ware possible to conceive, materials considered.* –January 1895, *CGL.*

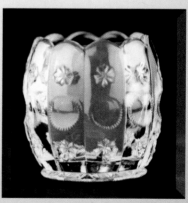

Clear

OMN: unknown

AKA: BULGING BARS

DATE: unknown

COLORS: clear, $90.00.

SIZE: 2½" tall x 2¼" wide

NOTES: This toothpick cannot be documented as Dalzell, since it has not been found in company catalogs. It was attributed to Dalzell, Gilmore & Leighton by the late William Heacock because of its similarity to a known Dalzell wine.

Clear

Satin ruby opalescent

OMN: FLORADINE

DATE: November 1888, for introduction as the new pattern of 1889

COLORS: satin ruby with opalescent white flowers, $1,500.00+; all other base colors with opalescent white flowers, $2,500.00+.

SIZE: 2⅜" tall x 2⅜" wide

NOTES: Floradine was made in the same shape molds as Oriental (Onyx), but today it is much more difficult to find. Both Floradine and Oriental are difficult to find in good condition as the glass is subject to easy breakage. Since the tops of the toothpicks were finished by grinding and polishing, heights may vary. There is a darker version of the color which is sometimes called cinnamon and also has white opalescent flowers. *Dalzell, Gilmore & Leighton Co. opened up the New Year with some of the handsomest novelties ever produced in this country which are destined to have an immense run. Among these is something entirely new being ruby and opalescent with raised figures of flowers and leaves, producing an effect of great beauty but which is indescribable."* –January 1889, CGL.

Clear

OMN: IVANHOE, No. 65D

DATE: 1897

COLORS: clear, $135.00.

SIZE: 2⅝" tall x 2⅛" wide

NOTES: This pattern was made in a full line of tableware.

Dalzell, Gilmore & Leighton Glass Co.

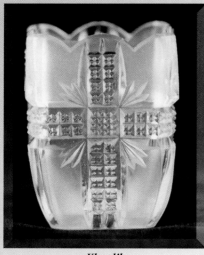

Klondike

75 D Toothpick.

OMN: No. 75D

AKA: KLONDIKE (when decorated)

DATE: 1898

COLORS: clear, $245.00; clear with amberette stain and satin panels, $625.00.

SIZE: 2⅜" tall x 1¾" wide

NOTES: *...a brand new line called Amberetta...which is probably the most original and unique in design of any shown this season. The shapes are generally square, though there are some rectangular and oval pieces, and there are narrow bands of neat small figuring crossing one another at the bottom, coming up the sides and going horizontally around each of the articles. They have this in plain crystal and also with the figured part in amber, and the effect is very striking and brilliant. They have it in transparent glass as well as satin finish... There are about 50 pieces altogether.* –January 1898, *CGL.* No. 75D refers to the clear pieces in this tableware pattern. Collectors have long called the amber and satin decorated pieces Klondike. Most pieces in the pattern are square. The pattern was continued in production while Dalzell was part of National Glass. Amberette is a generic term used by many Victorian companies to describe amber stain. This piece was possibly made in emerald green.

Clear

OMN: ORIENTAL

AKA: ONYX, FINDLAY ONYX

DATE: 1889

COLORS: cream, platinum flowers, $625.00.

SIZE: 2⅜" tall x 2⅜" wide

NOTES: Oriental (Onyx) is a wonderful art glass produced for tableware. The cream color with the platinum flowers is the most easily found variety, but there are rare examples of pieces in the pattern in various other color combinations, such as amber over cream and raspberry over cream. Shards dug at the factory site contain at least 30 different color combinations. Whether all of these were made commercially or were simply experimental is not known today. Known colors included in collections today include black, black with opal flowers, orange, peach, apricot, lemon, and opaque green with purple flowers. The Oriental ware was patented, the patent covering the design and the method of manufacture. The multiple layers of this exotic glass seem to create internal stresses in the glass, so that today it is fragile and often found with damage. Since the tops of these toothpicks were ground and polished, some height differences are likely. This piece was also made with flowers in other colors.

Cream with platinum flowers

DITHRIDGE & SON
PITTSBURGH, PENNSYLVANIA
1862 – 1873
(CONTINUED AS DITHRIDGE & CO. UNTIL 1890)

DITHRIDGE & CO.
JEANNETTE, PENNSYLVANIA
1890 – 1900

Dithridge and Co. evolved from the Curling & Price Glass Co., which had founded the Fort Pitt Glass Works in 1827. In 1862, Edward Dithridge became the sole owner of the firm, which specialized in kerosene lamp chimneys.

The firm reorganized in 1867 as Dithridge & Son. Another reorganization in 1873 changed the name to Dithridge & Co. In 1878, tableware and novelties were added to the product line. The company was well known for its many styles of table lamps. In 1890 the factory was moved to Jeannette, Pennsylvania, continuing the old designation of the Fort Pitt Glass Works but still using the company name of Dithridge & Co.

The factory became well known for its opal glass, and made many novelties, lamps, salt shakers, condiment sets, dresser sets, and toothpicks. Tableware patterns include Sultana, Astoria, Versailles, and Edgewood.

Opaque blue

OMN: unknown

AKA: CREASED BALE

DATE: 1894

COLORS: opaque colors: blue, $90.00; green, $85.00; ivory, $90.00; opal, $85.00; pink, $90.00.

SIZE: 2⅛" tall x 2⅛" wide

OMN: No. 59

AKA: HEART

DATE: 1894

COLORS: opaque colors: blue, $95.00; ivory (custard), $85.00; opal, $65.00; pink, $85.00.

SIZE: 2½" tall x 2¼" wide

Pink and blue

57

Dithridge & Co.

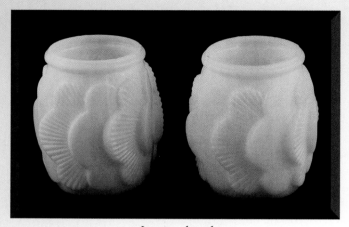

OMN: No. 50

AKA: SUNSET

DATE: 1894

Ivory and opal

COLORS: opaque colors: blue, $85.00; green, $85.00; ivory (custard), $110.00; opal, $85.00; pink, $90.00.

SIZE: 2¼" tall x 2⅛" wide

OMN: SWIRL

AKA: PRINCESS SWIRL

DATE: 1896

COLORS: opaque colors: blue, $90.00; opal, $65.00; pink, $90.00; blue, plated (cased), $115.00; opal, plated (cased), $110.00; pink, plated (cased), $115.00.

SIZE: unknown

NOTES: The pattern is shown as the salt shaker in the lower right of the 1896 ad.

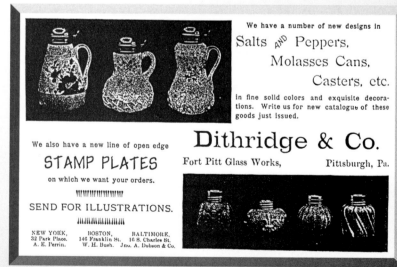

We have a number of new designs in

Salts AND **Peppers,**

Molasses Cans,

Casters, etc.

In fine solid colors and exquisite decorations. Write us for new catalogue of these goods just issued.

We also have a new line of open edge

STAMP PLATES

on which we want your orders.

SEND FOR ILLUSTRATIONS.

Dithridge & Co.

Fort Pitt Glass Works,   Pittsburgh, Pa.

NEW YORK,   BOSTON,   BALTIMORE.
32 Park Place.   146 Franklin St.   16 S. Charles St.
A. E. Perrin.   W. H. Bush.   Jno. A. Dobson & Co.

DOYLE & CO.
PITTSBURGH, PENNSYLVANIA
1855 – 1891

In 1855 William Doyle, Joseph Doyle, and others organized Doyle & Co. in Pittsburgh's South Side. The factory was destroyed by fire in 1878 and was rebuilt immediately. During this period, its products included barware, novelties, stemware, and tableware. Chimneys for kerosene lamps were manufactured at the Phillipsburgh Glass Works in Monaca, Pennsylvania. In 1891, the factory joined the U.S. Glass combine and was designated Factory P.

Patterns made by Doyle include Red Block, Doyle's Shell, Paneled Forget-Me-Not, and Hobnail with Thumbprint Base.

OMN: No. 150

AKA: HOBNAIL WITH THUMBPRINT BASE

DATE: mid-to-late 1880s

COLORS: clear, $28.00; amber, $45.00; blue, $60.00.

OMN: No. 500

AKA: HONEYCOMB, DOYLE'S

DATE: unknown

COLORS: clear, $32.00; blue, $65.00; canary, $70.00.

SIZE: 2¼" tall x 2" wide

Clear

DUGAN GLASS CO.
INDIANA, PENNSYLVANIA
1904 – 1913

By 1904 the National Glass Co. had disbanded and ceased the manufacture of glass. When it began selling the old factories, Thomas Dugan and others purchased the old Northwood Glass Works at Indiana, Pennsylvania. Production of glass was continuous at this site since Thomas Dugan was the new general manager, the same position he had held with National Glass Co. Dugan marked some National wares with its trademark, a *D* within a diamond.

The company made novelties, lamps, and tableware in clear and opalescent colors. Some known patterns include Erie and Victor. Dugan also continued some of the patterns originally made by Northwood/National.

OMN: ERIE

AKA: BEADED OVALS IN SAND

DATE: Ca. 1906

COLORS: clear, $135.00; clear with gold decor, $145.00; blue, $235.00; blue with gold decor, $250.00; green, $190.00; green with gold decor; $210.00; green with enamel decor, $215.00.

SIZE: 2⅜" tall x 2" wide

NOTES: Still available in 1906. Also made without the small circles of beads on the base, possibly due to a worn mold.

Green with enameled flowers and gold decoration, clear

OMN: VICTOR

AKA: JEWELED HEART

DATE: 1905

Green with gold decoration   *Blue with gold decoration*

COLORS: clear, $125.00; clear opalescent, $165.00; blue, $190.00; blue opalescent, $295.00; green, $180.00; green opalescent, $240.00; ivory (custard), $2,800.00+.

SIZE: 2⅜" tall x 2" wide

NOTES: Some of these toothpicks are found with the Dugan trademark. *The second line, the Victor, also in imitation cut, appears in no less than twelve different styles. Three plain colors, three different styles of decoration, three opalescents, and three kinds of "flashes."* –January 1905. This toothpick has been reproduced by L. G. Wright in clear decorated, ruby, amethyst, green, and amber as its Sweetheart pattern. The old is distinguished by the ridge under the base. The old has 24 beads around the base, while the new has only 20.

GEO. DUNCAN & SONS
PITTSBURGH, PENNSYLVANIA
1874 – 1891

Geo. Duncan & Sons began when Mr. Duncan bought out the widows and remaining heirs of the D. C. Ripley Co. of Pittsburgh's South Side. His son, James E., and son-in-law, A. H. Heisey, ran the company successfully, making many desirable tableware patterns and novelties.

In 1891, the company joined U.S. Glass and was designated Factory D. After suffering a disastrous fire in 1892, the plant closed and was not rebuilt, although U.S. Glass used the remaining buildings as a decorating shop for many years.

James E. Duncan started his own glass company, which became known as Duncan & Miller, in Washington, Pennsylvania, in 1893. A. H. Heisey started his glass company, A. H. Heisey & Co., in Newark, Ohio, in 1896.

Geo. Duncan & Sons made a distinction between amber and old gold, old gold being a softer, paler version of amber. Patterns made include the popular Snail, Shell and Tassel, Block, Three Face (all toothpicks in this pattern are *new*!), and Beaded Swirl. The colors in the listings are the names used by Geo. Duncan & Sons.

See also Duncan & Miller.

Canary

OMN: CHAIR, No. 2

DATE: 1886

COLORS: clear, $125.00; amber, $155.00; old gold, $155.00; blue, $185.00; canary, $195.00.

SIZE: 3½" tall x 2⅛" wide

NOTES: Duncan's chair is shaped somewhat like an old-fashioned bath tub and sometimes is referred to as a sitz bath toothpick. The pattern used is not Daisy and Button, but a variation called Daisy and Square. Duncan also made another chair with a solid seat.

OMN: GYPSY KETTLE

DATE: 1886

COLORS: clear, $35.00; amber, $65.00; old gold, $65.00; blue, $80.00; canary, $90.00.

SIZE: 2⅜" tall x 2½" wide at top

NOTES: Original Duncan price lists do not list a use for this piece, although it might be a match holder, as it is slightly larger than most toothpicks. Many other companies made a variety of kettles. Duncan's has the Daisy and Square motif, not a true Daisy and Button, and has no feet.

Amber

Amber

HAT TOOTHPICK.
PATENTED.

OMN: HOBNAIL HAT

DATE: 1885

COLORS: clear, $22.00; amber, $32.00; old gold, $32.00; blue, $50.00; canary, $50.00; clear with amber ribbon, $95.00.

SIZE: 2⅝" tall x 3⅛" wide

Clear with amber band

NOTES: These hobnail (Daisy and Button) hats were made in four sizes: salt, toothpick, spoon, and celery. Similar hats have been made more or less continuously since Duncan brought out this novelty in 1885. Duncan hats usually have a ground bottom, clearly visible on examination. The toothpick size was continued by U.S. Glass.

Amber, canary, and blue

OMN: LITTLE GERMAN BAND CAP

DATE: 1886

COLORS: clear, $60.00; amber, $110.00; old gold, $110.00; blue, $130.00; canary, $135.00.

SIZE: 1⅞" tall x 2½" wide

NOTES: The original catalogs illustrating this piece do not give a function. It is collected by both toothpick and open salt collectors.

OMN: POLKA DOT HAT

DATE: 1884

COLORS: clear, $65.00; amber, $130.00; old gold, $130.00; blue, $152.00; canary, $165.00.

SIZE: 2¼" tall x 3¾" wide at brim

NOTES: One of the earliest toothpicks made. Since each has a hand-tooled brim, sizes may vary, as do shapes.

Blue and amber

GEO. DUNCAN'S SONS & CO.
WASHINGTON, PENNSYLVANIA
1893 – 1900

DUNCAN & MILLER GLASS CO.
1900 – 1955

The new tableware factory of Geo. Duncan's Sons & Co. went into operation for the first time last Thursday, February 9, and made an excellent start. They had intended to be ready earlier, but the extreme cold of January retarded the building operations and kept them back several weeks at least. There is no more complete glass factory in the country and it is finished in every detail with brand new machinery and equipments. The buildings are of brick, with dressed stone foundations, and strength, solidity, and perfect adaptation to glass making purposes are features of all of them. The factory proper, or blow-house, is 96 feet square, with iron roof, and is admirably designed for light and ventilation. It has a 16 pot furnace, four glory holes and eight fifty foot lears; also mold oven. The pot arch is separate from the main building, but sufficiently near for convenience and is connected with it by an iron bridge. The other buildings are constructed around an open space, this plan being adopted to lessen the danger from the extension of fire should any break out, and also to give more light and air to the various departments contained in them. There is a basement 12 feet in the clear under all the buildings and they are three stories in height, each story being 12 feet high also. In the basement is the blacksmith shop and engine room, the latter fitted with a powerful and smooth running engine which furnishes the motive power for the whole concern. The mold shop is especially commodious, being 30 x 100 feet in dimensions and containing new lathes and other machinery all through. The engraving and cutting are over the mold shop and of the same size, and the storing room for packages which is also of ample dimensions is adjacent to them. The mixing room is furnished with solid oak bins for sand and other materials for mixing purposes and here also are the fireproof vaults for the storage of material. These are built in the strongest possible manner and pointed with cement. The packing room is 40 x 150 feet and directly above it is a warehouse for loose goods of the same size. There is a railroad siding 800 feet long connecting the works with the Pan-Handle railroad, and a large covered platform is being built alongside this to facilitate shipments. The office building is detached from the main building and is elegantly fitted up in polished wood. There are four rooms for office work down stairs and the sample room occupies the entire second floor. It has light on all four sides, and is splendidly finished, the walls and ceiling as well as floors being of highly varnished wood. The company have plenty of room for increasing the plant, should such become necessary, as their lot is 300 x 400 feet only about one quarter of which they have in use now. The location is a very pretty one, being near that of the Washington County fair grounds and a paved street runs right out to it. Besides the Pan-Handle Railroad, connecting the place with the entire Pennsylvania system, the Baltimore & Ohio Railroad also runs to the town and the facilities for transportation are all that can be wished for. Natural gas is plentiful in this district and the factory is operated with this fuel exclusively. There is plenty of petroleum about the place too. The products of the works will be tableware and bar goods, including blown tumblers. ... They will continue to add to their line as they go along. Washington is the county seat of Washington Co., and a thriving town of about 12,000 inhabitants. It has first class hotels, is well paved and lighted and is only about an hour's ride from Pittsburgh. –February 1893, CGL.

After leaving U.S. Glass, James E. Duncan, along with his brother Harry, built a new, modern factory in Washington, Pennsylvania. Trading on the good will and reputation of his father's company, Geo. Duncan & Sons, the new company was named Geo. Duncan's Sons & Co. J. Ernest Miller, their master moldmaker, was a partner in the firm, and following a reorganization in 1900, the company became Duncan & Miller Glass Co.

It is announced on good authority that James E. Duncan, formerly of George Duncan & Sons, Harry B. Duncan, J. Ernest Miller, and others will erect a large tableware factory at Washington. A sixteen-pot furnace is projected, and everything will be on an extensive scale. It is said that work on the new building will be commenced at once. –August 1892, CGL.

The factory operated successfully for many years with the Duncan family in charge of the company. In 1955, the company was bought out by Tiffin Glass of Tiffin, Ohio, and molds were moved to either the Tiffin plant or the Glassport, Pennsylvania, plant.

Duncan & Miller became well known for its attractive opalescent wares, swans, and popular tableware patterns. Some patterns include Homestead, Two Ply Swirl, Flower and Scroll, Mardi Gras, Teepee, Hobnail, Canterbury, and Early American Sandwich.

OMN: No. 40

AKA: BASSETTOWN

DATE: 1898

COLORS: clear, $75.00; clear with ruby stain, $165.00+.

SIZE: 2½" tall x 1⅞" wide

NOTES: Made in a full tableware line while the company name was Geo. Duncan's Sons & Co.

Clear

Clear

OMN: No. 50

AKA: BLOCK & ROSETTE

DATE: 1902

COLORS: clear, $110.00; clear with ruby stain, $350.00+; clear with rose stain, $385.00+; clear with gold decor, $170.00.

SIZE: 2⅜" tall x 2" wide

NOTES: *No. "50" is a beautifully figured hexagonal block rose pattern, strongly resembling cut, but quite out of the ordinary and very original. The line comprises about 75 pieces. It is made in crystal and crystal and gold. –January 1902.* Oriental Glass decorated this pattern with ruby stain.

OMN: No.56

AKA: BLOCKED THUMBPRINT BAND

DATE: 1904

COLORS: clear, $45.00; clear with ruby stain, $68.00; clear with gold decor, $48.00; clear with silver overlay, $75.00.

SIZE: 2¼" tall x 1¾" wide

NOTES: One of Duncan & Miller's colonial-inspired tableware lines. It is often seen with ruby stain.

Clear, cut

Clear with gold band and engraving

Clear with ruby stain

OMN: No. 39

AKA: BUTTON ARCHES

DATE: 1897

COLORS: clear, $22.00; clear with ruby stain, $45.00; clear with ruby stain and engraving, $45.00; clear with ruby stain and gold band, $45.00; clear with ruby stain and white band, $45.00; clear with gold band(s), $35.00; clear with gold, red, and enamel band, $45.00; clear with engraving, $38.00.

SIZE: 2¼" tall x 1¾" wide

NOTES: Made in a full tableware assortment while the company name was Geo. Duncan's Sons & Co. Decorations,

Clear with ruby stain

Clear with gold band

including the engravings, were done at the Oriental Glass Co. of Pittsburgh. *The Oriental Glass Co. are having a fine trade on their No. 39 ware. It is beautifully decorated in two styles — ruby, gold and crystal and gold.* –October 1901. *One of the Oriental's great leaders at present is their No. "39" pattern in ruby matt and gold matt, decorations that are very pleasing and attractive...* –January 1902. This toothpick remained in the Duncan & Miller line for many years, at least until 1927. Note that early examples have a serrated scalloped rim while in later examples the scallops are plain. Later production of this toothpick (and a few other pieces) was made in a pale milky white (clambroth) by Jefferson Glass Co. and probably ruby stain on clear.

OMN: No. 44

AKA: BUTTON PANEL

DATE: 1900

COLORS: Toothpick: clear, $70.00; clear with ruby stain, $265.00; clear with gold decor, $80.00. Toy spooner: clear, $70.00; clear with ruby stain, $245.00; clear with gold decor, $85.00.

SIZE: Toothpick: 2½" tall x 1⅞" wide. Toy spooner: 2⅝" tall x 1⅞" wide.

NOTES: Made in a wide variety of tableware items while the company name was Geo. Duncan's Sons & Co. Decorated by Oriental Glass Co. The toothpick and the toy spooner are almost identical, but the toothpick has a row of four buttons while the spooner has five.

Clear with ruby stain

Clear, toothpick and child's spooner

OMN: No. 58

AKA: CLOVER

DATE: 1905

COLORS: clear, $60.00; clear with gold decor, $70.00; clear with ruby stain, $175.00.

SIZE: 2⅜" tall, 1⅞" wide

NOTES: *"Prism and hob nail tells the story,"* according to Mr. Lindsay, the representative of the Duncan & Miller Glass Co., of his new line of general tableware. Some [pieces] are with figured foot or feet (which is grammatical when you are speaking of glass?). –January 1905. This is a more modern interpretation of old pressed glass patterns, using plain panels alternating with daisy and button panels. Clover was made in a full tableware line.

Clear

OMN: No. 48

AKA: DIAMOND RIDGE

DATE: 1901

COLORS: Toothpick: clear, $60.00; clear with gold ridges, $80.00; clear with gold top rim, $80.00. Bar glass: clear, $80.00; clear with gold ridges, $90.00; clear with gold top rim, $90.00.

SIZE: Toothpick: 2½" tall x 2" wide. Bar glass: 2⅝" tall x 2⅛" wide at top.

NOTES: The bar glass was also sometimes sold as a toothpick, as shown in early advertisements.

Clear, toothpick and bar glass

Clear, cut

OMN: No. 54

AKA: GABLE

DATE: 1903

COLORS: clear, $55.00; clear with engraving or cutting, $60.00.

SIZE: 2¼" tall x 1⅞" wide (without handles)

NOTES: A colonial type of pattern, most likely designed to compete with Heisey's various colonial lines and also those of other companies.

OMN: No. 20

AKA: GRATED DIAMOND & SUNBURST

DATE: 1894

COLORS: clear, $42.00; clear with ruby stain, $185.00+; clear with amber stain, $185.00+.

SIZE: 2⅜" tall x 2" wide

NOTES: Made while the company name was Geo. Duncan's Sons & Co. in a full tableware line. A trade announcement in January of 1895 stated that L. J. Rodgers of Pittsburgh was decorating Duncan's No. 20. Decorations listed were ruby stain, amber stain, gold, and colored enamels. Whether all these decorations were applied to the No. 20 toothpick was not clear. *No. 20, which made such a big hit last fall, contains 65 pieces...* –January 1895.

Clear

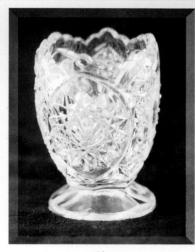

Clear

OMN: No. 63

AKA: HOMESTEAD

DATE: 1907

COLORS: clear, $95.00; clear with ruby stain, $240.00+.

SIZE: 2⅝" tall x 1⅞" wide

NOTES: This was a large line for Duncan & Miller. Some pieces, but not the toothpick, in the pattern were made by Tiffin/U.S. Glass after 1955 in several colors.

OMN: No. 68

AKA: KING ARTHUR

DATE: 1908

COLORS: clear, $80.00; clear with gold decor, $95.00.

SIZE: 2" tall x 1⅞" wide

NOTES: Tarentum made some pieces, at least the water set, in a pattern very similar to King Arthur, but in inferior, slightly yellowish glass. It is not known whether it made a toothpick.

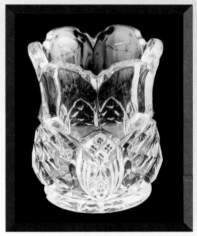

Clear

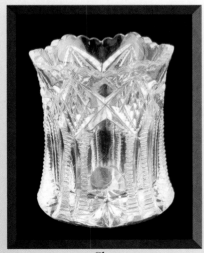

Clear

OMN: No. 52

AKA: LADDER WITH DIAMONDS

DATE: 1903

COLORS: clear, $60.00; clear with gold decor, $70.00; clear with ruby stain, $260.00.

SIZE: 2¼" tall x 2" wide

NOTES: *The Duncan & Miller Glass Co. W. B. Lindsay reports a brisk demand for this old established company's high grade of ware and has a good leader in the No. 52 imitation cut tableware set which has a fluted pillar effect and is embellished with heavy gold decoration. One hundred pieces constitute the new line. –January 1903.* Compare this with the Tarentum toothpick, Ladders with Diamonds. Duncan's pattern has large diamonds that are divided into many small diamonds around the top. Tarentum's has hobnails in this area. Duncan's Ladder with Diamonds was decorated by Oriental Glass Co. in ruby and gold.

Duncan & Miller Glass Co.

OMN: No. 42

AKA: MARDI GRAS

DATE: 1899

COLORS: Toothpick: clear, $45.00; clear with ruby stain, $175.00+; clear with gold decor, $55.00. Miniature rose bowl: clear, $40.00; clear with ruby stain, $135.00+; clear with gold decor, $50.00. Toy spooner: clear, $40.00; clear with ruby stain, $140.00+; clear with gold decor, $50.00.

SIZE: Toothpick: 2½" tall x 2" wide. Toy spooner: 2⅝" tall x 2" wide. Miniature rose bowl: 2⅛" tall x 2½" wide.

NOTES: Made while the company name was Geo. Duncan's Sons & Co. A very popular pattern made in a wide variety of pieces, including a child's table set, the spooner of which is often confused for a toothpick. Note that the miniature rose bowl is made from the toothpick mold and the top is hand tooled inward.

Clear, toy spooner and toothpick

Clear with silver overlay

OMN: No. 65

AKA: POLISHED MIRRORS

DATE: 1907

COLORS: clear, $42.00; clear with gold decor, $50.00; clear with silver overlay, $50.00.

SIZE: 2⅜" tall x 2" wide

NOTES: A colonial style, almost reminiscent of cut glass toothpicks with the large faceted areas around the base.

Clear with engraved gold band

Clear

OMN: No. 55

AKA: QUARTERED BLOCK

DATE: 1903

COLORS: clear, $55.00; clear with gold on top half, $60.00.

SIZE: 1⅜" tall x 1½" wide

NOTES: This tableware pattern was made in a wide variety of pieces, including kerosene lamps, in several sizes.

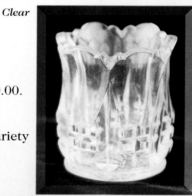

Clear with ruby stain

OMN: No. 24

AKA: QUARTERED BLOCK & DIAMONDS

DATE: 1895

COLORS: clear, $42.00; clear with ruby stain, $185.00+; clear with amber stain, $185.00+.

SIZE: 2½" tall x 1¾" wide

NOTES: This was a huge tableware line advertised as having 95 pieces. No. 24 was made by Geo. Duncan's Sons & Co. before it became Duncan & Miller. *It is a fine imitation of cut ware, in diamond and palm figure, and shows up splendidly in the brilliant metal used.* –January 1895. From the introduction, trade journal reports indicate that L. J. Rodgers of Pittsburgh was decorating Duncan's No. 24. Decorations listed include ruby stain, amber stain, gold, and enamels. It was not clear whether all of these were done on No. 24.

Clear with gold

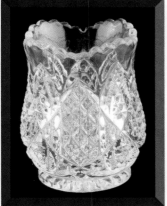
Clear

Clear, vase shape

OMN: No. 30

AKA: SCALLOPED SIX POINT

DATE: 1896

COLORS: Toothpick: clear, $40.00; clear with ruby stain, $165.00; clear with gold decor, $50.00. Vase shape: clear, $40.00; clear with ruby stain, $165.00; clear with gold decor, $50.00. Miniature rose bowl: clear, $40.00; clear with ruby stain, $165.00; clear with gold decor, $50.00.

SIZE: Toothpick: 2½" tall x 2" wide. Vase shape: 2" tall x 2¼" wide. Miniature rose bowl: 2⅛" tall x 2½" wide

NOTES: *The large, heavy punch bowl, a deep cut pattern, with bold, broad curved lines, handsomely filled in with a small, square cut figure, scalloped cut edge, plain rim and broad star bottom, finely balanced between the cut figure and plain surfaces...* –September 30, 1896. Designed by J. Ernest Miller. By December it was being advertised as being made in 175 pieces, available with gold decoration. Trade journals state that Oriental Glass decorated this pattern with ruby stain and gold. Made by Geo. Duncan's Sons & Co. in an immense tableware line. The toothpick also comes in a shape that looks like a tiny spittoon or vase. The toothpick mold was also used to form a miniature rose bowl. This is an odd name for this pattern as it has eight points, not six.

Clear

OMN: No. 75

AKA: STAR IN SQUARE

DATE: 1909

COLORS: clear, $110.00; clear with ruby stain, $240.00.

SIZE: 2¼" tall x 1⅝" wide

NOTES: This pattern was probably inspired by an old Geo. Duncan & Sons pattern called Zippered Block which is quite similar. This was a full tableware line.

Clear with ruby stain

OMN: No. 67

AKA: SUNBURST IN OVAL

DATE: 1908

COLORS: clear, $85.00; clear with gold decor, $95.00; clear with ruby stain, $500.00+.

SIZE: 2¼" tall x 1⅝" wide

NOTES: Made in a full line of tableware.

Clear with gold

69

OMN: No. 80

AKA: SUNFLOWER PATCH

DATE: 1912

COLORS: clear, $95.00; clear with allover ruby stain and gold, $265.00+.

SIZE: 2¼" tall x 1¾" wide

NOTES: Available in a full line of tableware. The allover ruby stain with gold highlights is difficult to find in any piece and quite desirable.

Clear

Clear

OMN: No. 61

AKA: SWEET 61

DATE: 1906

COLORS: clear, $48.00; clear with silver overlay, $75.00.

SIZE: 2¾" tall x 2⅛" wide

NOTES: An extensive colonial-styled line made by Duncan & Miller.

OMN: No. 28

AKA: TEPEE

DATE: 1896

COLORS: clear, $50.00; clear with ruby stain, $185.00+; clear with amber stain, $185.00+.

SIZE: 2⅜" tall x 2" wide

NOTES: *The new No. 28, an elegant scallop edged set of heavy cut glass imitation, is decidedly strong in the larger pieces, the prismatic color distributing effect of their sharp cutting showing up the brilliancy and purity of the metal to fine advantage, while their triangular nappies, comports, and the inthrown and dimple lipped olive dishes are among the best products of American pressed glassware. This set consists of 100 pieces... –January 1896.* A very popular tableware line with many pieces. This pattern was made while the company name was Geo. Duncan's Sons & Co.

Clear

Clear

Clear with ruby stain

OMN: No. 73

AKA: THUMBNAIL

DATE: 1909

COLORS: clear, $52.00; clear with gold decor, $60.00; clear with ruby stain, $195.00.

SIZE: 2⅜" tall x 2" wide

NOTES: Made in a full tableware line, often with gold decoration around the tops of pieces, resulting in very showy pieces.

Clear with gold

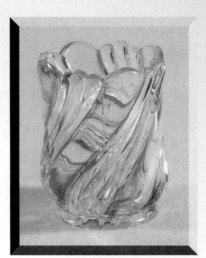

Clear with rose and gold

OMN: No. 51

AKA: TWO PLY SWIRL

DATE: 1902

COLORS: clear, $60.00; clear with gold decor, $72.00; clear with rose stain, $175.00; clear with ruby stain, $175.00.

SIZE: 2⅜" tall x 1⅞" wide

NOTES: *No. "51" is also a thing of beauty, being an oval twist fluted pattern, alternated with imitation cut flutes. There are about 60 pieces in this line. It is very rich and effective with the oval flute decorated in gold. It is also made in rose decoration-the color being put on the oval flute. –January 1902. Oriental Glass decorated Two Ply Swirl with ruby stain.*

OMN: No. 46

AKA: ZIPPER EDGE PANELS

DATE: 1900

COLORS: clear, $95.00; clear with ruby stain, $225.00+.

SIZE: 2¼" tall x 1⅞" wide

NOTES: Made while the company name was Geo. Duncan's Sons & Co. This pattern was an early colonial-inspired pattern.

OMN: No. 2005

AKA: ZIPPER SLASH

DATE: 1894

COLORS: clear, $28.00; clear with ruby stain, $52.00; clear with amber stain, $60.00; clear with engraving, $30.00; clear with enamel & satin, $38.00; clear with amber stain and satin finish, $95.00.

SIZE: 2¼" tall x 2" wide

NOTES: *A full tableware line of Geo. Duncan's Sons & Co. The old favorite No. 2005 is there in amber stain and engraved, and will hold its own still against anything of the kind in the field.* –January 1895.

Clear with satin finish and enamel decoration

Clear with satin finish and amber leaves

Clear with amber stain and satin finish leaves

Clear with ruby stain

EAGLE GLASS & MANUFACTURING CO.
WELLSBURG, WEST VIRGINIA
1895 – 1917

This company was organized in 1895 by brothers James, Joseph, H. W., and Samuel Paull in Wellsburg (Lazearville), West Virginia. In 1902 a fire occurred. The factory was damaged, but it was rebuilt. In 1911 the company went through a reorganization, but it continued in business until 1917. At that time the company stopped making glass, but it continued to make metal ware.

Much of the glassware production was of opal glass novelties, toothpicks, salt shakers, vanity sets, lamps, syrups, and sugar shakers.

OMN: BOWKNOT

AKA: BUNDLED CIGARS

DATE: 1899

COLORS: clear, $38.00; amber, $50.00; blue, $50.00; opal, $52.00; opal with gold decor, $58.00.

SIZE: 2⅛" tall x 1⅞" wide

NOTES: Has been reproduced in many colors. Some toothpicks have the legend "Wheeling, The Stogie City" on the bottom. Advertised in Butler Bros. catalog of 1892 as "Our 'Beauty' Match or Toothpick Stand Beautiful beyond words. Assorted in three colors. Price, 37 cents a dozen."

Opal with gold decoration

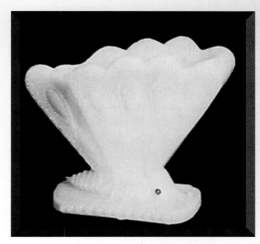

Opal

OMN: BUTTERFLY

DATE: 1899

COLORS: opal, $55.00.

SIZE: 2¾" tall x 1¼" wide x 3⅜" long

NOTES: According to company literature, this is a match container.

OMN: No. 15

AKA: FIBER BUNDLE

DATE: 1897

COLORS: blue opaque, $68.00; opal, $58.00; opal with gold decor, $72.00.

SIZE: 2" tall x 2⅛" wide

NOTES: *...in figured and decorated we have...gold corded vase toothpicks.* –February 1897.

Opal with gold decoration

Opal with enamel

OMN: No. 45

DATE: 1899

COLORS: opal, $48.00; opal, enamel decorated, $68.00.

SIZE: 2¼" tall x 2⅛" wide

ENTERPRISE MANUFACTURING CO.
AKRON, OHIO
EXACT DATES UNKNOWN

This company manufactured several novelties in the 1880s, including Luminous Match Safes.

Amber

OMN: BABY MINE

DATE: 1883

COLORS: clear, $38.00; clear, satin finish, $42.00; amber, $50.00; blue, $65.00; green, $60.00; opal, $68.00.

SIZE: 3½" tall x 4" long

NOTES: "Baby Mine" is embossed on the elephant's belly, readable from the top opening. Known in a wide variety of color shades. This was originally a candy container with a sliding tin top.

EVANSVILLE GLASS CO.
EVANSVILLE, INDIANA
1904 – 1907

This little-known company was organized by Jacob Rosenthal and William Barris and began producing glass in 1904. In less than a year it reorganized, and it declared bankruptcy by 1907.

Products made include novelties and tableware. The best-documented pattern of this company is Fernette.

Clear

OMN: FERNETTE

DATE: 1906

COLORS: clear, $42.00.

SIZE: 2½" tall x 2½" wide

NOTES: After the dissolution of Evansville Glass Co., at least some of the molds were moved to the second Canton Glass Co., as records indicate this pattern was made by Canton in 1920. This is not the company that joined National Glass as has been suggested in the past, since this was the second company to bear the name of Canton Glass. The molds and machinery from the first Canton Glass Co., which had joined National Glass, were moved to the Cambridge, Ohio, plant. See discussion under Canton Glass Co.

FEDERAL GLASS CO.
COLUMBUS, OHIO
1900 – 1980

The career glassmakers Robert and George Beatty organized Federal Glass in 1900 as a bottle plant. In 1906, they began producing tableware. They were quite successful, since the company remained in business until 1980.

Over the years they made bottles, canning jars, jellies, tableware, bar goods, and novelties. They are well known for Depression glass patterns, which they made in the late 1920s and 1930s.

OMN: No. 1905

AKA: FEATHERED POINTS

DATE: ca. 1905

COLORS: clear, $38.00.

SIZE: unknown

OMN: No. 1910

AKA: INDIAN SUNSET

DATE: ca. 1910

COLORS: clear, $38.00.

SIZE: unknown

FENTON ART GLASS CO.
MARTINS FERRY, OHIO — 1905 – 1907
WILLIAMSTOWN, WEST VIRGINIA
1907 – PRESENT

The Fenton Art Glass Co. was begun by two brothers, Frank L. and John W. Fenton. The company opened in 1905 strictly as a decorating company. *The Fenton Art Glass Co., of Martins Ferry, O., doing business in the old West Virginia plant, has been incorporated under the laws of the state of Ohio, with $20,000 capital stock. The company organized for business a few months ago and are doing a general decorating, enameling, gilding and designing of glassware business. Their line consists of tableware, bar bottles, lemonade sets, and novelties and the new company has already worked up a splendid trade which is constantly increasing.* –July 1905. In 1907, the company began to make glass after moving to Williamstown, West Virginia.

While Fenton made some tableware, most of its products throughout the years were decorative pieces. These became popular because of unusual colors and decorations. Fenton produced much early carnival glass. For a time, Jacob Rosenthal of Indiana Tumbler & Goblet worked at Fenton, bringing his formula for chocolate glass with him. A modest amount of chocolate glass was made by Fenton at this time and, more recently, in the 1980s.

Fenton is still in business, making mainly decorative items and figurines that are often elaborately decorated.

OMN: unknown

AKA: URN, FENTON'S

DATE: ca. 1920s

COLORS: blue, $65.00; canary, $65.00; green, $62.00.

SIZE: 2½" tall x 2⅛" wide across top

NOTES: There may be other colors, and these may also have been made with an iridescent finish. This looks more like a tiny vase than a true toothpick.

Blue

FINDLAY FLINT GLASS CO.
FINDLAY, OHIO
1889 – 1891

The Findlay Flint Glass Co. was organized in 1889 with the following officers: W. B. Ely, president; J. Q. Ashburn, vice president; C. W. Klein, secretary; and E. F. Dunn, treasurer. William McNaughton was hired as manager of the factory.

After operating less than two years, Findlay Flint suffered a disastrous fire on June 6, 1891, which completely destroyed the factory. It was never rebuilt.

In its short life, Findlay Flint made several notable patterns, including No. 9 Block & Double Bar, Dot (Stippled Forget Me Not), Pillar, No. 19, Spur Hobnail, and Shell. Novelties made include the Squash condiment set, the Butterfly toothpick, the Drawers toothpick, and the Elephant Head mustard or toothpick.

Clear

OMN: No. 9

AKA: BLOCK & DOUBLE BAR

DATE: 1889

COLORS: clear, $168.00.

SIZE: 2¼" tall x 2½" wide

NOTES: This is either a toothpick or the base of a mustard. Pieces of this pattern, mainly tumblers, are known with ruby stain.

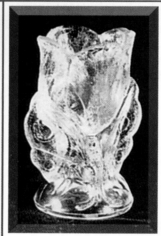

Clear

OMN: BUTTERFLY

AKA: BUTTERFLY & TULIP

DATE: 1889 – 1891

COLORS: clear, $370.00+.

SIZE: 3⅛" tall x 2¼" wide

Clear

OMN: DOT

AKA: STIPPLED FORGET ME NOT

DATE: 1890

COLORS: clear, $135.00.

SIZE: 2⅜" tall x 1⅝" wide

NOTES: A child's set was made in this pattern, but it lacks the leaves and flowers common to other pieces. The child's spooner also has a small foot, while the toothpick sits flat. This pattern was made in a full tableware assortment, and pieces are known in opal, blue, and amber, so be aware that the toothpick may also have been made in these colors.

Child's spooner, clear

Clear

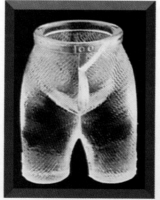

OMN: DRAWERS

DATE: 1889 – 1891

COLORS: clear, $120.00.

SIZE: 2⅞" tall x 2¼" wide

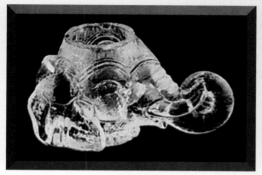

Clear

AKA: ELEPHANT HEAD

DATE: 1889 – 1891

COLORS: clear, $115.00; amber, $225.00; blue, $275.00.

SIZE: Old: 2⅜" tall x 2" wide x 4⅜" long. New: 2½" tall x 4⅜" long.

NOTES: This novelty may have been a mustard container, as small lids that fit the top are known. It has been reproduced by the Crystal Art Glass Co. of Cambridge, OH (Degenhart), in a wide variety of colors. Findlay Flint made it only in the three colors listed, so any other colors are reproductions. The major differences between the two are: 1. Tusks are shorter and do not go though the front loop of the trunk on the original. 2. Dot from the headdress is directly in front of the eye on the original. On the new the dot is above the level of the eye. 3. Between the headdress and the loop of the trunk are three large folds of skin on the original. The reproduction has four folds.

OMN: MILLER

AKA: HERRINGBONE RIB

DATE: 1891

COLORS: clear, $350.00+.

SIZE: 2¾" tall x 2" wide

Clear

NOTES: *Their latest novelty is the "Miller" mustard or toothpick. It is an imitation of a teapot and is named after the inventor, J. A. Miller, who is boss mold maker at the works. It will no doubt be a big seller.* –April 1891, *CGL.* Since Findlay Flint burned completely in early June of 1891, this is perhaps the most elusive toothpick made by the company. Very few examples are known.

FOSTORIA GLASS CO.
FOSTORIA, OHIO — 1887 – 1891
MOUNDSVILLE, WEST VIRGINIA
1891 – 1986

This company was organized in 1887 by Lucian Martin, W. S. Brady, Charles Beam, Charles Foster, and Otto Jaeger. At least three of these men had formerly been associated with Hobbs, Brockunier & Co. of Wheeling, West Virginia.

In 1891 the company moved to Moundsville, and existing molds were sent from Fostoria to the new factory. According to local lore, the molds for the popular Victoria pattern were not transferred, and their fate is not known.

The company remained successful for many years, making the transition from pressed tableware to dinnerware sets and blown ware in the late 1920s. The company had with many popular etchings. Early patterns made by the company include Bedford, Diana, Valencia, Robin Hood, Priscilla, Rococo, Wedding Bells, Sylvan, Atlanta, and others. The most enduring pattern made was American, some pieces of which are still produced today by Indiana Glass Co.

OMN: ALEXIS, No. 1630

DATE: 1909

COLORS: clear, $58.00.

SIZE: 2¼" tall x 2⅛" wide

No. **1630** Toothpick

NOTES: This toothpick was reproduced as a souvenir in pink and yellow in the mid-1980s. Also reissued in red, sometimes with the original Fostoria paper label.

Clear on metal stand

Clear

OMN: AMERICAN, No. 2056

DATE: 1915

COLORS: clear, $48.00.

SIZE: 2¼" tall x 1⅜" wide at top

NOTES: Fostoria made this pattern for a great length of time. It is generally accepted that the earliest toothpicks were ground and polished on the bottom rim and later ones were not.

OMN: ATLANTA, No. 500

DATE: 1896

COLORS: clear, $60.00; clear with engraving No. 133 (Floral), $70.00; clear, satin finish, $70.00; opal, $78.00; opal, enamel decor, $95.00; opal with satin finish, $120.00.

SIZE: 2" tall x 1¾" wide

Opal with enamel decoration

Clear

OMN: BEDFORD, No. 1000

AKA: LONG PUNTY

DATE: 1901

COLORS: clear, $45.00.

SIZE: 2¼" tall x 2¼" wide

NOTES: Note that the actual toothpick appears to have been necked in by comparison to the catalog illustration.

OMN: BRAZILIAN, No. 600

DATE: 1898

COLORS: clear, $48.00; emerald green, $125.00.

SIZE: 2⅝" tall x 2" wide

NOTES: *The No. 600 Brazilian ware is their banner line this season. The pattern is rich and elaborate and the glass as pure in color as it is possible for glass to be.* –January 1898, *CGL.* Also known with metal cage.

Clear

600 Toothpick.

Clear with metal cage

OMN: BRILLIANT, No. 1001

DATE: 1901

COLORS: clear, $48.00.

SIZE: 2½" tall x 2½" wide at top

NOTES: Made in a tableware line.

Clear

OMN: CAMEO, No. 604

AKA: APPLE & GRAPE IN SCROLL

DATE: 1898

COLORS: green, $280.00; opal $280.00.+

SIZE: unknown

NOTES: Made in a tableware line.

Green

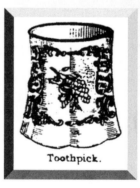

Toothpick.

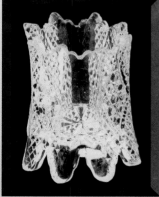

OMN: CARMEN, No. 575

DATE: 1897

COLORS: clear, $60.00; clear with amber stain, $145.00; opal, $170.00.

SIZE: 2" tall x 1¾" wide

NOTES: *In shape and design it differs materially from other leading patterns, and is a combination of a plain and figured pattern [with] the cut diamond on a cut field alternating with plain spaces...* –January 1897, *CGL.* Made in a tableware line. Decoration No. 501 consists of an amber stain flower on plain panels.

575 Toothpick.

Clear

Clear

OMN: COLONIAL, No. 2222

DATE: 1920

COLORS: clear, $38.00.

SIZE: 2¼" tall

NOTES: Some pieces of this pattern were made in amber, blue, and green.

OMN: COLONIAL PRISM, No. 2183

DATE: 1918

COLORS: clear, $38.00.

SIZE: 2¼" tall x 1¾" wide

NOTES: Made in a full tableware pattern. Known with notched edges.

Clear

Clear

OMN: CZARINA, No. 444

AKA: DIAMOND POINT & FAN

DATE: 1894

COLORS: clear, $32.00.

SIZE: 2¾" tall x 2" wide

OMN: No. 1819

AKA: DANDELION; THISTLE

DATE: 1911

COLORS: clear, $70.00; clear with ruby stain, $400.00.

SIZE: 2⅛" tall x 2⅛" wide

NOTES: Listed as "I. C." in catalogs, meaning either intaglio cut or imitation cut.

Clear

OMN: No. 88

AKA: DIAMOND MIRROR

DATE: 1888

COLORS: clear, $125.00.

SIZE: 2⅜" tall x 2⅛" wide

NOTES: Made while the company was still in Fostoria, Ohio.

Clear

Clear with satin and enamel decoration

OMN: DIANA, No. 601

DATE: 1898

COLORS: clear, $42.00; clear, decorated, $55.00.

SIZE: 2⅜" tall x 2⅛" wide

NOTES: *Other patterns they show are No. 601 Diana, a plain line. –January 1898.*

Opal

OMN: No. 1018

AKA: DRAPED BEADS

DATE: 1898

COLORS: clear, $28.00; opal, $52.00; opal, enamel decor, $65.00.

SIZE: 2" tall x 1¾" wide

NOTES: Not part of a full tableware pattern; only a toothpick, salt shaker, and possibly a syrup were produced.

1018 Tooth Pick

OMN: EDGEWOOD, No. 675

DATE: 1898

COLORS: clear, $40.00.

SIZE: 2⅝" tall x 2⅛" wide

NOTES: Made in a full tableware pattern.

Clear

81

Clear

OMN: ESSEX, No. 1372
DATE: 1905
COLORS: clear, $38.00.
SIZE: 2¼" tall x 2⅜" wide
NOTES: Made in a full tableware pattern.

OMN: FLEMISH, No. 1913
DATE: 1913
COLORS: clear, $45.00.
SIZE: 2⅛" tall x 2¼" wide
NOTES: Made in a full tableware pattern.

Clear

Clear

OMN: FRISCO, No. 1229
DATE: 1903
COLORS: clear, $42.00.
SIZE: 2⅜" tall x 2⅛" wide
NOTES: Some pieces of Frisco were reissued by Fostoria 1950 – 1959 in opal.

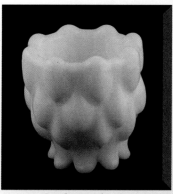

Opal reproduction

Clear

OMN: HARTFORD, No. 501
DATE: 1896
COLORS: clear, $65.00; clear with ruby stain, $155.00.
SIZE: 2⅝" tall x 2¼" wide
NOTES: Made in a tableware line.

OMN: HAT (TAPERED BLOCK)

DATE: 1896

COLORS: clear, $28.00.

SIZE: unknown

NOTES: There are two different styles of Tapered Block Hats, the difference being that Fostoria's has a smooth, plain brim while the National/Rochester Hat has blocks on the brim.

Hat Toothpick.
Packed 2½ gro. in bbl.

Clear

OMN: No. 1300

AKA: HEAVY DRAPE

DATE: 1904

COLORS: clear, $88.00; clear with gold decor, $155.00.

SIZE: 2⅜" tall x 2⅜" wide

NOTES: Made in a full tableware line.

No. 1300.
Toothpick.

No. 1299. Toothpick.

OMN: No. 1299

AKA: LONG BUTTRESS

DATE: 1904

COLORS: Clear $32.00.

SIZE: 2¼" tall x 2⅜" wide

NOTES: This varies from U.S. Glass Co.'s Mayflower (Portland) in that the outer surfaces are concave rather than flat.

Clear

Clear

OMN: LOUISE, No. 1121

AKA: STARRED JEWEL; SUNK JEWEL

DATE: 1902

COLORS: clear, $52.00; clear with gold decor, $62.00.

SIZE: 1⅜" tall x 1½" wide

NOTES: *They have two brand new lines… No. "1121" is one of the lucky hits of the year and is conceded to be one of the handsomest lines yet brought out. It is an artistically figured pattern and deservedly occupies a position at the top of the list. It is particularly adapted for the Western trade and is sure to have a big run. –January 1902.*

No. 1121. Toothpick

Clear

No. 1515 Toothpick

OMN: LUCERE, No. 1515

DATE: 1907

COLORS: clear, $38.00.

SIZE: 2⅛" tall x 2⅜" wide

NOTES: Made in a full tableware line.

Emerald green

576 Toothpick.

OMN: PERSIAN, No. 576

AKA: CROWN & SHIELD

DATE: 1897

COLORS: clear, $68.00; emerald green, $145.00.

SIZE: 2⅝" tall x 1⅞" wide

NOTES: *...an imitation cut pattern, combination curved and straight incut lines, filled in with diamond points...* –January 1897.

Clear

Emerald with gold

OMN: PRISCILLA, No. 676

DATE: 1899

COLORS: clear, $60.00; clear with gold decor, $60.00; emerald green, $155.00; emerald green with gold decor, $168.00.

SIZE: 2¼" tall x 2¼" wide

NOTES: Made in a full tableware line. Difficult to find in emerald green.

Clear

OMN: UNKNOWN

AKA: PYRAMIDS, INVERTED IMPERIAL

DATE: 1902

COLORS: clear $35.00.

SIZE: 2⅜" tall, 2⅜" wide

NOTES: The *Inverted Imperial* name should be phased out, as it incorrectly suggests the pattern was made by the Imperial Glass Corp.

OMN: REGAL, No. 2000

DATE: 1914

COLORS: clear, $42.00; clear with cutting, $45.00.

SIZE: 2" tall x 2" wide

NOTES: Made in a full tableware line.

Clear with cutting

OMN: ROSBY, No. 1704

DATE: 1910

COLORS: clear, $38.00.

SIZE: 2" tall x 2¼" wide

NOTES: Made in a full tableware line. Some pieces were reissued in 1969.

Clear

OMN: unknown

AKA: ROSE URN

DATE: 1900

COLORS: opal, $60.00.

SIZE: 2¾" tall x 3" wide

NOTES: Not part of a tableware pattern. Brought out with a line of opal novelties.

OMN: SOVEREIGN, No. 1641

DATE: 1909

COLORS: clear, $48.00; clear with gold decor, $52.00.

SIZE: 2⅛" tall x 2" wide

NOTES: Catalog illustration shows the angled motif to the left rather than the right as on the toothpick. Some pieces, but not the toothpick, were reissued in 1969 as Sovereign.

Clear

Fostoria Glass Co.

Clear

OMN: No. 1626

AKA: SWEET SIXTEEN

DATE: 1909

COLORS: clear, $45.00; clear with allover light marigold stain, $55.00.

SIZE: 2⅜" tall x 2¼" wide

NOTES: This was sold as a toothpick and also as an individual sugar with a matching individual cream.

Clear

OMN: SYLVAN, No. 1119

DATE: 1902

COLORS: clear, $28.00; clear with gold decor, $32.00.

SIZE: 2" tall x 2⅛" wide

NOTES: *They have two brand new lines of tableware... "1119" is a beautiful imitation cut pattern and quickly takes the eye of the Eastern buyer. This line is made in rich gold decoration and is a line that will keep its place in the front rank of anything shown this year. –January 1902.*

No. 1119.
Toothpick.

Clear

OMN: TUXEDO, No. 1578

DATE: 1908

COLORS: clear, $70.00.

SIZE: 3" tall x 2⅜" wide

NOTES: Made in a full tableware line.

No. 1578
Toothpick.

Clear with satin finish

OMN: No. 183

AKA: VICTORIA

DATE: ca. 1888

COLORS: clear, $175.00; clear with satin finish, $195.00.

SIZE: 2⅜" tall x 2⅛" wide. Bar glass: 2⅜" tall x 2" wide

NOTES: Made while the company was still in Fostoria, Ohio. Victoria also has a straight-sided bar glass in the pattern that is often included in toothpick collections. Also, some examples are found with a metal cage. Most pieces of this extensive tableware pattern have "Pat'd." in the bottoms of glass pieces.

Clear in metal cage

Clear bar glass with satin finish

Clear

OMN: VIGILANT, No. 403

DATE: 1896

COLORS: clear, $38.00; clear with carnival type stain, $42.00; clear with engraving, $42.00; clear with silver overlay, $52.00.

SIZE: 2⅞" tall x 2¼" wide

NOTES: Original catalogs indicate this pattern was decorated with Engraving No. 122 and Etching Nos. 32 and 41.

Clear with silver overlay

Clear

OMN: VIRGINIA, No. 1467

DATE: 1906

COLORS: clear, $45.00.

SIZE: 2⅛" tall x 2¼" wide.

NOTES: Also known with a metal wrap.

No. 1467.
Toothpick.

Clear

OMN: VOGUE, No. 2106

DATE: 1916

COLORS: clear, $38.00.

SIZE: 2¼" tall x 1¾" wide

Clear with rose stain

OMN: WEDDING BELLS, No. 789

DATE: 1900

COLORS: clear, $65.00; clear with gold decor, $65.00; clear with rose stain, $138.00.

SIZE: 2¼" tall x 2¼" wide

NOTES: *The Fostoria Glass Co., of Moundsville, W. Va., have been getting heaps of orders for their new No. 789 Wedding Bells pattern since they introduced it to the trade. The shapes are unquestionably novel and unique and the line occupies a place among the new things of the season distinctively its own. –January 1900.* Catalogs indicate that this pattern was "Patent Applied For."

GILLINDER & SONS
PHILADELPHIA, PENNSYLVANIA — 1861 – 1888
GREENSBURG, PENNSYLVANIA — 1888 – 1891

Gillinder & Sons was founded in 1861, and it primarily made window glass and lamp chimneys (blown ware). In 1888, it moved its pressed glass factory to Greensburg, Pennsylvania. This pressed ware factory joined U.S. Glass as Factory G in 1891. The Philadelphia works did not join U.S. Glass.

OMN: unknown

AKA: FAN FOOTED SCROLL

DATE: 1899

COLORS: clear, $42.00; opal, $58.00.

SIZE: unknown

NOTES: As can be seen from the smoking set illustrated, this is a match holder, not a toothpick.

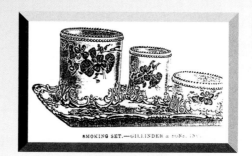

SMOKING SET.—GILLINDER & SONS, INC.

Clear with satin finish

OMN: JUST OUT

DATE: ca. 1876

COLORS: clear with satin finish, $125.00

SIZE: 3" tall x 2½" wide x 4½" long

NOTES: Possibly made for the Centennial Exposition. Gillinder made many clear satin figurines and novelties for the Exposition. "Just Out" is embossed on the sides of the base.

No. 2 MATCH HOLDER
2¼ inches high.

OMN: No. 2

AKA: LAMAR

DATE: 1897

COLORS: opal, $85.00; opal, enamel decorated, $125.00.

SIZE: unknown

NOTES: This was marketed as a match holder.

Opal, enamel decoration

OMN: No. 446

AKA: SCROLL & BULGE; BAROQUE SCROLL

DATE: 1897

COLORS: opal, $52.00; opal with bisque decor, $55.00.

SIZE: 2½" tall x 2" wide

NOTES: This is illustrated in an original 1897 ad that states the decoration is "bisque effect."

Opal with bisque decoration

GREENSBURG GLASS CO.
GREENSBURG, PENNSYLVANIA
1890 – 1900

The Greensburg Glass Co. was chartered in 1889 and began production of glass in 1890. The original manager of the plant was George Swift, who died shortly after the opening of the plant. After a series of reorganizations, Julius Proeger became general manager in 1893. *The company make all kinds of glassware for table use, from individual salt cellars, tumblers, and goblets, to large pitchers, bowls, fruit and cake dishes, etc...various styles of plain, figured, and engraved ware. –May 1893, CGL.*

In 1899, the company joined the National Glass Co. as Factory No. 8, Greensburg Glass Works. At that time, the Melrose molds were moved to Factory No. 18 (Royal), and this pattern continued in production at the new factory.

The company primarily made stemware, bar goods, novelties, and tableware. Patterns made include Aurora, Florida, Melrose, Corona, Frances, Murano, and Tacoma. Trade journal reports credit Oriental Glass Co. with applying ruby stain to several Greensburg patterns, including Corona and Florida.

OMN: CORONA

AKA: SUNK HONEYCOMB

DATE: August, 1893

COLORS: clear, $38.00; clear with engraving, $48.00; clear with ruby stain, $78.00.

SIZE: unknown

NOTES: Made in a full tableware line. In January 1895, the company indicated that this pattern was made in plain and engraved. Some pieces of Corona were made by McKee after a mold sale.

Clear with ruby stain

Clear with ruby stain and gold

OMN: FLORIDA

DATE: 1893

COLORS: clear, $68.00; clear with ruby and amber stain, $365.00; emerald with gold decor, $290.00; canary, $385.00; canary opalecscent, $425.00.

SIZE: 2¼" tall x 1¾" wide

NOTES: Florida was advertised first in December of 1892 as the new pattern for the coming year. The original description of the pattern stated, "The flower [of] the Florida pattern is in cameo style." The ruby and amber decoration was applied by Oriental Glass of Pittsburgh. In January 1895, the company reported that Florida was available in "plain and etched." Etched at that time meant satin finished.

Canary opalescent

Clear with amber stain

OMN: TACOMA

DATE: 1895

COLORS: clear, $42.00; clear with amber stain, $95.00; clear with ruby stain, $110.00.

SIZE: 2½" tall x 1⅞" wide

NOTES: Tacoma was made in 45 pieces in January 1895, according to trade journal reports. Early in 1895, the Oriental Glass Co. decorated Tacoma with ruby stain. After the demise of National Glass, molds of this pattern were apparently moved to at least two factories: Model Flint at Albany, Indiana (ca. 1900 catalog), and the McKee Glass Works.

A. H. HEISEY & CO.
NEWARK, OHIO
1896 – 1957

The new Model Glass Works of A. H. Heisey & Co., located in this city [Newark, Ohio] are nearing completion, and when finished will deserve their name, as they will in plan, convenience, and equipment be second to none in the country. Mr. A. H. Heisey, the head of the firm, deserves the credit for all this, as he has drawn upon his knowledge of the business, the fruits of an experience of many years, to bring the new plant as nearly as possible to perfection. This same knowledge will come into advantageous play in the management of the new enterprise, which can be counted upon, under Mr. Heisey's direction, to win success by the output. Mr. Heisey is still young and vigorous, full of vim and energy, of well balanced judgment, and possessing every qualification necessary to win success. The new factory building is in size 90x90 feet, the working floor being 12 feet above ground level. It will be equipped with one 16 pot furnace, arranged with 48 arches, and having four Nicholson gas producers connected with it. The stack is 112 feet high from ground to top. The lehrs and glory holes are connected with one of the improved Nicholson gas producers. There are six lehrs, 56 feet long, with 60 inch pans. The lehr and mold room will be 55x90 feet, with four brick arches underneath to be used for storage of materials, etc. The warehouse is 60x152 feet, three stories high. Fine offices will be located in a building separate from the factory. The roof of the factory, lehr and mold rooms, is of iron. All the lumber used, such as posts, joists, flooring, etc., are of native hard wood, principally oak, insuring the greatest security against fire. The entire plant will be heated by steam, and lighted by electricity from a plant installed in the works. The entire works are being constructed under the supervision of John Nicholson, Jr., and will be under roof by November 15, weather permitting, and are expected to employ about 250 hands. The present mold shop is located in one of the machine works of Newark, where twelve mold makers are busy at work on two handsome lines of tableware for the spring trade. Everything about the works is conveniently arranged. The facilities for the receipt of raw materials and fuel and the shipment of ware are unsurpassed, a switch from the Panhandle Railroad reaching each side of the factory. The location is within the city limits, and is beautiful. Electric street cars run by the property, making it easy of access. –November 1895.

In 1895, Augustus H. Heisey organized the A. H. Heisey & Co., with his sons, George Duncan, Edgar Wilson, and Thomas Clarence. Prior to this he had been a partner in Geo. Duncan & Sons and a director and head of the Commercial Department of U.S. Glass.

Heisey adopted the familiar *H* in a diamond trademark that was used extensively on most Heisey wares after 1901. A. H. Heisey served as president; eventually, Wilson succeeded him. After Wilson's death, his brother Clarence Heisey served as president until the company closed. All assets, including patterns, patents, molds, machinery, and good will were purchased by the Imperial Glass Corporation of Bellaire, Ohio, which continued some of the popular Heisey patterns.

Following the demise of Imperial Glass, the Heisey Collectors of America purchased the remaining Heisey molds except for those for Old Williamsburg, which were retained by Lancaster Colony/Indiana.

All toothpicks listed below were part of full tableware lines made by Heisey. Heisey did not make novelty toothpicks.

Popular Heisey patterns include Fandango, Fancy Loop, Peerless, Pillows, Prince of Wales, Plumes, and Winged Scroll. Many more were made during the post-toothpick period.

Clear

OMN: No. 150

AKA: BANDED FLUTE

DATE: 1907

COLORS: clear, $80.00; clear with gold decor, $90.00.

SIZE: 2⅜" tall x 1¾" wide

NOTES: The company listed this item as both a toothpick and a bar glass. Any sham in the bottom of the glass makes it a bar glass, not a toothpick. Usually marked with the Diamond H.

OMN: No. 1295

AKA: BEAD SWAG

DATE: uncertain, but ca. 1900 or slightly earlier

COLORS: clear, $55.00; clear with gold decor, $70.00; clear with gold and engraving, $75.00; clear with ruby stain, $60.00; opal, $125.00; opal with enamel decor, $160.00; emerald, $390.00+; emerald with gold, $425.00+.

SIZE: 2⅛" tall x 2⅛" wide

Opal, enamel flowers

NOTES: Not marked with the Diamond H. This toothpick has been reproduced in very opaque opal and custard, but decorated with hand painted flowers. However, the walls of the original are thin and of the same thickness throughout. The repro has very thick walls at the bottom with a straight interior. This pattern was decorated by Oriental Glass: *No. 1295, opal decorated; No. 1295, ruby and gold; No. 1295, gold and engraved.* –January 1900. In January of 1902, Oriental Glass reported it was decorating No. 1295 Bead Swag in ruby and gold. Also mentioned was "a very pretty wild rose pattern that sets it off beautifully."

Clear with ruby stain

OMN: No. 1235

AKA: BEADED PANEL & SUNBURST

DATE: September, 1897

COLORS: clear, $175.00; clear with gold decor, $175.00; clear with ruby stain, $310.00; clear with amber stain, $290.00; clear with other stains, $310.00.

SIZE: 2½" tall x 2" wide

NOTES: *They call it No. 1235 and it is the most elegant design we have yet seen in pressed glassware. The pieces are ornamented with fluting supplemented by chrysanthemums, which are as perfect representation of those pretty flowers as it is possible to make in glass.* –September 1897. Decorated by Oriental Glass in crystal and gold, crystal and ruby, or green and gold, according to trade announcements. The punch bowl in this pattern was made in emerald, opal, and Ivorina verde (custard). Pieces in this pattern are usually marked with the Diamond H, but not always.

Clear with Maiden Blush stain

Clear

OMN: COLONIAL, No. 400

DATE: ca. 1909

COLORS: clear, $135.00.

SIZE: 2¾" tall x 2¼" wide

NOTES: Often confused with the much more common Peerless toothpick. The difference is this toothpick has eight panels while Peerless has only six. This Heisey toothpick was also included in the No. 331 line, called Colonial Panel by collectors.

Clear

OMN: CONTINENTAL, No. 339

DATE: 1903

COLORS: clear, $138.00; clear with gold decor, $140.00; clear with engraving, $138.00; clear with ruby stain, $285.00+.

SIZE: 2⅜" tall x 2" wide

NOTES: *The new pattern, No. 339, or "Continental," of A. H. Heisey & Co., Newark, O., is a variation on the famous No. 300, the "pattern without a peer." In some respects it is an improvement on the 300, many of the pieces being more graceful and lighter, and more in the style of cut glass. The edge is lighter and made with plain scallop, while on the 300 the scallop is crimped. –January 1903.* Marked with the Diamond H.

Clear

OMN: No. 1200

AKA: CUT BLOCK

DATE: 1896

COLORS: clear, $70.00; clear with ruby stain, $115.00; clear with engraving, $110.00; clear with amber stain, $250.00.

SIZE: 2⅜" tall x 2¼" wide

NOTES: The first Heisey pattern. None of the pieces in this full tableware line are marked with the Diamond H. Toothpicks are often found as souvenir items. L. J. Rodgers of Pittsburgh decorated this pattern with amber and ruby stains.

Clear with ruby stain

Toothpick.

Toothpick, emerald

OMN: No. 1205

AKA: FANCY LOOP

DATE: 1896

COLORS: clear, $85.00; clear with gold decor, $85.00; clear with allover pale marigold stain, $280.00+; clear with lavender loops, $300.00+; emerald, $275.00; emerald with gold decor, $325.00+.

SIZE: Toothpick: 2⅛" tall x 2⅛" wide.
Bar: 2⅝" tall x 2" wide at top.

NOTES: *The Ransthorne Printing & Engraving Co. have just gotten out a handsome illustrated catalogue for A. H. Heisey & Co., of Newark, Ohio, showing 108 pieces of their new 1205 pattern, one of the handsomest designs ever put on the market by any American glass manufacturer. –1896. The design is imitation cut, containing both the round bead and faceted, diamond incut on the cross lines, filled in with minute hob nail facets. –1897.* Trade journal reports state the Oriental Glass Co. decorated Fancy Loop in clear with gold. It is unusual to find any piece of Fancy Loop with the Diamond H, but some do exist.

Bar glass, emerald

OMN: No. 1201

AKA: FANDANGO

DATE: 1896

COLORS: clear, $90.00; clear with gold decor, $95.00.

SIZE: 2½" tall x 1⅞" wide

NOTES: Illustrated in ads in January 1896, one of the first two patterns made by the new company. *The new 1201 pattern, made in excellent crystal glass, has met with a very large demand from the very start, and compelled the firm to get out their ware at other factories until their own factory was started.* –April 1896. The first pieces of both Fandango and Cut Block were most likely made at the Robinson Glass Co. in Zanesville, Ohio. Made in an extensive tableware line, and not marked with the Diamond H. Amber and ruby stain decorations were done by L. J. Rodgers of Pittsburgh. Some pieces still appeared in a Butler Brothers catalog in 1898.

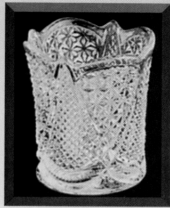

Clear with gold decoration

Clear

OMN: No. 352

AKA: FLAT PANEL

DATE: 1908

COLORS: clear, $75.00; clear with silver overlay, $90.00.

SIZE: 2⅜" tall x 1¾" wide

NOTES: Many items were made in this pattern, and they are usually marked with the Diamond H. This toothpick often has a fully ground and puntied bottom.

TOOTHPICK

TOOTHPICK
GROUND BOTTOM

OMN: No. 433

AKA: GREEK KEY

DATE: 1912

COLORS: clear, $700.00+.

SIZE: 2⅜" tall x 2¼" wide

NOTES: One of the most popular of the Heisey colonial patterns. Made in many interesting pieces, most of which are marked with the Diamond H. The toothpick and the bar glass without a sham are made from the same mold, although Heisey sold these designated as both. If the glass has a sham bottom, it is definitely a bar glass, not a toothpick.

Clear

OMN: KALONYAL, No. 1776

DATE: 1906

COLORS: clear, $450.00; clear with gold decor, $450.00; clear with ruby stain, $750.00.

SIZE: 2⅜" tall x 1⅞" wide

NOTES: This elusive pattern was made in a full tableware line and is usually marked with the Diamond H. Ruby stain is especially hard to find in this pattern.

A. H. Heisey & Co.

Clear

Clear with ruby stain and gold

OMN: No. 160

AKA: LOCKET ON CHAIN

COLORS: clear, $900.00+; clear with gold decor, $950.00+; clear with ruby stain and gold decor, $3,100.00+; emerald, $2,800.00+; emerald with gold decor, $2,900.00+; canary, $3,500.00+.

SIZE: 2¼" tall x 2" wide

NOTES: Prices for pieces with unusual colors and decorations are driven by supply and demand, and so are only estimates of what collectors would pay for examples.

OMN: No. 353

AKA: MEDIUM FLAT PANEL

DATE: 1909

COLORS: clear, $60.00; clear with silver overlay, $75.00.

SIZE: 1" tall x 1¼" wide x 3¾" long

NOTES: Heisey's only sanitary toothpick, a lay-down style. A huge colonial line with most items marked with the Diamond H.

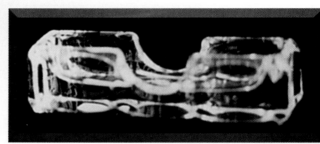

Clear

Clear with gold decoration

OMN: No. 315

AKA: PANELED CANE

DATE: 1901

COLORS: clear, $110.00; clear with gold decor, $125.00.

SIZE: 2¼" tall x 2" wide

NOTES: *The other new pattern is No. 315, a figured design of much elegance, also shown in plain crystal and crystal and gold.* –January 1901. First advertised in January of 1901 and made in a full tableware assortment. Pieces, including the toothpick, are usually marked with the Diamond H.

Clear

OMN: No. 300

AKA: PEERLESS

DATE: 1900

COLORS: clear, $75.00; clear with gold decor, $85.00.

SIZE: 2¼" tall x 1⅞" wide

NOTES: *...two new lines... These are Nos. 300 and 305... These patterns are very rich and ornate and there are full lines of both. They have them in plain crystal; also decorated in gold and colors, if so desired...* –January 1900. No. 305 is the pattern called Punty and Diamond Point (see page 96). Soon after the introduction, Heisey advertised this pattern as "The Pattern without a Peer," certainly the source of the name by which it is now known. *...their superb and matchless Colonial pattern, No. "300." This line has been on the market for three years and is running as strong now as ever. They keep adding to it right along...* –January 1902.

Clear

OMN: No. 325

AKA: PILLOWS

DATE: 1901

COLORS: clear, $375.00; clear with gold decor, $395.00.

SIZE: 2⅜" tall x 1¾" wide

NOTES: *Among the new things for this season are No. 325 pattern, imitation cut, in plain crystal and crystal and gold. –January 1901.* Most pieces of this large tableware line are marked with the Diamond H. A few rare pieces of the pattern are known with ruby stain, so this decoration is a possibility for the toothpick. Also a few rare pieces are known in rose, a pink similar to flamingo. But the toothpick is not known in this color.

Clear with gold

OMN: No. 1255

AKA: PINEAPPLE & FAN

DATE: 1898

COLORS: clear, $125.00; clear with gold decor, $138.00; clear with ruby stain, $210.00; emerald, $310.00; emerald with gold decor, $325.00.

SIZE: 2¼" tall x 2¼" wide

NOTES: *Their new pattern, No. 1255, of which there is a full line of about 80 pieces... They have this elegant pattern decorated in green and gold as well as in plain... –January 1898.* One of the early Heisey patterns found in emerald green. It was made in a full tableware assortment.

Emerald with gold

Pieces are not marked with the Diamond H as the pattern was made before the trademark was used. Several rare pieces of the pattern are known in a deep "ink blue," a deep dark emerald green (almost black), and canary opalescent. While toothpicks haven't been found in these colors, be aware that toothpicks could exist in these unusual colors and would be extremely rare.

Clear

OMN: No. 1255

AKA: PLAIN BAND

DATE: 1897

COLORS: clear, $42.00; clear with engraving, $68.00; clear with gold, $68.00; clear with ruby stain, $85.00; clear with colored stain (any), $95.00.

SIZE: 2½" tall x 2½" wide

TOOTHPICK

NOTES: *...such has been the demand for their new No. 1225 pattern that 17 shops have been put to work on it to keep up the supply. The line is a departure from the beaten path and gets far enough away from both the extremely plain and the figured and imitation cut patterns... The line, exclusive of the finished diverse shapes, embraces 75 pieces, and is made both plain and engraved. Besides being made plain and engraved, the line has edge touched with gold [on] the beads or pearls... The bulbous lower part of the bodies are filmed by a new process with a thin casing of iridescent colors in pink, light green and bright silver, showing a light tinge of blue... –April 1897. They have the 1225 line in new decorations of gold band and engraved... –January 1898.* Note the beaded top on the toothpick holder. A similar piece is a custard which has a smooth top rim. This custard item is often found in Ivorina Verde (custard), but the toothpick is not. This was a popular pattern for several years, so pieces are found both with the Diamond H and without it. The toothpick is also a spoon to a child's table set.

OMN: PRINCE OF WALES, PLUMES, No. 335

DATE: 1902

COLORS: clear, $195.00; clear with gold decor, $200.00; clear with ruby stain, $325.00.

SIZE: 2⅜" tall x 2" wide

NOTES: *They have two new lines — one figured, the other plain. The figured pattern is No. 335. The pattern is called Prince of Wales Plume, and it is a beauty. It is an imitation cut, heavy glass, clean and perfect and highly polished... It is also decorated in gold and is a very effective line from every point.* –January 1902. This pattern was made in a full tableware assortment. Many items in this pattern were decorated by the Oriental Glass Co. of Pittsburgh in ruby and gold with ruby. Most pieces are marked with the Diamond H.

Clear with ruby stain

TOOTHPICK

OMN: PRISCILLA, No. 351

DATE: 1907

COLORS: clear, $55.00; clear with cutting, $60.00; clear with silver overlay, $60.00.

SIZE: 2¼" tall x 1¾" wide

NOTES: One of Heisey's most popular Colonial patterns, made in a wide variety of tableware pieces. Almost all items are marked with the Diamond H.

TOOTHPICK
GROUND BOTTOM

Clear with cutting

Clear

OMN: No. 357

AKA: PRISON STRIPE

DATE: 1906

COLORS: clear, $400.00; clear with gold decor, $415.00.

SIZE: 2⅜" tall x 1⅞" wide

NOTES: Another Heisey pattern made in a full tableware line with most pieces being marked with the Diamond H. Somewhat difficult to find.

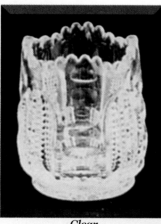

OMN: No. 305

AKA: PUNTY & DIAMOND POINT

DATE: 1900

COLORS: clear, $315.00.

SIZE: 2⅜" tall x 2" wide

NOTES: Several decorations were listed in original company material and included several luster colors and gold, either on the top edges or, mainly, in the punties. These are original company decorations, but we have not seen toothpicks with these decorations. Most pieces of the pattern are marked with the Diamond H.

Clear

OMN: No. 1220

AKA: PUNTY BAND

DATE: 1897

COLORS: clear, $58.00; clear with ruby stain, $72.00; clear with engraving, $68.00; Ivorina Verde (custard), $78.00; Ivorina Verde with enamel decorations, $90.00.

SIZE: 2¼" tall x 2⅛" wide

NOTES: *A combination of plain and figured line, the plain surface predominating, making it as plain set, or for engraving and decorations.* –January 1897. Decorated in ruby by Oriental Glass Co. in 1898. This toothpick was made in two styles, one with a scalloped top and another with a beaded top. Toothpicks may or may not be marked with the Diamond H.

Clear with ruby stain

OMN: PURITAN, No. 341

DATE: 1904

COLORS: clear, $135.00; clear with silver overlay, $148.00; clear with allover satin, $165.00.

SIZE: Standard: 3½" tall x 1⅞" wide. Flared: 3⅜" tall x 2½" wide at top.

NOTES: *The Puritan line of Colonial pressed tableware warrants everything good that is said about it. Every solitary piece in this immense line is a delight unto itself.* –January 1904.

Flared top and standard top, clear

OMN: QUEEN ANNE, No. 365

DATE: 1907

COLORS: clear, $700.00+; clear with gold decor, $750.00+; clear with ruby stain, $1,000.00+.

SIZE: 2⅜" tall x 2¼" wide

NOTES: One of the few early Heisey patterns to be both numbered and named by the company. Made in a full tableware line and marked with the Diamond H.

OMN: No. 310

AKA: RING BAND

DATE: 1900

COLORS: Ivorina Verde, $68.00; Ivorina Verde, flower decor, $115.00+; Ivorina Verde with gold, $115.00+.

SIZE: 2⅜" tall x 2" wide

NOTES: *Oriental Glass Co....Their No. "310" Ivorina Verde line decorated in a beautiful American beauty rose pattern is very rich and artistic. These goods are all done in new patterns, burned in, and will always retain their color and beauty.* –January 1902. This is an unusual pattern (full tableware line) in that it is mainly found in Ivorina Verde (custard) glass rather than clear. Most pieces, including the toothpick, are marked with the Diamond H. Enamel decorations and gold were added to Ring Band by Oriental Glass Co. of Pittsburgh.

Ivorina Verde with enameled flowers

A. H. Heisey & Co.

Clear

OMN: No. 343

AKA: SUNBURST

DATE: 1904

COLORS: clear, $215.00; clear with gold decor, $225.00; clear with ruby stain, $350.00+.

SIZE: 2¼" tall x 1¾" wide

NOTES: Found in a full tableware assortment. Most pieces are found marked with the Diamond H, although the toothpick may also be found unmarked.

OMN: No. 56

AKA: SWEET SCROLL

DATE: ca. 1898

COLORS: opal, $400.00+.

SIZE: 2⁷⁄₁₆" tall, 1¾" wide

NOTES: This was one of several opal novelties made by Heisey. It was originally a match holder. Marked with the Diamond H and the number 56.

OMN: TOURAINE, No. 337

DATE: 1902

COLORS: clear, $265.00; clear with gold decor, $280.00; clear with ruby stain, $365.00; clear with engraving, $360.00.

SIZE: 2⅜" tall x 1⅞" wide

NOTES: *They have two new lines – one figured, the other plain… The new line, No. "337, Touraine," is a plain pressed pattern with an imitation cut star in the bottom. It looks almost like blown ware and is amazingly free from flaws or mold marks. It is made plain, engraved, and with gold band decoration. –January 1902.* Decorated by Oriental Glass Co. with ruby stain and with gold decorations. Many pieces of the pattern are marked with the Diamond H. The bar glass differs from the toothpick in that the toothpick has a bottom ring, while the bar glass is flat.

Clear

OMN: No. 379

AKA: URN

DATE: 1907

COLORS: clear, $180.00; clear with gold on base and top rim, $200.00.

SIZE: 2¼" tall x 2" wide

NOTES: A severe colonial style pattern made in many different pieces, usually marked with the Diamond H. Pieces in this pattern were available with a plain pressed rim and base, but also with both base and top rim ground and polished. Be careful that the tops (and bottoms) of your toothpicks have three ribs. Sometimes repairs can remove these rings.

TOOTHPICK

Clear with gold on base and top rim

Clear

OMN: WALDORF-ASTORIA, No. 333

DATE: 1901

COLORS: clear, $100.00; clear with silver overlay, $115.00.

SIZE: 2⅛" tall x 2" wide

NOTES: A full tableware line in colonial style, usually all pieces are marked with the Diamond H. Differs from other colonial types in that it has a small belt of plain glass through the middle.

OMN: No. 1280

AKA: WINGED SCROLL

DATE: 1899

COLORS: clear, $225.00; clear with gold decor, $235.00; emerald, $325.00; emerald with gold decor, $335.00; Ivorina Verde, $220.00+; Ivorina Verde with gold, $225.00+; Ivorina Verde with enamel flowers, $228.00+; opal, $725.00+; opal with gold decor, $730.00+; canary (vaseline), $1,200.00+.

SIZE: Toothpick: 2¼" tall x 2⅛" wide. Match holder: 2⅛" tall x 2⅛" wide

NOTES: Advertised in January of 1899. Announcements were made that Oriental Glass was decorating No. 1280 in ivory and gold. Pieces in this line are not marked with the Diamond H. Winged Scroll also has a smoking set that includes a match holder that is sometimes collected as a toothpick. It is approximately the same size as the toothpick but has straight sides. A slightly larger straight-sided piece is the cigarette holder. Both of these are much more difficult to find than the toothpick.

Clear with gold decoration

Emerald with gold decoration

Ivorina Verde with gold decoration, match holder and toothpick

JOHN B. HIGBEE GLASS CO.
BRIDGEVILLE, PENNSYLVANIA
1907 – 1918

John B. Higbee, J. W. Higbee, and R. G. West organized the John B. Higbee Glass Co. and built the factory at Bridgeville, Pennsylvania. After a rather troubled business history plagued by bankruptcies and reorganizations, the business was closed in 1918.

Principal products produced included tableware and novelties. Pieces made by this company often have the trademark, a bee with "H I G" on the wings and body.

Clear

OMN: ALFA

AKA: REXFORD

DATE: 1908

COLORS: clear, $35.00

SIZE: 2¼" tall x 2⅛" wide

NOTES: Also made by the New Martinsville Glass Co. Also made with a cupped-in top rim.

Clear

OMN: No. 205

AKA: ESTELLE

DATE: 1910, 1916

COLORS: clear, $38.00; clear with etched decoration, $45.00; clear with marigold luster, $45.00.

SIZE: 2⅛" tall x 1⅞" wide

NOTES: Also made by the Paden City Glass Co. of Paden City, West Virginia.

OMN: HAWAIIAN

AKA: HAWAIIAN LEI, GALA

DATE: 1913

COLORS: clear, $38.00.

SIZE: 2⅛" tall x 2⅛" wide

NOTES: This is a spoon to a toy table set. Has been reproduced, especially in colors. This pattern also has a cube-sugar holder, sometimes collected as a lay-down toothpick.

Clear

Clear

OMN: MADORA

DATE: ca. 1910

COLORS: clear, $50.00.

SIZE: 2¼" tall x 2⅛" wide

HOBBS, BROCKUNIER & CO.
WHEELING, WEST VIRGINIA
1845 – 1888

HOBBS GLASS CO.
WHEELING, WEST VIRGINIA
1888 – 1891

The history of Hobbs, Brockunier & Co. is convoluted due to a number of changes in the company name over the years. The factory was established in 1845 and was then known as the Wheeling Glass Works in South Wheeling.

Hobbs, Brockunier & Co. was organized in 1863 by John L. Hobbs, his son John H. Hobbs, Charles W. Brockunier, and William, Leighton, Sr. The company became well known because of Leighton's lime glass formula and the various colors and treatments developed by Leighton and his son, William Jr. The firm was the most successful American glass company to produce both tableware and art glass of consistently high quality.

In 1888, the company was reorganized under a new charter and named the Hobbs Glass Co. After joining the U.S. Glass Co. in 1891, the company became Factory H.

Art glass colors produced by Hobbs, Brockunier & Co. includes the famous Coral (Wheeling Peachblow), Spangled, Neapolitan, and others. Well-known patterns made by the company include Polka Dot (Inverted Thumbprint), Dew Drop (Hobnail), Murano, Hobnail (Daisy & Button), and many others.

OMN: CORAL, No. 331

AKA: SEAWEED

DATE: 1891

COLORS: clear opalescent, $195.00; blue opalescent, $350.00; ruby opalescent, $350.00.

SIZE: unknown

NOTES: Hobbs Glass Co. originated this pattern. Beaumont apparently was able to secure some of the Hobbs molds and continued production in many of the same shapes originally made by Hobbs. Seaweed became Beaumont's No. 54 pattern.

OMN: CORAL

AKA: WHEELING PEACHBLOW

DATE: 1886

COLORS: amberina, plated, $800.00.

SIZE: 2¼" tall x 2⅜" wide

NOTES: Catalogs list this only as a mustard with a metal top. There is no true toothpick holder listed in old catalogs. Both the original manufacturer's name and the collector's name are derived from the color, not the pattern shape.

Mustard base

Hobbs, Brockunier & Co.

Rubina satin

OMN: DEW DROP, No. 323

AKA: HOBNAIL

DATE: 1885

COLORS: clear, $25.00; clear with Frances decor, $88.00; clear with No. 7 decor, $88.00; amber, $58.00; canary, $65.00; marine green, $70.00; rubina, $185.00; rubina satin, $230.00; sapphire (blue), $78.00.

SIZE: 2⅜" tall x 1⅝" wide

NOTES: Hobbs made many other colors and color combinations in this pattern, including ruby sapphire and ruby amber. Many pieces were found in both glossy and satin finishes and often with a translucent alabaster lining. These toothpicks might be found in any of these variations. The toothpicks were also sold with a small pitcher as a child's toy water set.

Clear with Frances decoration

Marine green

OMN: HOBNAIL, No. 101

AKA: DAISY & BUTTON

DATE: 1885

COLORS: clear, $28.00; clear with Frances decor, $88.00; clear with No. 7 decor, $88.00; amber, $38.00; amberina, $195.00; canary, $65.00; marine green, $68.00; sapphire (blue), $68.00.

SIZE: 2⅞" tall x 2⅛" wide

NOTES: This is shown in original catalogs as a toy tumbler, but is today widely known as a toothpick. Reproductions in this toothpick were made by L. G. Wright in vaseline, pink, ruby, blue, green, amber, amberina, and amethyst. A variation with hobnails (dew drops) was made by Fenton in a wide variety of colors.

Clear with amber daisies

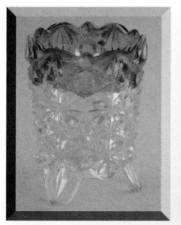

Clear with No. 7 decoration

Sapphire blue

Amberina

Ruby

OMN: No. 331

DATE: 1889

COLORS: clear, $95.00; ruby, $180.00.

SIZE: 2⅜" tall x 2½" wide

NOTES: Some molds for this pattern were used in Coral (Seaweed).

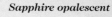

Sapphire opalescent

Clear with Frances decoration

OMN: No. 326

AKA: SWIRL

DATE: 1889

COLORS: Regular: clear, $65.00; clear with Frances decor, $195.00; clear with No. 7 decor, $190.00. Swirl Windows: clear opalescent, $250.00; sapphire opalescent, $385.00; ruby opalescent, $385.00.

SIZE: 2½" tall x 2" wide

NOTES: Frances decoration consists of a satin finish on a portion of the glass and an amber stained rim at the top. No. 7 decoration also has an amber stained top rim, but the body of the glass remains clear. The opalescent colors are made in what is now called Windows Opalescent.

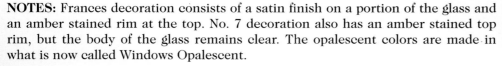

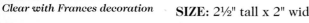

Ruby opalescent

Clear

OMN: No. 115

AKA: WHEELING

DATE: 1887

COLORS: clear, $65.00; clear with various enamels, $75.00; clear with various engraving, $75.00.

SIZE: 2" tall x 2" wide at top

NOTES: This is a toy tumbler, not a true toothpick.

IMPERIAL GLASS CO.
BELLAIRE, OHIO
1904 – 1984

There has been considerable speculation concerning the immense plant of the Imperial Glass Co. at Bellaire. O., owing to the delay in getting the factory in shape for operations, but it is understood that the management expect to be making glass by the last of October or the middle of November of this year.

A large mold making force is busily engaged getting out a diversified line of molds and there will be no delay in this branch. The Imperial was booked to start last September, but the company have been greatly handicapped on account of the contractors being unable to get material for building purposes.

The factory building is to be 268 x 413 feet in size. In the foundation 7000 cubic feet of concrete has been used, 1,500,000 bricks and 13,000 tons of structural iron. There will be three 14-pot furnaces and a continuous tank equal to 60 pots. When completed, it will in all probability be one of the best equipped plants in the United States, and will be a magnificent addition to Bellaire's many industries. –April 1903, *CGL*.

Edward Muehlman, J. N. Vance, and James Anderson organized the Imperial Glass Co. in 1904 with Arthur Bennett as manager. From the first, the company was proud of the fact that all their patterns were new with molds made at their mold shop. In 1909 they began making some colored glass. Early in its life, Imperial made an iridized line of semi-art glass that is avidly collected today.

The Elite Glass Works is one of Bellaire's newest and most progressive smaller industries, and now bids fair to expand... The plant has been in operation for several weeks under the management of the owner, Robert Englehardt, who for the past ten years has been a partner in the Wheeling Glass Decorating Co., turning out a similar line of ware... The glass used is the product of the big Imperial plant and is artistically decorated and ornamented at the Elite works. Vases, bowls and souvenirs of great variety are being finished with the "irridescent" [sic] effect and are so attractive that they are meeting with ready sale in every market. –October 1906, *CGL*. More research needs to be done concerning this arrangement with Imperial in order to know which items were decorated at Elite.

In the late 1950s the company purchased the assets of the Cambridge Glass Co. and the A. H. Heisey & Co., including molds, and made several patterns from each company. After several owners who did little to preserve and build up the company, bankruptcy was declared in 1984, and the company ceased business.

Patterns made by Imperial include many early pressed patterns in imitation cut glass styles, including File, which has falsely been attributed to the Columbia Glass Co. of Findlay, Ohio. By the 1930s, Imperial had introduced its extremely popular Candlewick and Cape Cod patterns. These patterns remained popular until the company closed.

OMN: COLONIAL, No. 600

AKA: CHESTERFIELD

DATE: 1910

COLORS: clear, $42.00.

SIZE: 2¼" tall x 3¾" wide across handles.

NOTES: Sometimes marked with Imperial's iron cross trademark. Imerial reissued the toothpick in several colors in 1966.

600 — Toothpick
44 dozen in barrel

OMN: No. 402, also No. 402½ in other catalogs

AKA: FASHION

DATE: 1914

COLORS: clear, $48.00.

SIZE: unknown

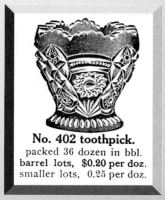

No. 402 toothpick.
packed 36 dozen in bbl.
barrel lots, $0.20 per doz.
smaller lots, 0.25 per doz.

Marigold carnival

OMN: unknown

AKA: FLUTE

DATE: 1913

COLORS: clear, $35.00; marigold carnival, $78.00; purple carnival, $90.00; canary with marigold carnival, $125.00; green carnival, $95.00.

SIZE: 2½" tall x 1¾" wide

Purple carnival

Clear

OMN: No. 3

AKA: GATHERED KNOT

DATE: ca. 1905

COLORS: clear, $40.00.

SIZE: 2⅜" tall x 2" wide

NOTES: Reproduced in colors.

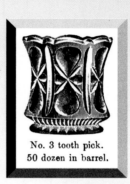

No. 3 tooth pick.
50 dozen in barrel.

179. Oval Toothpick

OMN: No. 179

DATE: ca. 1920s

COLORS: crystal, $38.00; Rose Marie (pink), $62.00; Imperial Green, $60.00.

SIZE: unknown

NOTES: Catalogs indicate this footed and handled toothpick is oval. This item probably has not been recognized as a toothpick holder, since its form is so unlike most toothpicks.

Clear

OMN: No. 612

AKA: PANEL, STAR & HOB

DATE: ca. 1904

COLORS: clear, $40.00; amber, $48.00.

SIZE: unknown

NOTES: Has been reproduced in colors.

612. Toothpick

Dark purple carnival, new

OMN: unknown

AKA: OCTAGON

COLORS: clear, $30.00; marigold carnival, $40.00; blue carnival, $52.00.

SIZE: Repro: 2½" tall x 2⅝" wide at top

NOTES: Heavily reproduced by Imperial in the 1960s and later. When decorated with either gold or cranberry stain, it was part of the line sold as Collector's Crystal at that time. Old toothpicks are noticeably thinner and lighter in weight than new ones. If you have a color other than those listed above, your toothpick is probably new.

No. 9 tooth pick.
50 dozen in barrel.

OMN: No. 9

AKA: PECORAH

DATE: ca. 1905

COLORS: clear, $45.00; clear with gold decor, $45.00.

SIZE: 3" tall x 1¼" wide at body

Clear with gold decor

OMN: No. 1

AKA: THREE IN ONE

DATE: 1904

COLORS: clear, $40.00.

SIZE: unknown

NOTES: In the 1960s, this toothpick was heavily reproduced by Imperial in many opaque and transparent colors, including carnival finishes. The old toothpick was made in only clear.

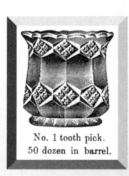

No. 1 tooth pick.
50 dozen in barrel.

INDIANA GLASS COMPANY
DUNKIRK, INDIANA
1904 – 2002

Indiana Glass Co. leased the National Glass Co.'s works No. 1 (Beatty-Brady) in 1904 and started manufacturing glass. Along with the lease of the factory, the company was able to obtain some molds from the defunct No. 9 (Indiana Tumbler & Goblet) and No. 11 (Model Flint) factories of National. National Glass was in receivership and suffering financial hardship, so assets were sold to settle debts in an attempt to keep the company solvent. This company still exists, having survived several reorganizations.

In the beginning, mainly jelly glasses were made, but after acquiring the molds from National, Indiana Glass began producing tableware. Two of its patterns were Nogi and Togo.

OMN: COLONIAL

DATE: 1908

COLORS: clear, $35.00; clear with cutting, $40.00.

SIZE: 2⅜" tall x 1¾" wide

Clear with cutting

OMN: unknown

AKA: GAELIC

DATE: 1908

COLORS: clear, $30.00; clear with stain, $45.00; clear with enamel decor, $45.00.

SIZE: 2" tall x 2" wide

Clear with enamel decoration

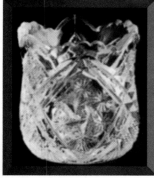

OMN: JUNO

AKA: STAR WHORL, DOUBLE PINWHEEL

DATE: 1905

COLORS: clear, $32.00; clear with gold decor, $40.00.

SIZE: 2¼" tall x 2¼" wide

NOTES: *The Juno line, comes decorated in a border of gold, a new honor, I am told, and a flattering one, for tank glass.* –January 1905

Toothpick

Clear

OMN: No. 300

AKA: OVAL STAR

DATE: unknown

COLORS: clear, $40.00.

SIZE: 2⅜" tall x 2¼" wide

One set packed complete in pasteboard box
Packs 2½ doz. Sets to barrel

Clear

OMN: No. 453

AKA: POINTED GOTHIC

DATE: 1920s

COLORS: clear, $32.00.

SIZE: 2⅜" tall x 1¾" wide

Clear

INDIANA TUMBLER & GOBLET CO.
GREENTOWN, INDIANA
1894 – 1903

The Indiana Tumbler & Goblet Co. of this place [Greentown, IN] expect to be making glass not later than June 10. Their buildings are all of brick except the office, and of the following dimensions: Factory proper, 72 x 72 feet; packing room, 100 x 50 feet; mold shop 52 x 46 feet; and barrel factory, 20 x 30 feet. The office is a frame building of three rooms located 25 feet from the main building and is finished in hard wood and otherwise conveniently arranged. When the plant is completed it will have a melting capacity of 18 pots; at present time there are one 10 pot furnace and four lears finished. They are going to make a full line of tumblers, beer mugs, jellies, and stemware. The company have their own gas well right at the factory and have also 400 acres of gas land right in the heart of the Indiana field. They have secured the services of the best set of glassworkers that can be had and expect to give thorough satisfaction in regard to the material and workmanship of their product. This place is on the Clover Leaf R. R., one of the best roads in the state of Indiana. Everything about the factory is fitted up in the most thorough and effective manner, the equipments are as complete as the best skill and long experience in the business can make them, and the management is such as to secure the confidence of the trade from the start. Under these conditions the prospects of the new company for a prosperous future seem to be most favorable in all respects. –May 1894, CGL.

The Indiana Tumbler & Goblet Co. began producing glassware in 1894 under the management of the Jenkins family: David C., Sr., David C., Jr., Thomas, and Lewis, Jr. The elder David Jenkins formerly owned the Columbia Glass Co. of Findlay, Ohio.

Indiana Tumbler & Goblet produced barware, jelly glasses, novelties, and tableware and began making colored glassware in 1897. In 1899, the company joined the National Glass Co. combine and was designated Factory No. 9, Indiana Tumbler & Goblet Works. While under the National management, Jacob Rosenthal created the famous chocolate glass and holly amber glass that were made at Greentown. Other companies in the National combine, notably McKee, also made at least small quantities of chocolate glass. Other unusual colors included the opaque Nile Green. After the company was destroyed by fire in 1903, Rosenthal left to work for Fenton in Williamstown, West Virginia. Jenkins went on to establish Indiana Glass at Kokomo, Indiana.

Some patterns made include Austrian, Columbia, Dewey, Teardrop & Tassel, Herringbone Buttress, and Cord Drapery.

See also National Glass Co., Factory 9.

Clear with gold decoration

OMN: AUSTRIAN, No. 200

DATE: 1897

COLORS: clear, $38.00; clear with gold decor, $42.00; canary, $155.00; chocolate, $210.00.

SIZE: 2⅞" tall x 2⅛" wide

NOTES: *The Austrian, or 200 line, just got out by the Indiana Tumbler & Goblet Co., of Greentown, Ind., is without doubt the prettiest pattern of pressed glassware it has been our good fortune to see for a long time. –July 1897, CGL.* Made in 35 pieces, according to trade journal reports. Dr. Ruth Herrick, early researcher of this factory's glass, reported that she had dug shards of this pattern in clear, light amber, blue, canary, emerald green, chocolate, and Nile Green.

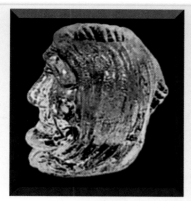

OMN: unknown

AKA: OLD WITCH; OLD WOMAN

DATE: unknown

COLORS: clear, $88.00; chocolate, $550.00+; Nile Green, $310.00.

SIZE: Repro: 2⅝" tall x 2¾" wide

NOTES: Originals are very rare. St. Clair reproduced this toothpick in several colors, including an opaque green similar to Nile green.

Clear

Opaque green

Nile Green

OMN: ST. BERNARD

AKA: DOG'S HEAD

DATE: unknown

COLORS: clear, $148.00; clear with satin finish, $168.00; Nile Green (opaque), $258.00.

SIZE: 2⅜" tall x 3½" wide

NOTES: Other dogs' heads were made by Riverside and McKee. Reproductions, some in old colors, were made by St. Clair. New items have 12 whiskers on the left side and 14 on the right, while the old have 12 on each side.

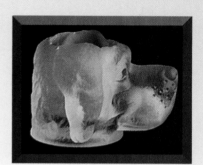

Clear with satin finish

JEFFERSON GLASS COMPANY
STEUBENVILLE, OHIO — 1900 – 1907
FOLLANSBEE, WEST VIRGINIA
1907 – EARLY 1930s

The Jefferson Glass Co. was organized in 1900 by Harry Bastow, George Mortimer, Grant Fish, and J. D. Sinclair. In the list of factories which have their home in Steubenville, the Jefferson Glass Co. stands prominent. This concern was incorporated four years ago under the laws of Ohio with a capital of $50,000. They manufacture crystal, colored, and opalescent tableware, lemonade sets, and novelties, decorated in gold and enamel… The plant is located at No. 324 North Seventh Street, covering a large portion of an entire city block, the factory being thoroughly up-to-date, equipped with all modern machinery and operating one 12-pot furnace and one day tank. They employ 200 hands and two traveling men on the road…–September 1905, CGL.

A. G. Frohme and George Caldwell became owners of the company in 1907 and moved the business from Steubenville to Follansbee. *Announcement was made this week that the Jefferson Glass Co., of Steubenville, O., have decided to erect a plant at Follansbee, W. Va. This move has been brought about, it is stated, by the fact that in their present location the company have no property on which to enlarge their present plant. The new plant will contain a 16-pot furnace and five lehrs, and it is reported that in*

addition to the present line of decorated glassware the company will branch out into the manufacture of other lines of tableware. Building operations will be commenced in the near future and the new plant will be ready for operation some time next fall. –May 1906, CGL.

B. W. Jacobs became the general manager in 1908. He formerly had worked at the Ohio Flint Glass Co. of Lancaster, Ohio. When he joined Jefferson, the rights to the Chippendale pattern and his process for finishing glassware termed "Krys-Tol" were brought to the new company. Krys-Tol was eventually made by the Central Glass Co. also.

Patterns made by the company include Iris, Vogue, Tokyo, Chippendale, Diamond Peg, Ribbed Drape, and Dolly Madison. *Every lover of fine colored glass articles should see their line… Their lustres are beautiful and the blendings and tints are unique. Many of these tints have never been brought out before. They are showing about 75 new patterns in wine, ruby, blue, emerald, etc. –January 1902, CGL.*

Be aware that not all patterns generally credited to Jefferson are documented by catalog illustrations or ads.

OMN: unknown

AKA: BUTTON ARCHES

DATE: ca. 1910

COLORS: clear, $28.00; clear with ruby stain, $52.00; Clambroth, $60.00.

SIZE: 2¼" tall x 1¾" wide

NOTES: This is a copy of the Duncan & Miller Button Arches. This toothpick and several other pieces of Button Arches are shown in an old Jefferson catalog. Most of these items were made for souvenir ware.

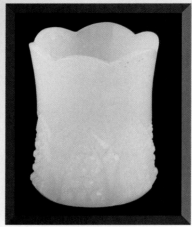

Clambroth

Green

OMN: No. 270

AKA: COLONIAL

DATE: 1908

COLORS: clear, $42.00; blue, $80.00; blue with gold decor, $95.00; green, $80.00.

SIZE: 2½" tall x 2⅛" wide

Blue with gold decoration

OMN: No. 140

AKA: DIAMOND PEG

DATE: 1894

COLORS: clear, $38.00; clear with ruby stain, $78.00; ivory, $85.00; ivory with enamel, $115.00.

SIZE: 2¼" tall x 2" wide

NOTES: Pieces of this pattern were marked "Krys-Tol." This pattern has been attributed to McKee because of a mold sale, but only the pitcher and some stemware were shown in a McKee catalog. McKee probably did not make the toothpick.

Ivory with enamel decoration

Green

Blue

OMN: No. 231

AKA: DOUBLE CIRCLE

DATE: 1905

COLORS: clear, $52.00; blue, $120.00; green, $105.00.

SIZE: 2½" tall x 1⅞" wide

Blue opalescent

OMN: No. 251

AKA: IDYLL

DATE: 1907

COLORS: clear, $68.00; blue, $190.00; green, $172.00; clear opalescent, $230.00; blue opalescent, $345.00; green opalescent, $570.00.

SIZE: 2½" tall x 1⅞" wide

Clear opalescent

Blue and green

Wine with gold decoration

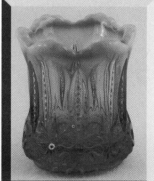

Blue opalescent

OMN: IRIS

AKA: IRIS WITH MEANDER

DATE: 1904

COLORS: clear, $48.00; blue, $138.00; green, $118.00; green with gold decor, $128.00; clear opalescent, $152.00; blue opalescent, $235.00; green opalescent, $215.00; canary opalescent, $252.00; wine, $135.00; wine with gold, $148.00.

SIZE: 2½" tall x 2" wide

NOTES: 1904 ads announced that the pattern Iris was available in "flint [clear], blue and canary opalescent. Also in Gold Decorated Crystal, Blue, Green, Wine."

Green with gold decoration

Jefferson Glass Co.

OMN: No. 254

AKA: JEFFERSON, FIGURE 8

DATE: 1907

COLORS: clear, $68.00; clear with rose stain, $155.00.

SIZE: 2¼" tall x 2" wide

Clear

Green with flat top

OMN: unknown

AKA: JEFFERSON OPTIC

DATE: 1910

COLORS: clear, $24.00; clear with enamel decor, $42.00; clear with ruby stain, $70.00; apple green, $52.00; apple green with enamel decor, $65.00; blue, $55.00; blue with enamel decor, $65.00; dark green, $50.00; dark green with enamel decor, $65.00; electric blue, $65.00; electric blue with enamel decor, $85.00; ivory, $70.00; wine, $60.00; wine with enamel decor, $68.00.

SIZE: 2¼" tall x 1¾" wide

NOTES: As can be seen in the photographs, toothpicks were made with scalloped tops and flat tops.

Clear with enamel decoration   *Clear with enamel decoration*   *Clear with ruby stain*   *Blue with enamel decoration*

Blue with enamel decoration   *Wine with enamel decoration*   *Green with enamel decoration*

OMN: No. 250

AKA: RIBBED DRAPE

DATE: 1906

COLORS: clear, $88.00; clear with enamel decor, $125.00; blue, $190.00; blue with enamel decor, $245.00; green, $185.00; green with enamel decor, $240.00; ivory, $270.00; ivory with enamel decor, $285.00.

SIZE: 2½" tall x 2" wide

Green with enamel decoration

Blue with enamel decoration   *Ivory with enamel decoration*

OMN: No. 221

AKA: RIBBED THUMBPRINT

DATE: 1905

COLORS: clear, $42.00; clear with ruby stain, $88.00; ivory, $190.00; ivory with enamel decor, $210.00; light green $65.00.

SIZE: 2½" tall x 1⅞" wide

Clear with ruby stain

Ivory with enameled flowers

OMN: unknown

AKA: RING & BEADS

DATE: 1910

COLORS: clear, $38.00; apple green, $75.00; blue, $80.00; ivory, $80.00; wine, $75.00.

SIZE: 2½" tall x 2" wide

NOTES: The wider items are individual sugars.

Green with gold on beads

Wine with enamel decoration

Blue with enamel decoration   *Toothpick*   *Wine with sanded finish and enamel decoration*

113

Jefferson Glass Co.

Clear opalescent

OMN: unknown

AKA: SWAG WITH BRACKETS

DATE: 1903

COLORS: clear, $42.00; blue, $80.00; canary, $85.00; green, $80.00; clear opalescent, $120.00; blue opalescent, $175.00; canary opalescent, $190.00; green opalescent, $165.00; wine, $78.00; wine with gold decor, $90.00.

SIZE: 2½" tall x 2⅛" wide

NOTES: This toothpick has been reproduced in several colors. On the old, the notches at the top are rounded; the notches on the new come to points. Reproduced by Degenhart and subsequently Boyd of Cambridge, Ohio, in many colors.

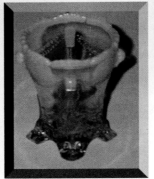

Canary opalescent

Wine with gold decoration

Blue with gold decoration

OMN: TOKYO, No. 212

DATE: 1904

COLORS: clear, $48.00; blue, $90.00; green, $90.00; clear opalescent, $128.00; blue opalescent, $260.00; green opalescent, $255.00.

SIZE: 2⅜" tall x 2" wide

NOTES: Some pieces in this pattern have been reproduced by the Fenton Art Glass Co., but not the toothpick.

Blue opalescent

Green opalescent

Wine with enamel decoration

OMN: VOGUE

AKA: SCALLOPED SKIRT

DATE: 1904

COLORS: clear, $48.00; clear with enamel decor, $52.00; blue, $120.00; blue with enamel decor, $130.00; green, $98.00; green with enamel decor, $115.00; wine, $98.00; wine with enamel decor, $120.00.

SIZE: 2½" tall x 2" wide

Green with enamel decoration

Blue with enamel decoration

KING, SON & CO.
PITTSBURGH, PENNSYLVANIA
1869 – 1891

This factory was known as the Cascade Glass Works. It was founded by David C. King and his son, William Campbell King, in 1869. This unlucky factory suffered two major fires within five years. In 1891 King, Son & Co. joined the U.S. Glass combine and became Factory K, and William King became a director of U.S. Glass. He remained with the company until his retirement.

King, Son & Co. introduced colors into their line in 1884. They made primarily tableware and novelties.

Blue

OMN: No. 362

AKA: DOG HOUSE

DATE: mid-to-late 1880s

COLORS: blue, $85.00; green, $85.00; amber with gold, $85.00.

SIZE: 2" tall x 2" wide

NOTES: This is the bottom to a mustard, but the lid is rarely found today.

OMN: DOUBLE SHOE, No. 326

DATE: mid-to-late 1880s

COLORS: clear, $45.00; amber, $140.00; blue, $140.00; opaque light blue, $160.00.

SIZE: 1¾" tall x 2¾" long

NOTES: Possibly an individual salt rather than a true toothpick. May be a match holder for burnt and unused matches, but it seems rather short for that purpose.

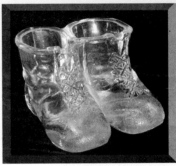

Clear

Clear

OMN: LONDON

AKA: PICKET

DATE: late 1880s

COLORS: clear, $70.00; canary, $135.00; light green, $130.00; clear satin, $100.00.

SIZE: 3" tall x 2" wide

NOTES: According to old King catalogs, this is a match vase and the original name is London.

OMN: No. 254

DATE: 1884

COLORS: clear, $42.00; canary, $65.00; apple green, $65.00.

SIZE: unknown

NOTES: Catalogs indicate this was made either plain or with a vertical optic.

Optic canary, plain canary

OMN: No. 346

AKA: SHEAF OF FLOWERS

DATE: late 1880s

COLORS: clear, $50.00.

SIZE: unknown

NOTES: Catalog pictures are not good, but the design appears to be a sheaf or bouquet of flowers tied in the middle. Named by authors.

OMN: No. 352

AKA: SHELL CORNUCOPIA

DATE: late 1880s

COLORS: clear, $45.00; amber, $60.00; blue, $60.00.

SIZE: unknown

NOTES: Named by authors. Also made with a lid and designated an ink.

OMN: SOCK

AKA: BABY'S BOOTEE

DATE: late 1880s

COLORS: clear, $38.00; amber, $52.00; blue, $60.00; light amber, $60.00; opaque light blue, $68.00; pale blue, $45.00; opal, $50.00.

SIZE: 2⅝" tall x 3⅝" long

NOTES: Possibly also made in apple green as King, Son & Co. is known to have made this color. No specific designation of toothpick was listed in catalogs.

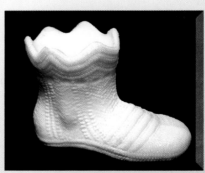

Opal

KOKOMO GLASS MANUFACTURING COMPANY
KOKOMO, INDIANA
1900 – 1906

D. C. JENKINS GLASS CO.
KOKOMO, INDIANA
1906 – 1923
ARCADIA, INDIANA (SECOND PLANT)
1913 – 1932

The Jenkins family, David C. Sr., David C. Jr., and Addison, organized the Kokomo Glass Manufacturing Co. in 1900, and the plant started making glass in 1901. A fire in 1905 completely destroyed the factory, but it was rebuilt in 1906. *A disastrous fire visited the plant of the Kokomo Glass Mfg. Co., Kokomo, Ind., last Sunday evening. The fire is said to have originated in the basement of the south wing... By hard work the [fire] department managed to save the cooper shop, a small building separated from the main structures, and the producer gas plant. The walls of the factory were of brick construction, but all the interior structural work was of wood. The heat from the furnaces had dried every stick of timber under the roof until it was ready to flash into flames at the first touch of fire and this explains the rapidity with which the blaze spread and the completeness of the work of destruction.* –June 1905, CGL. In 1906 David C. Jenkins, Sr., retired, and the company was reorganized as the D. C. Jenkins Glass Co. In 1913, it purchased a vacant glass house at Arcadia, Indiana, as a second factory and continued making the same products, especially opalescent glass.

A few of its patterns include Dewdrop and Raindrop, Paneled Cherry, Paneled Grape, Sunburst, Boxed Star, and Thistle Blow.

Clear

OMN: No. 215

AKA: FALCON STRAWBERRY

DATE: uncertain

COLORS: clear, $55.00.

SIZE: 2⅜" tall x 1½" wide

OMN: No. 707

AKA: GRAPE WITH THUMBPRINT

DATE: uncertain

COLORS: clear, $48.00.

SIZE: 2⅜" tall x 1¾" wide

Clear

Kokomo Glass Manufacturing Co.

Clear

OMN: No. 475
AKA: PANELED CHERRY
DATE: 1904
COLORS: clear, $48.00.
SIZE: 2½" tall x 1¾" wide

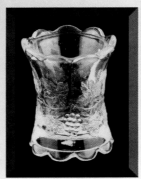

Clear

OMN: No. 807
AKA: PANELED GRAPE, LATE
DATE: 1910
COLORS: clear, $48.00.
SIZE: 2⅜" tall x 1¾" wide

Clear

OMN: unknown
AKA: PANELED SUNFLOWER
DATE: unknown
COLORS: clear, $52.00.
SIZE: 2½" tall x 1¾" wide
NOTES: This toothpick has two different tops, one with vertical striations and one plain.

OMN: No. 209
AKA: STARS & STRIPES, ZIPPER & DIAMONDS
DATE: ca. 1900
COLORS: clear, $30.00.
SIZE: 2¾" tall x 1¼" wide
NOTES: Made in the teens by Federal Glass Co., which called it Climax.

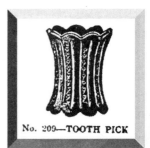

No. 209—TOOTH PICK

LaBelle Glass Co.
Bridgeport, Ohio
1872 – 1888

The LaBelle Glass Co. was organized in 1872 by Andrew H. Baggs, E. P. Rhodes, and F. C. Winship at Bridgeport, Ohio. Harry Northwood was hired as plant manager in 1886, but he remained at LaBelle for a very short time and likely had little impact on the company. While Mr. Northwood was an accomplished etcher and engraver, he has also been credited with being a chemist and metal maker. However, nothing in the trade journals was found to confirm this.

The history of this factory is a checkered one, since it had many problems during its lifetime. It was idle from 1884 to 1886. As with many factories, LaBelle reorganized, closed, and reopened. In September of 1887, it was destroyed by fire, rebuilt, and reopened in January 1888. Its final closing was in April of 1888 due to bankruptcy.

LaBelle made tableware, barware, and lamps. Several patterns were made. They include No. 849, No. 210, Queen Anne, No. 365 Bamboo, Baird, a Paragon ink set, No. 90 and No. 400 tea sets, and a Hammock novelty bouquet holder.

Ruby opalescent

OMN: unknown
AKA: LABELLE OPAL
DATE: 1886
COLORS: clear opalescent, $160.00; canary opalescent, $225.00; ruby opalescent, $225.00.
SIZE: 2¼" tall x 1¾" wide
NOTES: Long attributed to LaBelle, but we have found no catalog or ad showing this pattern.

Clear opalescent

LIBBEY GLASS CO.
TOLEDO, OHIO
1888 – PRESENT

The New England Glass Works, William L. Libbey & Son, Proprietors, came into existence in 1880 at the location of the former Boston Porcelain & Glass Co., which had been founded in 1818 by Deming Jarves.

In 1888 the firm moved to Toledo, Ohio, and the name was changed to W. L. Libbey & Son Company, Proprietors, New England Glass Works. In 1892 the name was shortened to Libbey Glass Co. This factory continues producing glass today with a different name and different focus.

Libbey is well known for maize and amberina.

We are indebted to our art glass experts for the information about, and pricing of, these toothpicks.

Clear satin

OMN: unknown

AKA: HAT

DATE: 1893

COLORS: clear, $95.00; clear satin, $105.00.

SIZE: 2" tall x 3" across brim

NOTES: Some pieces are embossed "World's Columbian Exhibition 1893" on the brim and "Libbey Glass Co., Toledo, Ohio" on the base.

OMN: MAIZE

DATE: 1889

COLORS: ivory with green leaves, $535.00; ivory with blue leaves, $560.00.

SIZE: 2¼" tall x 2⅛" wide

NOTES: The opal and ivory pieces are often decorated with enameled green or blue husks, sometimes outlined with gold. This line is blown, not pressed. Made at the Toledo plant.

Maize, ivory decorated

MCKEE & BROS.
PITTSBURGH, PENNSYLVANIA
1835 – 1888
JEANNETTE, PENNSYLVANIA
1888 – 1899

The Passing of the McKees:

With the formation of the National Glass Co. the identity, personality, individuality, and a certain amount of family history and family pride passes from off the stage of action. It would not be true to say that they pass into obscurity and forgetfulness, for no single individual or family active enough to have impressed either their individuality, personality or intellectuality upon so important an industry of the United States, can ever pass into oblivion. And, besides, for the same reason that "no man is great to

his valet," no man is, as a rule, great to his generation. The future alone can correctly and justly judge certain men who retire from active participation in glass affairs because of the coming of a more formidable economic force than the industrial world has heretofore witnessed. And these remarks apply with special force to the McKee family — H. Sellers, the father, and A. Hart and Tom, the sons.

For two generations the name of McKee has been a leader and beacon in the glass industry. They impressed themselves upon the industry to a larger and more

McKee & Bros.

prominent extent than most of their compeers, and were respected and feared as independents, as peacemakers, as chasers into whose eyes no competitor was ever known to throw dust, for they were always first at the start, and were never last at the finish. –November 1899, CGL.

The following is a review of H. Sellers McKee, reported in 1905:

H. Sellers McKee is perhaps better known as a glass manufacturer and investor in street railways. He has been president of the First National Bank of Birmingham for a number of years and is one of the largest stockholders in that institution. He was born on the South Side in 1845, until recently had lived all his life in Pittsburg. His present home is in New York, where he has resided for some time. He expects to make that city his permanent home. Mr. McKee attended the old Birmingham school and then began his business career. His father, Thomas McKee, established a glass business with his brother, Samuel McKee, on the South Side about 1835, and the firm of S. McKee & Co. was the pioneer glass firm on that side of the river, and perhaps in Pittsburg. Frederick, Stuart, and William McKee, brothers of H. Sellers McKee, built a flint glass factory at South Eighteenth Street and was a clerk in that firm for a number of years.

The name of the firm was McKee & Bros., and later the father sold his interest in the firm of S. McKee & Co. and joined his sons in business. After the death of his father in 1866, H. Sellers McKee became a partner in the firm of McKee & Bros. He acquired most of the holdings of his brothers in the business and in 1884, when his brother Stuart died, H. Sellers McKee was the largest owner of stock in the firm. When the Pittsburg & Lake Erie Railroad acquired the property at South Eighteenth, preparations were made to rebuild the glass house elsewhere. Jeannette was selected and the plant was erected there and put in operation about 1892.

Later Mr. McKee took his son, A. Hart McKee, as a partner and the name of McKee & Bros. was still continued. Later Mr. McKee and James A. Chambers formed the Chambers & McKee Glass Co., which manufactured window glass and the plant was built at Jeannette. The firm established the first tank factory in this part of the country and continued in business until the American Window Glass Co. was organized in 1899, when the control of the plant was secured by that company. At about this time the National Glass Co. was formed and bought the flint glass plant at Jeannette, conducted by H. Sellers McKee and his son, and since that time Mr. McKee has not been in the glass business. –March 1905, CGL.

The first of several McKee glass factories was the S. McKee & Co., established on the South Side of Pittsburgh in 1835 by Thomas McKee and his brother Samuel. This factory manufactured green bottles.

Frederick, Stuart, and William McKee (sons of Thomas) organized McKee & Bros. and built a flint glass factory at South 18th Street. H. Sellers, a younger brother, was a clerk in the firm. Later Thomas sold his interest in S. McKee & Co. and joined his sons at McKee & Bros. In 1866, Thomas died and H. Sellers McKee became a partner in McKee & Bros. H. Sellers acquired most of the holdings of his brothers; and in 1884, when his brother Stuart died, he was the largest stockholder in the firm. The property was acquired by the Pittsburgh and Lake Erie Railroad, so consequently a new plant was erected at Jeannette, Pennsylvania, in 1888. In 1899, the company became part of the National Glass Co. In 1904, National ceased making glass and leased its properties. The McKee & Bros. works were leased to the chartered firm of McKee-Jeannette Glass Co. The McKee family was not involved with this new company. It appears from existing McKee-Jeannette catalogs that many, if not all, the current National/McKee molds were included in the transfer of ownership, as many patterns were continued by McKee-Jeannette.

McKee & Bros. manufactured tableware, stemware, lamps, and novelties. From 1897 to 1902, it made many novelties and covered animal dishes in opal glass. Patterns include Oxford, Majestic, Gladiator, Celtic, National, Teutonic, Keystone, Nelly, Jubilee, Britannic, Empire, Germanic, Adonis, Masonic, Lone Star, Ionic, Sunbeam, Napoleon, Hiawatha, Doric, and many others.

See also McKee-Jeannette and National Glass Co., Factory No. 12.

Clear

OMN: APOLLO

DATE: 1899

COLORS: clear, $38.00; clear with rose stain, $98.00; rose pink, $130.00.

SIZE: 2¼" tall x 2" wide

NOTES: *Have you seen the Rose Pink of McKee & Bros.? It's a wonder what beautiful colors glassware is made in, anyway. But this Rose Pink is something new, and rare, for that matter, for they are the only firm that make it... How pretty their Apollo shape looks in this color... Either in crystal or rose pink it is handsome and has established itself as a favorite.* –February 1899, CGL. Still available in a 1902 catalog.

OMN: BOAR HEAD

DATE: ca. 1886

COLORS: clear, $125.00.

SIZE: unknown

NOTES: While this is a hang-on-the-wall match holder, it is an interesting item to add to collections. Colors are unknown at this time, although the standard McKee colors of the period should be expected.

BOAR HEAD

Opal

OMN: BOSTON BULL

DATE: 1899

COLORS: clear, $115.00; opal, $185.00.

SIZE: 2½" tall x 3½" wide

NOTES: Early ads indicate this was a match holder. Colors made are unknown at this time. This was made prior to the merger with National and was included in the 1902 National catalog.

Bull Dog Match Holder.

OMN: BRITANNIC

DATE: 1895

COLORS: clear, $42.00; clear with amber stain, $135.00; clear with ruby stain, $135.00.

SIZE: 2⅜" tall x 2⅛" wide

NOTES: *The second pattern of the series, the Britannic, embracing 100 pieces, was designed and made with the special view of pleasing the large jobbing trade. The shapes are new, and the metal as brilliant in quality as it is possible to make it.* –December 1894, *CGL.* Decorations of ruby and amber stains were applied to Britannic by the Mueller Glass Staining Co., of Pittsburgh, in 1895. Also decorated with colors and "tasteful engraving."

Clear with amber stain

Clear with ruby stain

Clear with ruby stain

121

Green and clear with ruby stain

No. 103 Champion Caster
(3 Bottles and Toothpick)

OMN: CHAMPION, No. 103

DATE: 1896

COLORS: clear, $42.00; clear with gold decor, $48.00; clear with ruby stain, $138.00; clear with amber stain, $138.00; emerald green, $90.00. Caster set: clear, $250.00; emerald green, $375.00.

SIZE: 2¼" tall x 2" wide

NOTES: *The "Champion" pattern lately completed by McKee & Bros., is being placed before the trade...*

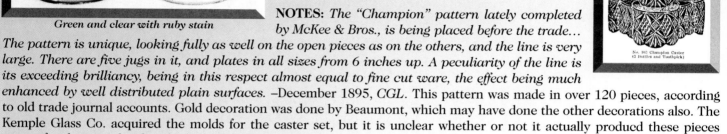

The pattern is unique, looking fully as well on the open pieces as on the others, and the line is very large. There are five jugs in it, and plates in all sizes from 6 inches up. A peculiarity of the line is its exceeding brilliancy, being in this respect almost equal to fine cut ware, the effect being much enhanced by well distributed plain surfaces. –December 1895, *CGL.* This pattern was made in over 120 pieces, according to old trade journal accounts. Gold decoration was done by Beaumont, which may have done the other decorations also. The Kemple Glass Co. acquired the molds for the caster set, but it is unclear whether or not it actually produced these pieces except for the cruet bottle, which was substantionally changed.

Clear

OMN: DORIC

AKA: FEATHER

DATE: 1896

COLORS: clear, $85.00; clear with ruby stain, $285.00; clear with amber stain, $285.00; emerald green, $325.00.

SIZE: 2¾" tall x 2" wide

NOTES: This pattern was continued by McKee while a part of National; it appears in a 1902 National Glass Co. catalog. This was a large tableware line.

Emerald green

OMN: IONIC

DATE: 1895

COLORS: clear, $32.00; clear with No. 400 engraving, $38.00.

SIZE: unknown

NOTES: *The Ionic is perfectly plain, and makes up well engraved. There are 40 pieces in this line.* –December 1894, *CGL.* The pattern, but not the toothpick, appears in the 1902 National Glass Co. catalog.

Ionic Set.
ENGRAVED NO. 400.
SUGAR AND COVER
SPOON.
CREAM.
BUTTER AND COVER

Clear with ruby stain

Clear with gold decoration

OMN: JUBILEE

AKA: HICKMAN

DATE: 1897

COLORS: clear, $48.00; clear with gold decor, $58.00; emerald green, $165.00; clear with ruby stain, $185.00.

SIZE: 2¼" tall x 2" wide

NOTES: Original McKee ads indicate this pattern was made in 189 items. This pattern was continued by McKee when it was a part of National Glass as it appears in a 1902 National Glass catalog.

Clear

OMN: KEYSTONE

DATE: 1897

COLORS: clear, $40.00; clear with ruby stain, $140.00; clear with engraving, $52.00; opal, $115.00; opal with enamel decor, $128.00.

SIZE: 2⅜" tall x 2" wide

NOTES: In 1899 the company offered an opal Keystone "match or toothpick" decorated with hand-painted flowers and "fine gilding" in a Cinderella assortment of opal decorated novelties. Appears in the 1902 National Glass Co. catalog.

Clear with ruby stain

OMN: LENOX

DATE: 1899

COLORS: clear, $175.00; clear with ruby stain, $400.00.

SIZE: 2⅜" tall x 2" wide

NOTES: Still in the National Glass Co. catalog in 1902.

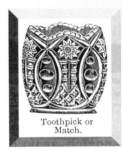

Toothpick or Match.

Clear

OMN: LONE STAR

AKA: SQUAT PINEAPPLE

DATE: 1898

COLORS: crystal, $52.00.

SIZE: 2¼" tall x 1⅞" wide

NOTES: This pattern was originated by McKee and continued by National Glass.

OMN: MAJESTIC in January 1894, PILGRIM in January 1897

DATE: 1894

COLORS: clear, $38.00; clear with ruby stain, $115.00.

SIZE: 2½" tall x 2" wide

NOTES: Note that both names are original with McKee & Bros. Apparently the name was changed after about three years, possibly to stimulate sales. Appears in the 1902 National Glass Co. catalog.

Clear with ruby stain

OMN: MASONIC

DATE: 1895

COLORS: clear, $42.00; clear with ruby stain, $130.00; clear with amber stain, $170.00.

SIZE: 2⅜" tall x 1⅞" wide

NOTES: *The Masonic pattern contains 120 pieces in all, which are pronounced by experts to be by all odds the best imitation of cut glass ever put upon the market...* –December 1894, *CGL*. The Mueller Glass Staining Co. were decorating this pattern with ruby stain and amber stain in January of 1895. By May, announcements were made that the company was shipping Masonic in amber stain to England. The pattern was also decorated with colors and "tasteful engraving."

Clear with amber stain

Clear with ruby stain

OMN: OWL HEAD

DATE: ca. 1886

COLORS: clear, $115.00.

SIZE: unknown

NOTES: While this is a hang-on-the-wall match holder, it is an interesting item to add to collections. Colors are unknown at this time, although the standard McKee colors of the period should be expected.

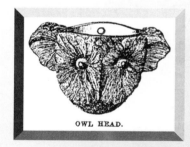

OWL HEAD.

OMN: PLUG HAT

DATE: probably the late 1880s

COLORS: clear, $65.00; amber, $72.00; blue, $78.00; clear with ruby stain, $85.00; blue opaque, $85.00, canary, $80.00.

SIZE: 2¼" tall x 3" wide across brim

NOTES: Catalogs call this a toothpick or match. This hat is identical to Cambridge's Saratoga Hat. It is possible that the mold was transferred to Cambridge after National ceased to exist.

Plug Hat Toothpick or Match

Amber

Opal

OMN: RAM HEAD

AKA: HOOPED BARREL (base only)

DATE: ca. 1886

COLORS: Base only: clear, $35.00; opaque blue, $68.00; ivory, $68.00; opal, $65.00. Mustard, complete: clear, $100.00; opaque blue, $145.00; ivory, $135.00; opal, $225.00+.

SIZE: unknown

NOTES: This mustard is often found without its lid, causing it to be misidentified as a toothpick. The name give to the base is Hooped Barrel. Without a catalog illustration, it would be difficult to determine that the ram's head lid went with the base. This example has metal bands. It is also known with a metal allover cage.

RAM HEAD. (ALSO MUSTARD, WITH COVER.)

Skull Match Holder.

OMN: RAMESES III (McKee), SKULL (National)

DATE: 1899

COLORS: clear, $75.00; opal, $250.00+.

SIZE: 2½" tall x 3½" long

NOTES: This was made by McKee shortly before the merger with National Glass, and was continued by National in its 1902 catalog.

Opal

Mustard, blue

OMN: STUMP

AKA: BIRD AND TREE

DATE: ca. 1886

COLORS: clear, $55.00; amber, $80.00; blue, $95.00; canary, $165.00.

SIZE: 2¾" tall x 2" wide

NOTES: This toothpick was also used as a base for a mustard and shown both ways in an old company catalog. This has been reproduced recently in colors never made originally.

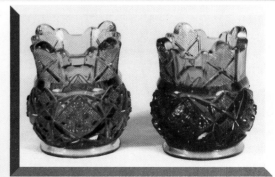

STUMP MUSTARD AND COVER. STUMP.

Note leaf lid for mustard.

OMN: SUNBEAM

DATE: 1898

COLORS: clear, $42.00; blue, $95.00; emerald, $80.00; emerald with gold decor, $85.00; clear with ruby stain, $175.00.

SIZE: 2½" tall x 2¼" wide

NOTES: *McKee & Bros. have already taken some remarkably big orders for their new Sunbeam pattern.... –January 1898, CGL.* The blue toothpick has been found with a flared top, so other colors may also be found like this. Still in wholesale catalogs in 1905.

*Emerald with gold decoration
and blue with gold decoration*

OMN: TEUTONIC

DATE: 1894

COLORS: clear, $42.00; clear with ruby stain, $120.00; clear with amber stain, $165.00.

SIZE: unknown

NOTES: This pattern was decorated with ruby stain and amber stain by the Mueller Glass Staining Co. of Pittsburgh in early 1895. Appears in the 1902 National Glass Co. catalog.

McKee-Jeannette Glass Co.
Jeannette, Pennsylvania
1904 – 1908

McKee Glass Co.
Jeannette, Pennsylvania
1908 – 1951

In 1904 Andrew Jackson Smith, Ernest Smith, and William Carle leased the McKee Glass Works from the National Glass Co. and organized the McKee-Jeannette Glass Co. From catalogs of the McKee-Jeannette company, it appears that some, if not all, of the National/McKee molds were included in the lease as many patterns originating with National/McKee were continued by McKee-Jeannette. After National Glass declared bankruptcy in 1908, the McKee-Jeannette firm reorganized and was renamed the McKee Glass Co. *The new McKee Glass Co. expect soon to take over the properties of the McKee-Jeannette Glass Co., which is* *still in the hands of receivers, Smith and Keltz. The company will have a capital of $125,000 and the stockholders include A. J. Smith, J. W. Keltz, D. B. Pilkey and other local capitalists. The business of the big plant under the receivers has been vigorously pushed and almost all old customers retained.* –December 1908.

In 1951 the company was purchased by the Thatcher Manufacturing Co., maker of bottles and containers.

The company is well known for its Prescut patterns, stemware, and novelties.

Clear

OMN: AZTEC

DATE: 1904

COLORS: clear, $28.00; clear with ruby stain, $72.00.

SIZE: 2⅛" tall x 1⅞" wide

NOTES: Part of Prescut lines. There are many reproductions in colors. The bar glass was also hand-tooled into a toothpick.

Toothpick.

OMN: No. 700

AKA: CHOKER

DATE: 1907

COLORS: Toothpick: clear, $48.00. Condiment set: clear, $185.00.

SIZE: unknown

NOTES: *The 700 Pattern made to meet the growing demand for Plain Patterns –1907.*

Clear with gold decoration

OMN: COLONIAL, No. 20

AKA: LEAN QUEEN (sanitary shape)

DATE: 1910

COLORS: Standard shape: clear, $42.00; clear with gold decor, $45.00. Sanitary shape: clear, $52.00; opal, $85.00.

SIZE: Standard shape: 2⅜" tall x 2¼" tall

NOTES: Made in two styles, the standard shape and a sanitary shape. The sanitary was previously named Lean Queen, but it is part of the No. 20 Colonial line.

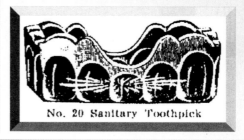

OMN: MARTEC

DATE: ca. 1904

COLORS: clear, $38.00.

SIZE: unknown

NOTES: The toothpick was not shown in catalogs we have seen. It is a flat, sanitary type. Marked "Prescut."

OMN: No. 410

DATE: 1917

COLORS: clear, $42.00.

SIZE: unknown

NOTES: Described in McKee catalogs as "innovation cut." The term referred to the process of making the pressed glass, not the specific pattern, as several lines were made that were all designated as Innovation Cut. Design patent given of No. 50590. Reproduced by St. Clair Glass in many colors and with a beaded top. The old has a smooth top.

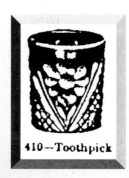

McKee-Jeannette Glass Co.

Clear

OMN: PEEK-A-BOO

DATE: ca. 1904

COLORS: clear, $65.00; amber, $78.00; blue, $85.00; canary $85.00.

SIZE: 3¾" tall x 1⅞" wide

NOTES: Many reproductions exist of this toothpick. It is unclear whether this toothpick originated with National/McKee or with McKee-Jeannette. Another size is 4" tall. Reproductions were made by Kemple, which called these Cherub. Reproduced with top row of blocks shorter than original. The reproductions also have concave undersides, not the hollow centers of the old pieces.

Amber

OMN: PURITAN

DATE: 1910

COLORS: clear, $45.00.

SIZE: unknown

NOTES: Very similar to Rock Crystal, but less ornate.

OMN: RAMONA

AKA: TIPTOE

DATE: ca. 1910

COLORS: clear, $68.00.

SIZE: 2⅜" tall x 2" wide

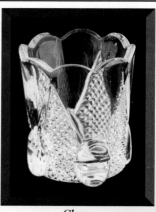

Clear

OMN: ROCK CRYSTAL

DATE: 1903

COLORS: clear, $52.00.

SIZE: 2⅜" tall x 2" wide

NOTES: New Martinsville and U.S. Glass also had patterns of this name. McKee continued production of Rock Crystal in newer shapes in the late 1920s and later, making many items in colors. During the period the toothpick was made, only clear was made in this pattern.

Clear

Clear

Amber

OMN: TAPPAN

DATE: 1915

COLORS: clear, $22.00; amber, $32.00.

SIZE: 2⅜" tall x 1¾" wide

NOTES: This is not a toothpick, but a spooner to a child's table set. This has also been reproduced, sometimes in unusual colors. Reproduced by Kemple.

OMN: TOLTEC

DATE: early 1900s

COLORS: Regular: clear, $42.00. Bar glass toothpick: clear, $42.00.

SIZE: unknown

NOTES: Part of the Prescut lines. reproduced by Kemple in colors. Note the bar glass, which has been hand tooled to make two styles of toothpick holders.

Toothpick

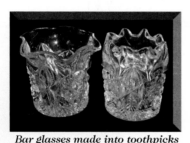

Bar glasses made into toothpicks

OMN: YUTEC

AKA: REGAL STAR

DATE: 1909

COLORS: clear, $42.00.

SIZE: unknown

NOTES: Part of the Prescut line. Has been reproduced by Kemple in a shorter version. The new has a ring around the base not present in the original.

MILLERSBURG GLASS CO.
MILLERSBURG, OHIO
1909 – 1911

The Millersburg Glass Co. started operations in 1909 under the direction of John Fenton, Robert Fenton, R. W. Stanley, and H. F. Weber. Bankruptcy loomed in 1911, and the firm was reorganized as the Radium Glass Co., producing carnival glass. This firm was in business for about six months.

Some Millersburg patterns include Ohio Star, Hobstar & Feather, and Millersburg Flute, along with several hard-to-find carnival pieces. Millersburg is known primarily for its carnival glass.

OMN: OHIO STAR

DATE: 1910

COLORS: clear, $135.00.

SIZE: 2" tall x 2" wide

Clear

MODEL FLINT GLASS CO.
FINDLAY, OHIO — 1888 – 1893
ALBANY, INDIANA — 1893 – 1899

The Model Flint Glass Co. was organized in 1888 with A. C. Heck as president, A. L. Strasburger as secretary, Andrew L. Stephenson as treasurer, and W. C. Walters as factory manager.

Gas shortages in the Findlay area caused the company to move to Albany in 1893. In 1899 Model Flint became one of the National Glass Co. factories, designated Factory No. 11. Popular patterns were continued at the Albany plant, and the factory also made opalescent glass during this period.

Patterns include No. 849 Square Waffle, No. 851 Deep Star, No. 857 Pillow Encircled, No. 861 Double Wave & Fan, Heck, No. 901 Indiana, Albany, Planet, and others. Model Flint's most famous novelty was the Lord's Supper bread plate.

See also National Glass Co., Factory No. 11.

OMN: FISH IN POND

DATE: unknown

COLORS: clear, $95.00.

SIZE: unknown

NOTES: Appears to match a salt shaker shown in a Model Flint catalog from the Albany plant. The stippled finish on the toothpick has caused some to call this "pseudo Pomona."

Clear

OMN: PEERLESS

DATE: 1898

COLORS: clear, $32.00; clear with gold decor, $42.00; emerald green, $80.00; emerald green with gold decor, $90.00.

SIZE: 2¼" tall x 1⅞" wide; wider version, 2⅜" tall x 2⅜" wide

NOTES: Made only at the Albany, Indiana, plant.

Emerald green with gold decoration

Toothpick.

OMN: PRIDE

AKA: BEVELED STAR

DATE: 1899

COLORS: clear, $65.00; amber, $145.00; emerald green, $145.00.

SIZE: 2½" tall x 2¼" wide

NOTES: Made only at the Albany, Indiana, plant. The top portion of the toothpick may be flared or straight.

Clear

Pride Toothpick.

Emerald green

Clear

OMN: STUMP

AKA: SERPENT, SERPENT ON STUMP, SNAKE ON STUMP

DATE: 1892

COLORS: clear, $40.00; amber, $70.00; blue, $88.00.

SIZE: 2⅝" tall x 2⅜" wide

NOTES: Made at both the Findlay and the Albany factories. Reproduced by L. G. Wright of West Virginia in blue, ruby, amber, amethyst, green, and possibly clear.

Stump Toothpick.

Blue

Clear

OMN: TWIST

AKA: SWIRL

DATE: 1892

COLORS: clear, $50.00; clear with satin finish, $62.00; clear opalescent, $160.00; canary opalescent, $210.00; blue opalescent, $210.00.

SIZE: 2⁷⁄₁₆" tall x 2⁵⁄₁₆" wide

NOTES: This is listed both as a toothpick and a child's spoon holder in company catalogs. Only clear pieces were made at the Findlay factory. All colors were made in Albany. The satin finished pieces sometimes are decorated with enameled rims.

C. F. MONROE
MERIDEN, CONNECTICUT
1892 TO APPROXIMATELY WORLD WAR I
(CA. 1914)

C. F. Monroe established his own decorating company in 1892. This company did not manufacture its own glass, but purchased blanks, mainly some from American companies, but also some from importers. Many of the salt and pepper shakers and probably toothpicks were manufactured for C. F. Monroe by the Rodefer Glass Co. of Bellaire, Ohio. Many decorated products are signed with a company backstamp.

Various well-known decorations were done by Monroe, including Wavecrest, Nakara, and Kelva.

Values of toothpicks decorated by this company are difficult to evaluate. The same toothpick holder with a different type of decoration may be worth more or less than those shown. We are indebted to our art glass experts for the descriptions and prices of these toothpicks.

OMN: unknown

AKA: BINOCULARS, OPERA GLASSES

DATE: 1893

COLORS: opal, decorated, $700.00+.

SIZE: unknown

NOTES: Shown in a 1893 ad from C. F. Monroe. Unusual double toothpick encased in a metal frame.

OMN: unknown

AKA: PETAL TOP

DATE: 1893

COLORS: opal, decorated, $265.00.

SIZE: unknown

NOTES: See illustration of this toothpick in original ad with Binoculars. Some have Wavecrest mark on base.

Opal with hand-painted floral decoration

OMN: unknown

AKA: SHORT CYLINDER

DATE: 1898

COLORS: opal, decorated, $285.00.

SIZE: 2¼" tall x 1⅞" wide

NOTES: Measurements do not include the metal frame. This piece is marked on the base with the Wavecrest signature.

Opal with enamel flowers, metal frame

Wavecrest mark on base

MOSAIC GLASS CO.
FOSTORIA, OHIO
1891 – CA. 1893

This factory had a checkered history of problems. It ceased production about 1893, and the factory site was destroyed by fire in 1895.

OMN: SWAN

DATE: 1891

COLORS: crystal, $95.00; amber, $165.00; blue, $185.00.

SIZE: unknown

NOTES: Designed by Jonathan Haley. Note this is listed as a toothpick, salt, or cologne bottle holder. This novelty was reproduced by St. Clair in chocolate glass and other colors. Reproduced in purple carnival.

MT. WASHINGTON GLASS CO.
BOSTON, MASSACHUSETTS
1837 – 1870
NEW BEDFORD, MASSACHUSETTS
1870 – 1894

This company has a complicated and varied history with openings, closings, and reorganizations throughout its history. It was formed in 1837 by Deming Jarves and his son George. William Libbey joined the firm in 1851. In 1861, the company reorganized and was renamed Libbey & Howe.

The company moved to New Bedford, Massachusetts, in 1870 and became Wm. L. Libbey & Co. William Libbey resigned in 1872 and went to the New England Glass Co. Many reorganizations followed, and the company name was at times the Mt. Washington Glass Co., the Pairpoint

Manufacturing Co., and the Pairpoint Corporation. In 1894 it merged with Pairpoint, manufacturer of metal mountings.

This company is known primarily for its art glass such as Burmese, Amberina, Pearl Satin, and others. In the following lists, we use the term *Lusterless* (an original company term) to describe opal with a satin finish. Many of the decorations on Mt. Washington blanks were done by the Smith brothers, both when they were employed by Mt. Washington and after they left to form their own decorating company.

A patent was held by the company in 1881 for Pearl Satin. Mt. Washington licensed Thomas Webb & Sons of England to also make this type of glass. Some was also made by the Phoenix Glass Co. Burmese was patented in 1885 and was also made by Thomas Webb & Sons of England.

Famous colors and decorations made by Mt. Washington include Crown Milano, about 1890, decorated glassware; Peach Blow, about 1886, pink shading to blue; and Royal Flemish, about 1890, decorated glassware.

The descriptions and values given below were provided to us by experts in art glass. Since the decoration is so integral to the value of these toothpicks, the values given are for the specific toothpick and decoration shown. Comment should be made about "unfinished or unfired Burmese." This is an incorrect term, as the glass referred to by these names is actually ivory (custard) glass with an allover acid finish.

See also Libbey Glass Co.

Decorated

OMN: unknown

AKA: BROWNIE

DATE: 1895

COLORS: opal decorated with Palmer Cox–type brownie, $700.00+.

SIZE: 2¼" tall x 2¼" wide

NOTES: Known with several different Palmer Cox–type Brownies.

OMN: unknown

AKA: BULB BASE, SQUARE TOP

DATE: unknown

COLORS: Burmese, diamond quilted, $600.00+; Lusterless Burmese, hand-painted pine cone decor, $625.00+; Lusterless Burmese, hand-painted florals, $600.00+; Lusterless Burmese, allover hand-painted florals, $650.00+; Lusterless Burmese, hand-painted oak leaf and blue dot decor, $650.00+; Pearl Satin (MOP), blue, $500.00+; Rose Amber, $400.00.

SIZE: 2⅝" tall x 2⅝" across top

NOTES: This shape was widely used by Mt. Washington for a variety of its patented glasses. The Pearl Satin (or mother-of-pearl) could also have been made by Thomas Webb & Sons of England, which had a license from Mt. Washington to make this glass. Webb was also licensed to make Burmese, called Queen's Burmese, with elaborate enamel decoration. Many of these toothpick holders have an optic effect that is now known as diamond quilted or Venetian Diamond.

Glossy Burmese, diamond quilted

Lusterless Burmese, hand-painted pine cone decoration

Lusterless Burmese, hand-painted forget-me-nots

Lusterless Burmese, hand-painted allover floral decoration

*Lusterless Burmese, hand-painted
oak leaf and blue dot decoration*

*Blue Pearl Satin
(mother-of-pearl)*

*Rose Amber (amberina),
diamond optic*

OMN: BEET

AKA: FIG, BEADED TOP

DATE: unknown

COLORS: Lusterless ivory, yellow highlights and enameled
flowers, $750.00+.

SIZE: 1⅞" tall x 2½" wide

NOTES: Fig-shaped salt shakers were referred to as Beets in an
original Mt. Washington catalog. At this point, it is hardly likely
that collectors will revert to the original name!

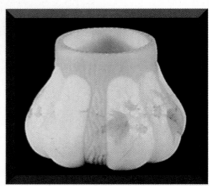

Lusterless ivory with enamel decoration

OMN: BEET

AKA: FIG, CRIMPED TOP

DATE: 1888

COLORS: Lusterless white with yellow wash and hand-painted floral decor,
$450.00+; Lusterless green with hand-painted leaves and berries, $1,500.00+;
Lusterless white with hand-painted ferns and flowers, $600.00+; Burmese with
hand-painted leaves and flowers, $800.00+; Burmese with peach highlights and
hand-painted flowers, $800.00.

SIZE: 2½" across base

NOTES: The toothpick at far left below is thought to be an experimental
greenish shade of Burmese. Original catalog illustrations of the Fig salt shaker
call it a beet, but this shape is so well known as a fig, and it also appears to be so
much more like a fig than a beet, that we endorse the use of the common name.

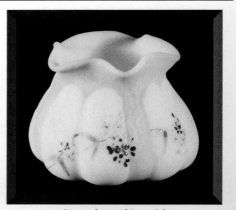

*Lusterless white with
yellow wash and hand-painted
floral decoration with blue dots*

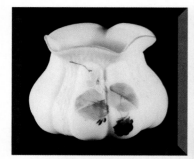

*Lusterless pale green with
hand-painted leaves and berries*

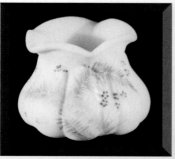

*Lusterless ivory with hand-
painted ferns and tiny flowers*

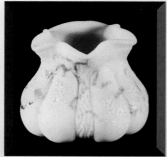

*Burmese with delicate hand-
painted leaves and flowers*

*Burmese with peach highlights
and hand-painted flowers*

OMN: unknown

AKA: FIG, TINY FINGERS

DATE: 1888

COLORS: canary with satin finish and hand-painted flowers, $2,800.00.

SIZE: 2½" across base

NOTES: It is unusual to find this form in colors other than lusterless white or Burmese. This is probably Royal Flemish.

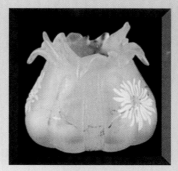

Canary with satin finish and hand-painted flowers

Lusterless white with blue tint and hand-painted daisies

OMN: unknown

AKA: FINE RIB, BEADED TOP

DATE: 1890

COLORS: Lusterless white with blue tint, hand-painted enameled daisies, $350.00+; Lusterless white with blue wash, hand-painted oak leaves and blue dot decor, $400.00+.

SIZE: 2¼" tall x 2½" across bottom

Lusterless white with blue wash and hand-painted oak leaves and blue dot decoration

OMN: unknown

AKA: FINE RIB, THREE LOBE TOP

DATE: 1890

COLORS: Lusterless white with rust interior, hand-painted floral branch, $400.00+.

SIZE: 2½" across bottom

Lusterless white with rust interior and hand-painted floral branch

Hand-painted autumn oak leaves and blue dots

OMN: unknown

AKA: FINE RIB WITH FLAT FINGERS, FLAT FINGERS

DATE: 1890

COLORS: Lusterless white with autumn oak leaves and blue dots, $950.00+; Lusterless white, yellow ground with hand-painted flowers, $680.00+.

SIZE: 2⁵⁄₁₆" tall x 2½" wide

Hand-painted opal with yellow ground, hand-painted small flowers, marked "CM"

Mt. Washington Glass Co.

Opal with hand-painted decoration

OMN: unknown

AKA: FOOTED LOBE

DATE: unknown

COLORS: opal with hand-painted decor, $450.00+; Burmese with hand-painted floral, $700.00+.

SIZE: 2¼" tall x 2¾" wide

*Burmese with
hand-painted floral spray*

OMN: unknown

AKA: HAT

DATE: 1888

COLORS: opal with imitation Burmese color and oak leaf and white dot, $700.00+.

SIZE: 2" tall x 2⅞" wide

*Imitation Burmese and
hand-painted oak leaf and
white dot decoration*

*Lusterless white decorated,
souvenir of 1893 World's Fair*

OMN: unknown

AKA: LITTLE LOBE

DATE: 1893

COLORS: Lusterless white, various decorations, $285.00.

SIZE: 2½" tall x 2¼" wide

NOTES: This toothpick holder was made under contract for Libbey at the time of the 1892/1893 World's Fair and is sometimes marked with the Libbey trademark. It bears a strong resemblance to Mt. Washington–made glass rather than Libbey glass of the period. "…the theory that Libbey commissioned items from other factories and decorators when its factory was unable to supply the enormous demand for souvenirs of the Fair." –*Libbey Glass* by Carl U. Fauster.

OMN: unknown

AKA: MELON

DATE: unknown

COLORS: Lusterless white with yellow wash and hand-painted florals, $280.00.

SIZE: unknown

NOTES: Decorated by Smith Bros. and signed with its rampant lion trademark.

*Lusterless white with yellow wash
and hand-painted floral decoration*

Glossy white with enamel decoration

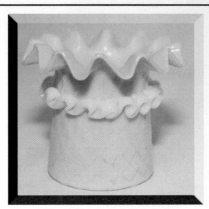

OMN: MUSHROOM, No. 535

DATE: 1891

COLORS: glossy white with enamel decor, $1,550.00+.

SIZE: Small: 1¾" tall x 2¾" wide across top x 1⅜" wide at base.

NOTES: These examples are usually decorated with hand-painted florals, often quite elaborate. There were two sizes made, and both appear in company literature as suitable for toothpicks, although the smaller size is also listed as a salt and the larger as a flower holder.

Lusterless white with hand-painted floral decoration

OMN: unknown

AKA: PARALLEL GREEK KEY

DATE: 1888

COLORS: Lusterless white, decorated, $470.00.

SIZE: 2½" tall x 2¼" wide

Burmese, hand-painted leaves and blue berries

OMN: unknown

AKA: RUFFLED TOP

DATE: unknown

COLORS: Burmese, $850.00+; glossy Burmese with rigaree, $1,250.00+.

SIZE: 2½" tall x 2¼" wide

Glossy Burmese, diamond quilted with rigaree

Pearl satin, amber

OMN: unknown

AKA: RUFFLED TOP, DOUBLE CRIMP

DATE: unknown

COLORS: amber plated with opal, $625.00.

SIZE: 2¾" tall x 2½" wide

NOTES: This may also have been made by Thomas Webb & Sons of England, or possibly, the Phoenix Glass Co.

Lusterless ivory with hand-painted
allover floral decoration

OMN: unknown

AKA: SIMPLE SCROLL, BEADED TOP

DATE: unknown

COLORS: Lusterless ivory with hand-painted allover floral decor, $650.00; Lusterless white with hand-painted floral decor, $625.00.

SIZE: 2½" wide at base

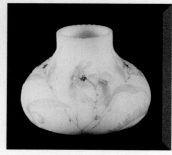

Lusterless white with
hand-painted floral decoration

Glossy white with
hand-painted bouquet

OMN: unknown

AKA: SIMPLE SCROLL, CRIMPED TOP

DATE: unknown

COLORS: glossy white with hand-painted floral decor, $375.00.

SIZE: 2½" wide at base

OMN: unknown

AKA: SIMPLE SCROLL, TINY FINGERS

DATE: unknown

COLORS: Lusterless white with yellow wash and blue iris, $1,600.00.

SIZE: 2½" wide at base

Lusterless white with yellow
wash and blue iris

Lusterless Burmese with
hand-painted flowers

OMN: unknown

AKA: SIMPLE SCROLL, 6 RUFFLED TOP

DATE: ca. 1886

COLORS: Lusterless Burmese with hand-painted flowers, $750.00; signed and decorated Crown Milano, $1,850.00.

SIZE: 2" wide at base

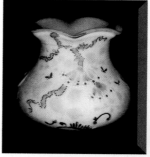

Signed Crown Milano, decorated

Crown Milano mark

OMN: unknown

AKA: SPIDER WEB

DATE: 1890

COLORS: Lusterless white, $135.00; Lusterless ivory with oak leaf and blue dot decor, $350.00; Lusterless white with yellow band, hand-painted decor, $335.00; Lusterless Burmese with oak leaf and blue dot decor, $485.00; Lusterless white with pink band, hand-painted flowers, $350.00.

SIZE: 2½" tall x 2" wide

NOTES: Decorations on these were often done by Smith Brothers, a firm specializing in glass decoration. Many types of decoration can be found on this toothpick, and prices will vary with the quality and type of decoration.

Lusterless ivory with
oak leaf and blue dot
decoration

Lusterless white
with oak leaf
and blue dot decoration

Lusterless white
with pink band and
hand-painted flowers

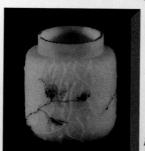

Lusterless white yellow band
and hand-painted decoration

Glossy Burmese, diamond quilted

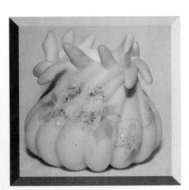

Peachblow with hand-painted flowers

OMN: unknown

AKA: SQUARE TOP

DATE: ca. 1886

COLORS: Burmese glossy, diamond quilted, $550.00; peachblow, hand-painted flowers, $4,000.00+; Burmese with leaves and blue berry decor, $550.00; Lusterless ivory with oak leaf and blue dot decor, $580.00.

SIZE: 2½" tall x 1⅞" wide at top

NOTES: This simple shape was made by both Mt. Washington and New England Glass. The types of glass of which the toothpicks were made are used to differentiate between the two. Examples of Mt. Washington peachblow are extremely rare.

Lusterless ivory with oak leaf and blue dot decoration

Burmese with leaves and blue berry decoration

OMN: unknown

AKA: STRAIGHT SIDES, CRIMPED TOP

DATE: 1886

COLORS: Lusterless white with Mt. Washington decor as shown, $465.00.

SIZE: 2⁷⁄₁₆" tall x 2⅛" wide

NOTES: Crown Milano decoration.

Lusterless white with hand-painted flowers

OMN: unknown

AKA: SWIRLED

DATE: 1890

COLORS: Lusterless white with enamel florals, $340.00.

SIZE: 2½" wide

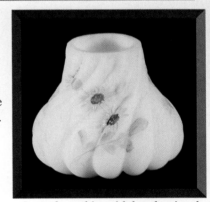

Lusterless white with hand-painted yellow brown-eyed Susans

Ruby satin with enamel decoration

OMN: unknown

AKA: SWIRLED, TINY FINGERS

DATE: 1890

COLORS: Lusterless white with yellow flowers, $1,600.00+; ruby satin with floral decoration, $1,600.00.

SIZE: 2¼" tall x 2½" wide

Lusterless white with yellow flowers

Mt. Washington Glass Co.

Burmese with diamond quilting

OMN: unknown

AKA: TRI-CORNER

DATE: ca. 1886

COLORS: glossy Burmese with diamond quilting, $650.00; rose amber, $425.00; peachblow, satin finish, $2,500.00+; peachblow with blue dot decoration, $5,500.00+.

SIZE: unknown

NOTES: New England Glass Co. (and possibly other firms) made a tri-corner toothpick also.

Rose amber

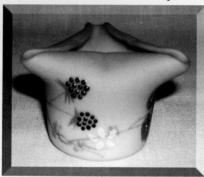

Peachblow with blue dot decoration

Lusterless white with yellow wash on top and hand-painted flower decoration

Lusterless white with blue wash on top and hand-painted flower decoration

Lusterless ivory with hand-painted daisies

Burmese with oak leaf and blue dot decoration

OMN: unknown

AKA: URN

DATE: ca. 1886

COLORS: Lusterless white with hand-painted decor, $350.00; Lusterless ivory with hand-painted daisies, $510.00; Burmese with oak leaf and blue dot decor, $550.00; amberina diamond quilted, $550.00.

SIZE: 2¾" tall x 2½" wide

NOTES: This is attributed to Mt. Washington primarily because of the hand-painted decorations. However, Challinor & Taylor produced a very similar shape and was well known for its decorations on opal.

Amberina diamond quilted

NATIONAL GLASS CO.
PITTSBURGH, PENNSYLVANIA
1899 – 1904+

National Glass Co. was organized as a combine to compete with the United States Glass Co. and was composed of many factories that had not joined that combine. The U.S. Glass Co. designated its factories by letter, so National designated its by number, as follows:

No. 1 — Beatty-Brady Glass Works, Dunkirk, Indiana

No. 2 — Canton Glass Works, Marion, Indiana

No. 3 — Central Glass Works, Summitville, Indiana

No. 4 — Crystal Glass Works, Bridgeport, Ohio

No. 5 — Cumberland Glass Works, Cumberland, Maryland

No. 6 — Dalzell, Gilmore & Leighton Glass Works, Findlay, Ohio

No. 7 — Fairmont Glass Works, Fairmont, West Virginia

No. 8 — Greensburg Glass Works, Greensburg, Pennsylvania

No. 9 — Indiana Tumbler & Goblet Works, Greentown, Indiana

No. 10 — Keystone Glass Works, Rochester, Pennsylvania

No. 11 — Model Flint Glass Works, Albany, Indiana

No. 12 — McKee & Bros. Glass Works, Jeannette, Pennsylvania

No. 13 — Northwood Glass Works, Indiana, Pennsylvania

No. 14 — Ohio Flint Glass Works, Lancaster, Ohio

No. 15 — Riverside Glass Works, Wellsburg, West Virginia

No. 16 — Robinson Glass Works, Zanesville, Ohio

No. 17 — Rochester Glass Works, Rochester, Pennsylvania

No. 18 — Royal Glass Works, Marietta, Ohio

No. 19 — West Virginia Glass Works, Martins Ferry, Ohio

After joining National, these factories were no longer individual entities, only various works of National. All patterns made during this period must be credited to National to be correct, although sometimes the factory number is known.

During its organization, National sponsored a contest for the best design for a new pattern. The pattern that won was called Prize and was manufactured in a full tableware line by the company. National had several factories specializing in lamps at this time.

Following a pattern of member factory closings, the members of management announced in 1904 that they were retiring from manufacturing. At this time, they leased the factories remaining in the combine.

The Cambridge Glass Co. was organized and owned by National Glass Co., but was incorporated as a completely separate entity. Although it was a separate company, it was under the control of National; Cambridge received the best of the molds and machinery, and probably workers from factories that went out of business in the combine.

Some well-known patterns made by National include Venus, Vulcan, Kismet, Navarre, Nautilus, Roanoke, Prize, Indiana, Reward, Eureka, Revere, Maypole, Toltec, Aztec, No. 575 Colonial, and Medallion.

The National Glass Co. combine issued a catalog around 1901 that included patterns currently being made by the member factories. Of great help in attributing patterns was the designation under each pattern as to which factory was producing the pattern.

Beatty-Brady Glass Works, No. 1

OMN: unknown

AKA: STIPPLED SANDBURR

DATE: 1902

COLORS: clear, $42.00.

SIZE: 2⅜" tall x 2¼" wide

NOTES: At least the tumbler was continued by Indiana Glass Co. and named Mars in its original catalog illustration.

Dalzell, Gilmore & Leighton, No. 6

Clear with gold decoration

Clear with ruby stain

OMN: DAPHNE, No. 81D

AKA: WELLSBURG

DATE: 1901

COLORS: clear, $62.00; clear with gold decor, $70.00; clear with satin, $70.00; clear with ruby stain, $300.00.

SIZE: 2⅜" tall x 2" wide

Clear with cutting

OMN: No. 85D

AKA: DELOS

DATE: 1901

COLORS: clear, $60.00; clear with cut stars, $85.00; clear with ruby stain, $300.00.

SIZE: 2⅜" tall x 2¼" wide

NOTES: This line of tableware had a rather long life; at least some pieces were offered for sale as late as 1905.

Clear

OMN: unknown

AKA: DEEP FILE

DATE: 1902

COLORS: clear, $75.00.

SIZE: 2⅜" tall x 1¾" wide

NOTES: This became Cambridge's No. 2502 after the molds were transferred from Dalzell, Gilmore & Leighton to the new Cambridge factory. It is likely that most of this pattern was made at Cambridge, not Findlay.

OMN: No. 77D

AKA: RETORT

DATE: 1899

COLORS: clear, $75.00.

SIZE: 2⅜" tall x 2⅛" wide

NOTES: Still in 1902 National catalog.

OMN: No. 79D

AKA: SERRATED TEARDROP, TEARDROP WITH EYEWINKERS

DATE: 1901

COLORS: clear, $68.00; clear with engraving, $85.00; emerald green, $325.00.

SIZE: 2⅜" tall x 2⅜" wide

Clear with engraving

OMN: SHEAF

AKA: SHEAF OF WHEAT

DATE: 1901

COLORS: National Glass/Dalzell: Clear, $95.00, blue, $225.00; National Glass/Indiana Tumbler & Goblet: amber, $152.00; chocolate, $500.00+; Nile Green, $325.00.

SIZE: 3" tall x 1⅓" wide

NOTES: A novelty toothpick with no other matching pieces. The sickle that protrudes from the sheaf is often damaged. Has been reproduced by St. Clair in colors, including chocolate.

Clear

Nile Green

Clear

OMN: unknown

AKA: TEARDROP & CRACKED ICE

DATE: ca. 1901

COLORS: clear, $142.00.

SIZE: 2⅜" tall x 2¼" wide

NOTES: The molds for this pattern were made by Dalzell, and possibly some production was done at its Findlay plant. However, most of the pattern was made at the new National plant at Cambridge, Ohio, where it was listed as No. 2501.

Indiana Tumbler & Goblet Works, No. 9

Clear

OMN: No. 300

AKA: BEADED PANEL

DATE: ca. 1902

COLORS: clear, $500.00.

SIZE: unknown

Chocolate

OMN: unknown

AKA: CACTUS, PANELED AGAVE

DATE: 1900 to 1903

COLORS: clear, $48.00; chocolate, $75.00.

SIZE: 2⅝" tall x 2⅛" wide

NOTES: Reproductions are known for this toothpick. At least two versions of the old exist, one with 15 cheverons and one with 18 cheverons.

Holly golden agate in family size and regular size

Holly white agate, $5,000.00

Holly pedestal version

OMN: HOLLY, No. 450

AKA: HOLLY AMBER

DATE: 1903

COLORS: Regular size: clear, $275.00; golden agate, $650.00+; white agate, $5,000.00+. Family size: golden agate, $1,000.00. Pedestal type: clear, $2,500.00; golden agate, $3,500.00+.

SIZE: 2⅜" tall x 2¼" tall

NOTES: This toothpick was made in three styles; the footed variety is extremely rare. There are many, many reproductions of this toothpick in various colors, including copies in golden agate.

Clear

OMN: INDIANA

AKA: CORD DRAPERY

DATE: 1901

COLORS: clear, $185.00.

SIZE: 2¼" tall x 2¼" wide at top

NOTES: The pattern comes in various Indiana Tumbler & Goblet Co. colors, so the toothpick might also be found in colors.

OMN: No. 400

AKA: LEAF BRACKET

DATE: 1900

COLORS: clear, $115.00; chocolate, $400.00+.

SIZE: 2⅝" tall x 1⅜" wide at top

NOTES: Available in a complete tableware pattern.

Chocolate

OMN: unknown

AKA: PICTURE FRAME

DATE: unknown

COLORS: clear, $175.00; amber, $400.00; chocolate, $1,800.00; Nile green, $1,800.00; teal blue, $600.00.

SIZE: 3½" tall x 2⅝" wide at front bottom

NOTES: This novelty item has "R. M." on the base, probably indicating it was made for a specific company and may have been a private mold. Some are known with mirrors on the front.

Chocolate

McKee & Bros. Glass Works, No. 12

Clear with ruby stain

OMN: EUREKA

DATE: 1901

COLORS: clear, $35.00; clear with ruby stain, $135.00.

SIZE: 2½" tall x 2" wide

NOTES: Still in a wholesaler's catalog in 1905.

OMN: GOTHIC

AKA: SPEARPONT BAND

DATE: 1902

COLORS: clear, $35.00; clear with ruby stain, $85.00; clear with gold, $40.00.

SIZE: 2⅜" tall x 1⅞" wide

NOTES: Made in a full tableware line.

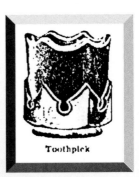
Toothpick

Clear with ruby stain

OMN: KISMET, No. 909

DATE: 1900

COLORS: clear, $48.00; clear with gold decor, $58.00.

SIZE: unknown

NOTES: ...*the Kismet, also in fine crystal, decorated in gold...*–January 1900, *CGL*. Pieces were made in amber, blue, and green, but it is not known if the toothpick was made in these colors. Still shown in the National 1902 catalog. See also Broken Pillar & Reed, Model Flint, No. 11 (National), p. 148.

Clear with ruby stain

OMN: NAOMI

AKA: RIB & BEAD

DATE: 1901

COLORS: clear, $38.00; clear with ruby stain, $135.00.

SIZE: 2⅜" tall x 2¼" wide

OMN: NAVARRE

AKA: PRINCE ALBERT

DATE: 1900

COLORS: clear, $55.00; clear with ruby stain, $200.00.

SIZE: unknown

NOTES: ...*the Navarre, of which there is also a full line.*–January 1900, *CGL*. Still included in the 1902 National Glass Co. catalog.

Clear

Clear with ruby stain

OMN: THE PRIZE, No. 500

DATE: 1900

COLORS: clear, $38.00; clear with ruby stain, $138.00; emerald green, $100.00; emerald green with gold, $115.00.

SIZE: 2¾" tall x 2½" wide

NOTES: Still included in the 1902 National Glass Co. catalog.

Emerald with gold decoration

OMN: RAINBOW

DATE: 1899

COLORS: clear, $42.00; clear with ruby stain, $135.00.

SIZE: 2¼" tall x 1¾" wide

NOTES: Still included in the 1902 National Glass Co. catalog.

Clear

OMN: STARS & STRIPES

DATE: 1899

COLORS: clear, $48.00.

SIZE: 2¼" tall x 2¼" wide

NOTES: Also made in a smoking set. The match holder is 1¾" tall and 1½" wide. The cigarette holder is 2¾" tall and 2⅜" wide.

Clear

Chocolate

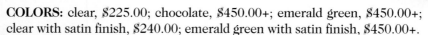

Sultan Toy Sugar and Cover   Sultan Toy Spoon   Sultan Toy Cream   Sultan Toy Butter and Cover

Sultan 4 Piece Set

OMN: SULTAN

AKA: WILD ROSE WITH SCROLLING

DATE: ca. 1901

COLORS: clear, $225.00; chocolate, $450.00+; emerald green, $450.00+; clear with satin finish, $240.00; emerald green with satin finish, $450.00+.

SIZE: 2¼" tall x 2⅛" wide at top

NOTES: The "toothpick" is actually a spooner from a child's set. Reproduced by Fenton in many colors, including chocolate; should have the Fenton oval logo on base if it is a Fenton piece.

Emerald green

OMN: UNION

AKA: SERRATED RIBS & PANELS

DATE: 1900

COLORS: clear, $45.00; clear with ruby stain, $140.00.

SIZE: 2⅛" tall x 2½" wide

Clear with ruby stain

Clear

OMN: VULCAN

DATE: 1900

COLORS: clear, $38.00; clear with gold decor, $45.00; clear with rose pink decor, $68.00.

SIZE: 2⅛" tall x 2⅛" wide

NOTES: *The Vulcan, a very large and comprehensive line in bright crystal glass, plain, and decorated in gold and rose pink...* –January 1900. Original catalogs call this a toothpick or match. This toothpick has been reproduced extensively by the Fenton Art Glass Co. in various colors, including opalescent blue and pink.

Model Flint Glass Works, No. 11

OMN: No. 909

AKA: BROKEN PILLAR & REED

DATE: 1899

COLORS: clear, $68.00; clear with amethyst stain, $135.00.

SIZE: unknown

NOTES: This appears to be the same pattern as Kismet, made at the McKee Works.

Clear opalescent, clear, clear with gold decoration, blue opalescent

OMN: MANILA

AKA: WREATH & SHELL

DATE: 1900

COLORS: clear, $65.00; clear with gold decor, $78.00; clear opalescent, $225.00; blue opalescent, $350.00; canary opalescent, $350.00.

SIZE: 2⅜" tall x 2" wide

OMN: PLANET

DATE: 1901

COLORS: clear, $50.00; clear with gold decor, $65.00.

SIZE: 2⅜" tall x 1⅝" wide at top

Clear

OMN: unknown

AKA: RIBBED SPIRAL

DATE: 1900

COLORS: clear opalescent, $115.00; blue opalescent, $150.00; canary opalescent, $150.00.

SIZE: 2⅜" tall x 2" wide

Clear opalescent

Canary opalescent

Northwood Glass Works, No. 13

OMN: No. 22

AKA: DIAMOND SPEARHEAD

DATE: 1902

COLORS: All the following in opalescent: clear, $45.00; blue, $135.00; canary, $135.00; dark blue, $165.00; green, $115.00.

SIZE: 2¼" tall x 1⅞" wide

NOTES: Included in the 1902 National Glass Co. catalog.

Clear opalescent

Blue opalescent

Dark blue opalescent   *Canary opalescent*   *Green opalescent*

OMN: NATIONAL

AKA: S REPEAT

DATE: 1903

COLORS: clear, $45.00; clear, gold decor, $48.00; amethyst, $95.00; amethyst with gold decor, $115.00; blue, $68.00; blue with gold decor, $88.00; green, $65.00; green with gold decor, $85.00.

SIZE: 2¼" tall x 1⅞" wide

Amethyst   *Blue with gold decoration*   *Green with gold decoration*

NOTES: Still available in 1906. This toothpick has been reproduced in many colors by L. G. Wright, including milk glass, amethyst, ruby, and purple slag.

OMN: NAUTILUS

AKA: ARGONAUT SHELL

DATE: 1900

COLORS: ivory, $385.00; ivory, decorated, $450.00+.

SIZE: 2¾" tall x 2⅜" wide

NOTES: *On the same floor is the new fancy table line, Nautilus, in ivory and gold, manufactured at the Northwood works, and fully up to the previous great record of that concern. –January 1900.* Copied from a china or porcelain pattern. Reproduced by L. G. Wright in blue satin, ivory decorated, and possibly other colors in a footed, pedestal version.

Ivory with gold and enamel decoration

Apple green

OMN: NESTOR

DATE: ca. 1902

COLORS: clear, $48.00; amethyst, $78.00; blue, $78.00; green, $75.00.

SIZE: 2⅜" tall x 2" wide

NOTES: Sometimes decorated with enamel decorations in various colors. This pattern has been attributed to Northwood, but we have found no documentation. A tray for the condiment set is known with the Northwood trademark.

Blue

Blue opalescent

OMN: NEW YORK

AKA: SHELL; BEADED SHELL

DATE: 1900 – 1910

COLORS: clear, $450.00; blue, $800.00+; green, $800.00+; yellow, $800.00+. Any of the above in opalescent, $800.00+.

SIZE: 2¼" tall x 1⅞" wide

OMN: unknown

AKA: QUILTED PHLOX

DATE: 1900

COLORS: blue opaque, $230.00; blue translucent, $350.00+; green opaque, $225.00; opal, $230.00; pink opaque, $230.00.

SIZE: 2½" tall x 2" wide across top, 2½" at widest portion

NOTES: Pieces of the pattern, including the toothpick, are also found in plated (cased) colors. Add 10% to above prices for plated colors.

Opaque green

Ohio Flint Glass Works, No. 14

OMN: ORINDA, No. 92

DATE: 1901

COLORS: clear, $42.00; clear with ruby stain, $148.00; opal, $92.00.

SIZE: 2¼" tall x 1¾" wide

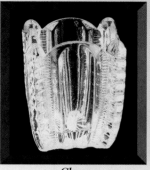

Clear with ruby stain

Clear

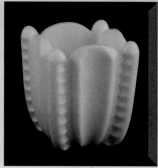

Opal

Riverside Glass Works, No. 15

15/510 Spoon Holder.

OMN: No. 510

AKA: BULL'S-EYE & BUTTONS

DATE: 1900

COLORS: clear, $45.00; clear with gold decor, $55.00; emerald green, $92.00; emerald green with gold decor, $120.00.

SIZE: unknown

NOTES: This pattern is shown in the 1902 National catalog.

Clear

AKA: INVERTED EYE

DATE: 1902

COLORS: clear, $48.00.

SIZE: 2⅝" tall x 2¼" wide at top

NOTES: Credited to Riverside by C. W. Gorham in *Riverside Glass Works,* as pattern No. 517, but we have not seen catalog proof of this attribution.

Clear

OMN: RADIANT, No. 512

DATE: 1901

COLORS: clear, $48.00.

SIZE: 2¾" tall x 2⅛" wide

Clear with gold decoration

OMN: REWARD, No. 511

DATE: 1901

COLORS: clear, $38.00; clear with gold decor, $60.00; clear with ruby stain, $145.00; emerald green, $138.00; emerald green with gold, $155.00.

SIZE: 2½" tall x 2⅛" wide

National Glass Co.

Flared Panels with plain base

Winsome

OMN: No. 550

AKA: WINSOME

DATE: 1903

COLORS: clear, $45.00; clear with gold decor, $60.00.

SIZE: 2½" tall x 2¼" wide

NOTES: Introduced as a new pattern in early 1903. A variation exists with a plain, rather than patterned, base and has been named Flared Panels.

Rochester Glass Works, No. 17

OMN: No. 1350

AKA: HAT, DAISY & BUTTON

DATE: 1902

COLORS: clear, $68.00.

SIZE: unknown

NOTES: While part of the National combine, Rochester made a Daisy and Button hat, pattern No. 1350. It may have been made earlier also. It appears almost identical to other D&B hats, but is shown with very straight sides. Other colors are likely, but we cannot document them at this time.

Canary

OMN: No. 1353

AKA: HAT, TAPERED BLOCK

DATE: 1902

COLORS: clear, $38.00; blue, $68.00; canary, $70.00.

SIZE: 2¼" tall x 2" wide

NOTES: Included in the 1902 National Glass Co. catalog, although it may have been made earlier. There are two varieties of Tapered Block pattern hats, the difference being that the National/Rochester one has blocks on the brim of the hat while the Fostoria hat brim is plain.

Royal Glass Works, No. 18

OMN: No. 315

AKA: NATIONAL PRISM

DATE: 1900 – 1920

COLORS: clear, $38.00.

SIZE: 2⅜" tall x 2⅛" wide

NOTES: Named by Mr. Millard, an early glass researcher and author.

Unknown Factory

It is possible that the following toothpicks and patterns were made by McKee while it was part of the National Glass combine, as McKee patterns are sometimes found in chocolate glass. However, with no catalog proof, we have elected to place them in this category.

Clear

OMN: unknown

AKA: CHRYSANTHEMUM LEAF

DATE: ca. 1901

COLORS: clear, $390.00; chocolate, $800.00+.

SIZE: 2⅜" tall x 2⅛" wide

OMN: No. 913

AKA: DIAMOND LIL

DATE: 1904

COLORS: clear, $38.00.

SIZE: unknown

NOTES: The factory origin of this toothpick is not known.

AKA: DIAMOND PYRAMID; BEADED TRIANGLE

DATE: ca. 1901

COLORS: clear, $38.00.

SIZE: 2⅜" tall x 2" wide

NOTES: Other pieces in the pattern are known in chocolate glass.

Clear

Ivory with enamel decoration

AKA: WILD ROSE WITH BOWKNOT

DATE: ca. 1901

COLORS: clear, $48.00; clear with satin finish, $65.00; chocolate, $280.00; ivory, $128.00; ivory with enamel decoration, $185.00.

SIZE: 1¾" tall x 1¾" wide at top

NEW ENGLAND GLASS CO.
BOSTON, MASSACHUSETTS
1818 – 1887

LIBBEY GLASS CO.
TOLEDO, OHIO
1888 – PRESENT

The New England Glass Co. reopened in 1888 as the New England Glass Works, William L. Libbey & Son, Proprietors. The original company was organized in 1818 by Deming Jarves.

In 1888 the company moved to Toledo, Ohio, and the name was changed to W. L. Libbey & Son Company, Proprietors, New England Glass Works. In 1892 the name was shortened to the Libbey Glass Co.

This company made the well-known amberina that was patented by Joseph Locke in 1883 and assigned to W. L. and E. D. Libbey. Some amberina was also made at Mt.

Washington despite the Libbey patent. Agata was patented in 1885. Pomona was patented in 1885. Plated amberina was patented in 1886. All were developed and patented by Joseph Locke.

Since New England Glass and Libbey made most of the amberina in this country, we have listed most of the amberina toothpicks that are unattributed in this chapter so that you can easily compare them. Be aware that not all are New England, and some might be imported. We thank our art glass experts for the descriptions and prices of toothpicks in this category.

OMN: AMBERINA

DATE: ca. 1883

COLORS: amberina, $700.00+.

SIZE: 2¾" tall x 1" wide at base

NOTES: Illustrated example has polka dot optic, today often called Inverted Thumbprint.

Polka dot optic

OMN: AMBERINA

DATE: ca. 1883

COLORS: amberina, $315.00.

SIZE: 2½" tall x 2½" wide

NOTES: May be Mt. Washington.

Amberina

Venetian diamond optic

OMN: AMBERINA, AGATA

DATE: ca. 1883

COLORS: amberina with optic, $475.00+.

SIZE: 2¾" tall x 1¾" wide at base

Amberina

OMN: AMBERINA, AGATA

AKA: TRI-CORNER

DATE: ca. 1883

COLORS: amberina, $500.00+; wild rose with agata decoration, $1,500.00.

SIZE: 2¼" tall x 1¾" wide

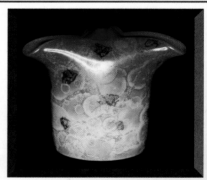

Wild Rose with Agata Decoration

OMN: unknown

AKA: AMBERINA, SQUARE TOP; AGATA, SQUARE TOP

DATE: ca. 1883

COLORS: amberina, $325.00; amberina with optic, $325.00; wild rose with agata stain, $1,300.00+.

SIZE: 2½" tall x 1¾" wide

NOTES: "Venetian diamond" is used today to refer to the diamond optic used as a decorative effect in amberina and other glass. The Venetian diamond example shown may be Mt. Washington's Rose Amber, because of the slight difference in color and the larger optic.

Agata

Amberina

Amberina, Venetian diamond (optic)

OMN: AMBERINA

AKA: SQUARE TOP, 2 HANDLED

DATE: ca. 1883

COLORS: amberina, $600.00+.

SIZE: unknown

NOTES: This toothpick has a polka dot optic, often erroneously called Inverted Thumbprint today.

OMN: unknown

AKA: GREEN OPAQUE

DATE: ca. 1887

COLORS: opaque green with decorated top, $1,500.00+; blue opaque, $1,500.00.

SIZE: 2" tall x 2¼" wide

Green opaque decorated with blue netting & gold

Clear with satin finish and amber stained top

OMN: POMONA

AKA: RIGAREE NECK

DATE: 1885

COLORS: clear, satin finish and amber stain, $450.00+.

SIZE: 2¼" tall x 2⅜" wide

NOTES: Pomona is a decoration. Several shapes are known.

OMN: POMONA

AKA: SQUARE TOP

DATE: 1885

COLORS: clear, pomona-type decoration, $450.00+.

SIZE: 2⅜" tall x 1¾" wide

OMN: POMONA

AKA: TRI-CORNER

DATE: 1885

COLORS: clear, pomona-type decoration, $500.00+.

SIZE: 2½" tall x 1⅝" wide

OMN: WILD ROSE

DATE: 1886

COLORS: any style, $1,200.00.

SIZE: 2¼" tall x 1⅞" wide

NOTES: Although widely known as New England Peachblow, the original company name was Wild Rose.

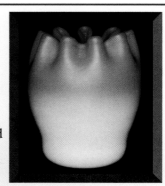

NEW MARTINSVILLE GLASS MANUFACTURING CO. NEW MARTINSVILLE, WEST VIRGINIA 1900 – 1944

Mark Douglas, David Fisher, and G. W. Motheny organized the New Martinsville Glass Mfg. Co. in 1900. Disasters plagued the company during its first seven years, including a flood, three fires, and two explosions. Reports in 1902 stated that Joseph Webb, the former glass maker for the Phoenix Glass Co., was now in charge of the glass making department at New Martinsville.

In 1937 bankruptcy was declared, and the company was reorganized as the New Martinsville Glass Co. G. R. Cummings purchased all the stock in the company in 1944 and changed the name to Viking Glass Co. The factory existed until mid-1998 as the Dalzell-Viking Glass Co.

Patterns include No. 600, Rock Crystal, Muranese, Nos. 100, 500 Wetzel, 700, and 88 Carnation.

Clear

Clear with ruby stain

OMN: CARNATION, No. 88

DATE: 1906

COLORS: clear, $68.00; clear with ruby stain, $285.00.

SIZE: 2⅝" tall x 1⅞" wide

Clear with gold decoration

OMN: FLORENE, No. 720

DATE: 1910

COLORS: clear, $40.00; clear with gold decor, $48.00; clear with ruby stain, $135.00; emerald green, $190.00.

SIZE: flared top, 2½" tall x 2¼" wide at top; straight top, 2½" tall x 1⅞" wide.

OMN: FRONTIER, No. 718

DATE: 1909

COLORS: clear, $40.00; clear with gold decor, $45.00; clear with ruby stain, $135.00.

SIZE: 2¼" tall x 1⅞" wide

Gold decoration

Clear

Spoon, ruby stained

OMN: No. 724

AKA: HEART IN SAND

DATE: 1915

COLORS: clear, $100.00; clear with ruby stain, $300.00.

SIZE: 2" tall x 2¼" wide at top

OMN: No. 704

AKA: PLACID THUMBPRINT

DATE: 1907

COLORS: clear, $38.00; clear with ruby stain, $130.00.

SIZE: unknown

NOTES: There is also a variation with no thumbprints.

Clear

OMN: No. 713

AKA: PLEATED MEDALLION

DATE: 1910

COLORS: clear, $48.00.

SIZE: 2¼" tall x 2⅛" wide

OMN: No. 721

AKA: STUDIO

DATE: ca. 1910

COLORS: clear, $38.00; clear with gold decor, $48.00.

SIZE: 2½" tall x 1¾" wide

Clear with gold decoration

Clear

OMN: TEASEL, No. 702

DATE: 1906

COLORS: clear, $48.00.

SIZE: 2⅞" tall x 2" wide

Cobalt

OMN: TOBIN, No. 711

AKA: LEAF & STAR

DATE: 1909

COLORS: clear, $60.00; clear with gold decor, $68.00; clear with ruby stain, $185.00; cobalt, $160.00.

SIZE: 3" tall, 1⅝" wide

NOTES: *The new pressed table line No. 711 of the New Martinsville (W. Va.) Glass Mfg. Co. will certainly find eager buyers. It is copied from a successful cut glass pattern, noticeable for the amount of uncut glass shown.* –June 1908.

Clear with ruby stain

NICKEL PLATE GLASS CO.
FOSTORIA, OHIO
1888 – 1891

The Nickel Plate Glass Co. was organized in 1888 by Peter Cassell, A. J. Smith, B. M. Hildreth, William Robinson, and J. B. Russell.

In 1891 the company joined the United States Glass Co. combine, becoming known as Factory N.

The factory made tableware, lamps, and novelties, much of it in opalescent ware. Patterns include No. 76 Richmond, No. 77 Royal, Frosted Circle, and No. 82 One-O-One (a pattern made in clear; do not confuse it with Challinor's No. 101). Opalescent patterns include Double Greek Key, No. 90 Swirl, and No. 94 Wide Stripe in clear, ruby, and blue.

OMN: unknown

AKA: DOUBLE GREEK KEY

DATE: 1889

COLORS: clear, $190.00; clear opalescent, $425.00; blue opalescent, $800.00+.

SIZE: 2½" tall x 2½" wide

NOTES: *Their new blown line of tableware and bar goods with key border, known as the Grecian key, is a very handsome pattern...* –January 1889. While some pieces of Double Greek Key are indeed blown, most pieces are pressed. The toothpick is blown. This pattern is not included in the July 1890 catalog, indicating it may possibly have been out of production by this time. This would account for the pattern's rarity today.

Blue opalescent

Ruby opalescent

OMN: No. 90

AKA: SWIRL

DATE: 1890

COLORS: clear opalescent, $185.00; blue opalescent, $325.00+; ruby opalescent, $325.00+.

SIZE: 2⅛" tall x 2¼" wide

NOTES: Illustrated in a July 1890 company catalog.

OMN: VENICIA

DATE: unknown

COLORS: green to clear, $95.00; green opaque, $125.00; rubina, $135.00; ruby, $85.00.

SIZE: 2½" tall x 2¼" wide

NOTES: Researchers of Fostoria, Ohio, glass attribute this pattern to Nickel Plate. We have not seen this in an original ad or catalog. This may well be a product of West Virginia Glass Co.

Rubina

Ruby opalescent

OMN: No. 94

AKA: WIDE STRIPE

DATE: 1890

COLORS: clear opalescent, $190.00; blue opalescent, $310.00; ruby opalescent, $310.00.

SIZE: 2¼" tall x 2¼" wide

NOTES: llustrated in a July 1890 catalog that stated this was made as "No. 94 Opalescent Ware in Ruby, White, and Blue."

NORTHWOOD GLASS WORKS
MARTIN'S FERRY, OHIO
1889 – 1893

NORTHWOOD GLASS CO.
ELLWOOD CITY, PENNSYLVANIA
1893 – 1896
INDIANA, PENNSYLVANIA
1896 – 1899

NORTHWOOD & CO.
WHEELING, WEST VIRGINIA
1902 – 1924

Harry Northwood was associated with several glass making companies that bore his name. The Northwood Glass Works was organized and operated at Martins Ferry, Ohio, by 1889. The factory name was changed to the Northwood Glass Co. when it moved to Ellwood City, Pennsylvania, in 1893. Facing bankruptcy in 1896, the company moved to Indiana, Pennsylvania. In 1899, this company joined the National Glass Co. combine and was designated Factory No. 13, Northwood Glass Works.

A great rush is on in the shipping department at the Northwood Glass Works of the National Glass Co., at Indiana, Pa. From 1,000 to 1,300 barrels of ware are shipped weekly and the coopers have to work at night in order to keep ahead of the packers. In the decorating department the decorators also have to work at night in the effort to keep up. –October 1901.

Soon after the Northwoods joined National, the comapny sent Harry and his brother Carl to England to manage its London office. In 1902 the Northwoods returned to America, and by the end of the year they had leased and reopened the old Hobbs, Brockunier & Co. factory at Wheeling, West Virginia. At this time, the name of the new company was H. Northwood & Co.

Products made over the years were primarily tableware and lamps. Some patterns that were made include Royal Ivy, Aurora, Royal Oak, Jewel, Apple Blossom, Crystal Queen, Klondyke, Alaska, Louis XV, Intaglio, Opaline Brocade, Venetian, Carnelian, Reliance, Mikado, Encore, Regent, Diadem, and Royal Art. In later years, goofus glass and carnival glass were made. The last Northwood company also produced several opaque colors in the 1920s. Not all patterns were made at all locations. Dates are needed to verify which location produced the glass. Collectors are accustomed to considering any of the products of all the Northwood factories as "Northwood," so we have not separated them into different factory entries, although this would normally be done with other companies. Each of the above factories was a distinct entity and should not be considered merely a part of one company.

See also National Glass Co., Factory No. 13.

Clear opalescent

OMN: AURORA, No. 285

AKA: OPALESCENT STRIPE, RING NECK MOLD

DATE: 1890

COLORS: clear opalescent, $230.00; rubina, $195.00; ruby opalescent, $390.00; blue opalescent, $425.00; rubina with etching, $210.00.

SIZE: 2⅛" tall x 2⅛" wide

NOTES: Made at Northwood Glass Works, Martins Ferry, Ohio.

Blue opalescent

Rubina

Northwoods Glass Works

OMN: unknown

AKA: CHRYSANTHEMUM BASE SWIRL

DATE: ca. 1893

COLORS: clear opalescent, $190.00; blue opalescent, $350.00+; ruby opalescent, $325.00+; ruby with opal frit, $380.00+; canary with opal frit, $350.00.

SIZE: 2⅛" tall x 2" wide

NOTES: Northwood produced a line of glass called Granite Ware with the overlay of opal frit.

Ruby opalescent stripe

Ruby with opal frit overlay

Canary with opal frit overlay

Blue opalescent stripe

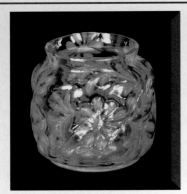
Blue opalescent

OMN: unknown

AKA: DAISY & FERN

DATE: 1895

COLORS: clear opalescent, $175.00; blue opalescent, $265.00; ruby opalescent, $350.00.

SIZE: 2⅛" tall x 2⅜" wide

NOTES: The toothpick was made in the same mold as Parian. Made at the Northwood Glass Co., Ellwood City, Pennsylvania.

OMN: GENEVA

DATE: 1899

COLORS: chocolate, $245.00; emerald green, $190.00; ivory, $145.00.

SIZE: 2½" tall x 2¼" wide

NOTES: Ivory pieces in this pattern are sometimes decorated in the same manner as Louis XV, with brown or green decoration done by Northwood. This pattern was still included in the 1902 National Glass Co. catalog, indicating it was being made by McKee.

Chocolate

OMN: unknown

AKA: INVERTED FAN & FEATHER

DATE: 1904

COLORS: ivory, $415.00; ivory with pink stain and gold, $450.00+; pink slag, $700.00+.

SIZE: 2⅜" tall x 1¾" wide

NOTES: Most likely begun by Northwood at Indiana, Pennsylvania, as salts and peppers are known with the Northwood mark. The pink slag was developed by Harry Bastow while working for National after Northwood's departure. Thomas Dugan refined the formula for this color. Later pieces in the pattern were made by Dugan in emerald green and opalescent blue. This toothpick has been reproduced in colors and also pink slag.

Pink slag

Ivory with gold and enamel decoration

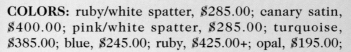

OMN: No. 333

AKA: LEAF MOLD

DATE: 1891

COLORS: ruby/white spatter, $285.00; canary satin, $400.00; pink/white spatter, $285.00; turquoise, $385.00; blue, $245.00; ruby, $425.00+; opal, $195.00; canary with ruby and white spatter, $315.00.

SIZE: 1¾" tall x 2¼" wide

NOTES: Made at the Northwood Glass Works, Martins Ferry, Ohio.

Canary with ruby and white spatter

Canary, satin finish

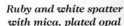

Ruby and white spatter with mica, plated opal

Canary satin

Blue plated with opal, satin finish

Ruby

Ruby spatter (top repaired)

OMN: No. 263

AKA: LEAF UMBRELLA

DATE: 1889

COLORS: ruby, $285.00; ruby spatter, $315.00; mauve satin, $290.00; blue, $275.00; blue, satin, $325.00; canary, $355.00; canary satin, $350.00; mauve, $280.00.

SIZE: 2½" tall x 2¼" wide

NOTES: Pieces are sometimes cased and sometimes with satin finish. Made at the Northwood Glass Works, Martins Ferry, Ohio.

OMN: LOUIS XV

DATE: 1898

COLORS: ivory with gold decor, $700.00+; ivory with brown stain, $1,500.00; ivory with green stain, $625.00.

SIZE: 2½" tall

NOTES: *The special pattern this year is one of the richest things ever put on the market in pressed glassware. It is called Louis XV after the luxurious and courtly king of France, and is made in ivory and gold... There is a low relief figure, just a breath, being a combination of Hogarth's graceful lines of beauty, into which a spray of color is thrown, which greatly increases the artistic effect. The edges are gracefully scalloped, and tipped with bright gold. The tiny curved feet, in imitation of sea shells, are in the style of the best English castor place laid on work, and are in gold decoration.* –August 1898. This pattern may be found with the block Northwood signature. Made at the Northwood Glass Co., Indiana, Pennsylvania.

Ivory with brown stain

Northwood Glass Works

Clear

OMN: MEMPHIS, No. 19

DATE: 1907

COLORS: crystal, $85.00.

SIZE: 2½" tall x 2⅜" wide

NOTES: This is also the base of a mustard. Pieces are signed "Northwood." Made at the H. Northwood & Co., Wheeling, West Virginia.

Clear mustard and cover

Blue opaque with gold decoration

OMN: PAGODA

AKA: CHRYSANTHEMUM SPRIG

DATE: 1899

COLORS: Ivory, $365.00; Turquoise Blue Opal, $550.00.

SIZE: 2½" tall x 2¼" wide

NOTES: Pagoda is the original name of this pattern. Turquoise Blue Opal is the original chemist's term for the opaque blue color. Items in this tableware pattern are often gold decorated. Items are signed Northwood in script, so it was developed by Northwood, but much of the production was by National and later by Dugan.

Ivory with gold decoration

Clear opalescent

OMN: unknown

AKA: PANELED SPRIG

DATE: 1889

COLORS: clear, $80.00; clear opalescent, $158.00; opal with enamel decoration, $130.00; ruby, $235.00; ruby with enamel decoration, $250.00.

SIZE: 2⅛" tall x 2⅛" wide

NOTES: Made at the Northwood Glass Works, Martins Ferry, Ohio.

Opal with enamel decoration

Ruby with enamel decoration

Blue with satin finish

OMN: PARIAN

AKA: PARIAN SWIRL

DATE: 1895

COLORS: clear with satin finish, $135.00; blue with satin finish, $225.00; rainbow with satin finish, $330.00; ruby with satin finish, $225.00.

SIZE: 2¼" tall x 2½" wide

NOTES: Used same mold as Royal Ivy and Daisy & Fern, thus the accepted attribution to the Northwood Company. Made at the Northwood Glass Co., Ellwood City, Pennsylvania.

Rainbow with satin finish

Pink and white spatter, satin finish

OMN: No. 245

AKA: RIBBED PILLAR

DATE: 1889

COLORS: pink/white spatter, $125.00; blue/white spatter, $225.00; ruby/white spatter, $235.00.

SIZE: 2¼" tall x 2⅛" wide

NOTES: Made at Northwood Glass Works, Martins Ferry, Ohio.

Blue and white spatter

OMN: ROYAL IVY, No. 287

DATE: 1890

COLORS: clear, $68.00; clear with amber stain, $550.00+; clear with satin finish, $85.00; craquelle, $350.00; rainbow spatter, $350.00; rubina, $95.00; rubina with satin finish, $125.00; ruby, $85.00; ruby with satin finish, $120.00; spatter, plated, $375.00.

SIZE: 2⅛" tall x 2⅛" wide

NOTES: Made as a tableware line. Often pieces are found with a satin finish; for these, add 10% to the above suggested values. Made at the Northwood Glass Works, Martins Ferry, Ohio.

Rainbow spatter

Rainbow spatter, plated with opal

Rubina

Rubina (top repaired)

OMN: ROYAL OAK, No. 315

DATE: 1891

COLORS: clear, $75.00; clear with amber stain, $275.00; clear with satin finish, $88.00; rubina, $125.00; rubina with satin finish, $130.00.

SIZE: 2" tall x 2¼" wide

NOTES: *The "Royal Oak," No. 315, is a square shape in bright ruby, flashed and etched, and crystal etched, with oak leaf in heavy relief and acorn knob.* –January 1891. Etched refers to what is now called satin glass. Made at the Northwood Glass Works, Martins Ferry, Ohio.

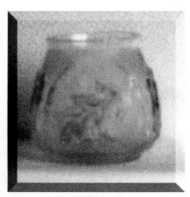

Clear with amber stain

We start the New Year with
Two new lines in rich colors.
New novelties in Flint Glass.
Fine Flint Water Sets.
A large line of Ruby-edge ware.
Machine Etched and Engraved.

NEW ROYAL OAK LINE.

NEW JEWEL LINE.

NORTHWOOD GLASS CO., **Martin's Ferry, O.**

AKA: SCROLL WITH ACANTHUS

DATE: ca. 1902

COLORS: clear, $165.00; clear with satin panels, $188.00; clear with enamel and gold decor, $168.00; blue, $185.00; blue with enamel and gold decor, $225.00; green, $195.00; purple mosaic (slag), $255.00.

SIZE: 2½" tall x 2⅛" wide

NOTES: There is no positive proof this is Northwood, but its existence in purple mosaic lends credence to the Northwood attribution since Northwood made this color while at Wheeling, West Virginia.

Clear with enamel and gold decoration

Blue with enamel and gold decoration

Purple mosaic (slag)

AKA: THREADED RUBINA

DATE: unknown

COLORS: rubina, $400.00+

SIZE: 2⅜" tall x 2¼" wide

NOTES: This toothpick is the same shape as the mold used for Leaf Umbrella. Possibly this was a reworked mold.

O'HARA GLASS CO., LTD.
PITTSBURGH, PENNSYLVANIA
1875 – 1891

The O'Hara Glass Co. originated from the reorganization of the James B. Lyon & Co. in 1875. In 1891, the company joined the United States Glass Co. and was given the designation Factory L.

Products included tableware in patterns such as No. 750, Cordova, Aldine, Prism Column, Waterfall, No. 500 Column Block, and No. 600 Reticulated Cord.

28 Candlestick.

OMN: No. 725 (O'Hara), No. 28 (U.S. Glass)

AKA: CANDLESTICK MATCH HOLDER

DATE: prior to 1891

COLORS: clear, $60.00; blue, $70.00.

SIZE: 2⅞" tall x 1¾" wide x 4" wide at base

NOTES: This item is included in later U.S. Glass Co. catalogs, indicating it was made by Factory C (Challinor). This was probably after O'Hara had been closed and the mold moved to Challinor.

Clear

Emerald and clear with ruby stain

Toothpick Holder.

OMN: CORDOVA

DATE: 1891

COLORS: clear, $38.00; clear with ruby stain, $130.00; blue, $200.00+; emerald green, $95.00.

SIZE: 3⅜" tall x 2" wide

NOTES: *The O'Hara Glass Co. ... have been getting out a stock of their new line and will be well provided when trade needs require them. Orders are scarce at present, but the "Cordova" will fetch them as soon as the dealers see it.* –December 1890. This pattern was patented December 16, 1890, and the toothpick still appeared in a Butler Brothers catalog in 1898. The blue and emerald green colors were made ca. 1898. Known with an allover metal cage. Ruby stain may be on top, on bottom, or all over.

OMN: No. 500

AKA: COLUMN BLOCK, PANEL & STAR

DATE: 1888

COLORS: clear, $48.00; amber, $155.00; blue, $160.00; canary, $165.00.

SIZE: 3⅛" tall x 1¾" wide

NOTES: Toothpicks are very rare in colors. The condiment and a cologne are illustrated in an 1888 catalog.

Clear

OMN: unknown

AKA: FINECUT BAND

DATE: prior to 1891

COLORS: clear, $55.00.

SIZE: unknown

NOTES: This small barrel-shaped item is a match holder to a smoking set. It is possible it was also made in the standard colors made by O'Hara. Named by authors.

Smoker's Set.

OHIO FLINT GLASS CO.
BOWLING GREEN, OHIO — 1891 – 1892
DUNKIRK, INDIANA — 1893 – 1899
LANCASTER, OHIO — 1899

Trade journals in 1905 reported extensively on Ohio Flint's new process for glass, called Krys-Tol. The report indicated that the new process was in the annealing of the glass at an extremely high temperature, producing a brilliant effect with a superior finish. Eventually the company sold the process and the trademark *Krys-Tol* to Jefferson Glass, which in turn eventually sold it to the Central Glass Works.

Some of the company's patterns include Diamond, Monroe, Kenneth, Azmoor, 1776 Colonial, and others, most of which are unidentified today.

Ohio Flint Glass Co.

OMN: FROG

AKA: FROG & SHELL

DATE: ca. 1897

COLORS: clear, $68.00; opal, $110.00; blue, $120.00, amber, $95.00.

SIZE: Reproduction: 2¾" tall, 3½" x 1⁹⁄₁₆" top opening, 3½" x 2¾" base, and 4" long.

NOTES: Many reproductions in colors never made originally were done by L. G. Wright Co. of West Virginia in milk glass, amethyst, green, amber, and blue. This company made many confusing items both from original molds and from new molds matching old patterns. This design was also used in Tufts silverplate.

Reproduction, green

OMN: GLORIA

AKA: unknown

DATE: 1907

COLORS: clear, $50.00.

SIZE: unknown

NOTES: *The Gloria is a cut pattern and must be seen to be properly appreciated. The special feature of this pattern is the concave panels, and with the chrysanthemums showing through an illuminated effect is produced seldom seen outside of cut glass... the toothpick holder, which is flat, so that the picks are lying down instead of standing...* –January 1907, CGL. Pieces in this pattern may be marked "Krys-Tol," as that name is featured prominently in the original ad.

A101. Leaf Tooth Pick Packs is doz. to the bbl.

OMN: LEAF

AKA: LEAF BUNDLE

DATE: ca. 1897

COLORS: clear, $50.00; amber, $75.00; blue, $75.00; opal, $95.00.

SIZE: 2⅝" tall x 1¾" wide at rim

NOTES: Found in a circa 1897 jobber's catalog with other Ohio Flint patterns. This particular catalog contained no patterns from any other company.

Clear

OMN: PEEK A BOO

AKA: GREENAWAY GIRLS

DATE: ca. 1897

COLORS: clear, $48.00; opal, $70.00; dark teal blue, $85.00.

SIZE: 2½" tall x 1⅝" wide, container only

NOTES: Another toothpick by the name of Peek A Boo exists and was made by McKee-Jeannette, so this should be referred to as Peek A Boo by Ohio Flint.

Clear

PADEN CITY GLASS CO.
PADEN CITY, WEST VIRGINIA
1916 – 1951

The Paden City Glass Co. was founded in 1916 by David Fisher, Charles Schupbach, D. J. McGrail, and W. J. McCoy.

Patterns made by the company include Tree, Estelle, Inna, Etta, and Webb. The company existed into the Depression era and is known for several Depression/elegant patterns in many colors.

No 205--Toothpick

OMN: No. 205
AKA: ESTELLE
DATE: ca. 1916
COLORS: clear, $30.00.
SIZE: 1⅜" tall x 1½" wide
NOTES: Included in a Paden City catalog.

Clear

OMN: No. 300
DATE: ca. 1917
COLORS: clear, $30.00.
SIZE: unknown
NOTES: Has been reproduced.

No. 300 Toothpick

No. 202 Toothpick

OMN: No. 202
AKA: TREE
DATE: 1918
COLORS: clear, $32.00.
SIZE: 2¼" tall x 1¾" wide
NOTES: This is made by several companies, and it is debatable which versions are reproductions and which are simply by different makers. Available in many colors in poor quality glass lacking detail.

Clear

QUEZAL ART GLASS & DECORATING CO.
BROOKLYN, NEW YORK
1901-1925

This company was founded by Martin Bach, Sr., and Thomas Johnson. These men had formerly worked at the Tiffany company, and the Quezal company showed strong Tiffany influence.

Quezal Art Glass made lustered glass in various techniques including peacock eye, pulled feather, leaves and flowers, and trailing. Other decorations included silver deposit and engraving. The company was well known for vases, light shades, and other decorative ware.

Martin Bach, Sr., died in 1924, and the company was reorganized but was closed in 1925.

OMN: QUEZAL VASE
DATE: ca. 1901
COLORS: iridescent multicolor, $600.00+.
SIZE: unknown

167

RICHARDS & HARTLEY FLINT GLASS CO.
PITTSBURGH, PENNSYLVANIA
1865 – 1884

RICHARDS & HARTLEY GLASS CO.
TARENTUM, PENNSYLVANIA
1884 – 1891

The Richards & Hartley Glass Co. was organized at Pittsburgh, Pennsylvania, in 1865 by Robert and William Hartley, Joseph Richards, and John Wilson. During this period the company made tableware, stemware, bar goods, and lamps.

In 1865 the company moved to Tarentum, Pennsylvania, and the name changed to Richards & Hartley Glass Co. In 1891 it joined the United States Glass Co. and became Factory E.

Patterns include Mikado, Hanover, Tremont, Thousand Eye, Hartley, Three Panel, Oval Loop, Clover, and Bar & Diamond.

Blue

OMN: CAT

AKA: KITTEN ON A PILLOW

DATE: mid-1880s

COLORS: clear, $100.00; amber, $130.00; blue, $130.00; canary, $138.00.

SIZE: 3½" tall x 2⅛" wide at top x 3" across base at widest part

NOTES: Shown in a Richards & Hartley catalog published prior to the merger with U.S. Glass. Also included in the 1891 U.S. Glass catalog. Has been reproduced.

CAT TOOTH PICK
IN AMBER, BLUE & CANARY

DARWIN TOOTH PICK

OMN: DARWIN

DATE: mid 1880s

COLORS: clear, $68.00; amber, $95.00; blue, $95.00; canary, $150.00.

SIZE: 2½" tall x 2" wide

NOTES: Included in a Richards & Hartley catalog prior to the merger with U. S. Glass. Also included in the 1891 U. S. Glass catalog.

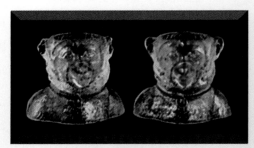

Clear and canary

Clear

OMN: No. 103

AKA: HAT, THOUSAND EYE

DATE: 1888

COLORS: clear, $65.00; amber, $75.00; apple green, $75.00; blue, $80.00; canary, $80.00.

SIZE: 2⅛" tall x 2¼" wide

NOTES: The Thousand Eye pattern was also made by Adams & Co., but the toothpick and the hat toothpick were shown only in the Richards & Hartley catalog. See Thousand Eye on next page for the standard toothpick shape in this pattern.

103 HAT.

Blue

OMN: MIKADO, No. 99

AKA: DAISY & BUTTON WITH CROSSBARS

DATE: 1885

COLORS: clear, $38.00; amber, $52.00; blue, $60.00; canary, $60.00.

SIZE: 2¼" tall x 2⅜" wide

NOTES: Included in the U.S. Glass Co. catalog in 1891. This toothpick does not match the rest of the pattern. If it were not for old catalogs, this would not be identified as Mikado.

Old version

AKA: RABBIT WITH BASKET

DATE: ca. mid-1880s

COLORS: Old: clear, $85.00; clear with ruby stain, $145.00; blue, $135.00. New: clear, $58.00; amber, $68.00; pale blue, $68.00; pink, $68.00.

SIZE: Old: 3⅜" tall x 2" wide. New: 3⅜" tall x 2" wide

NOTES: Note that the old toothpick has a basket composed of plain rings of glass. The newer toothpick has a basketweave pattern. The L. G. Wright Glass Co. made this toothpick in the 1960s in many colors. It is a newer toothpick made to resemble the old rabbit match made by Richards & Hartley and subsequently by Challinor while part of U.S. Glass. It has been seen in several newer colors, such as pale blue and pink.

Amber, L. G. Wright version

Blue, new L. G. Wright version

Amber

OMN: No. 103

AKA: THOUSAND EYE

DATE: 1888

COLORS: clear, $42.00; amber, $58.00; apple green, $65.00; blue, $65.00; canary, $70.00.

SIZE: 2" tall x 2" wide

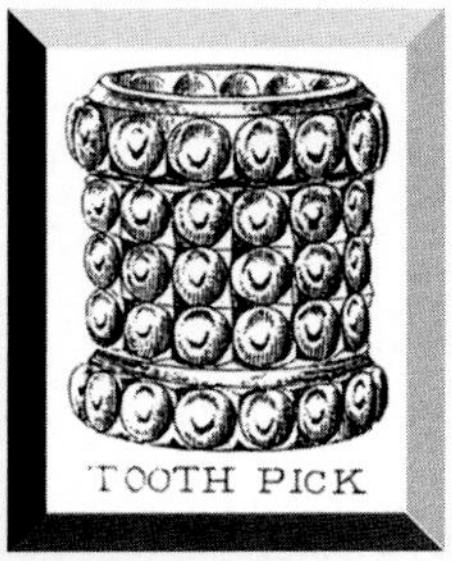

RIVERSIDE GLASS CO.
WELLSBURG, WEST VIRGINIA
1880 – 1907

Riverside Glass was organized in 1880 by J. E. Ratcliffe, John Dornan, and Charles Brady, former employees of Hobbs, Brockunier & Co. As with most glass factories, they had their problems with fires; but they appeared to be much more stable than many firms.

In 1899 the company joined the National Glass Co. and became known as Factory No. 15, Riverside Glass Works. Eventually the company went bankrupt, and some molds went to the Cambridge Glass Co. in Cambridge, Ohio.

Patterns include No. 348 America, No. 420, No. 434 Victoria, No. 436 Brilliant, Esther, X-Ray, Derby, No. 484 Croesus, No. 492 Empress, and Lily Langtry.

See also National Glass Co., Factory No. 15.

OMN: No. 420

AKA: BOX IN BOX

DATE: 1894

COLORS: clear, $50.00; clear with gold decor, $55.00; clear with ruby stain, $138.00; emerald green, $95.00; emerald green with gold decor, $115.00.

SIZE: 2¾" tall x 2⅜" wide

Green decorated with gold, clear with ruby stain

Clear with amber stain

OMN: BRILLIANT, No. 436

DATE: 1895

COLORS: clear, $60.00; clear with amber stain, $155.00; clear with ruby stain, $155.00; clear with engraving, $80.00.

SIZE: 2½" tall x 2¼" wide

NOTES: In April of 1895 it was reported that the Mueller Glass Staining Co., of Pittsburgh, was having good sales of this pattern in amber stain.

Emerald green with gold

OMN: CROESUS, No. 484

DATE: 1898

COLORS: clear, $85.00; emerald green, gold decor, $85.00; royal purple, gold decor, $95.00.

SIZE: 2⅝" tall x 2⅛" wide

NOTES: *The Riverside Glass Works of Wellsburg, W. Va., have out a new pattern which they have appropriately named the Croesus, No. 484. We need scarcely remind our readers that this was the name of a king of Lydia so famed for his wealth that his name has been handed down to posterity as the personification of riches... They have a full line of it, in plain, crystal, royal purple and gold, and emerald and gold. The tint of the latter is the finest we have ever seen. The purple is also exceedingly rich and the crystal is crystal indeed. –December, 1897. ...about 30 pieces in this line... –January 1898.* The quotation goes on to say that the 30 items were those made in color, while in plain crystal there were about 70 items available. This toothpick has been reproduced. After the closure of Riverside, at least some of the molds appear to have gone to McKee as the pattern is included in their catalogs. Clear is the most difficult to find.

Royal purple with gold

OMN: DERBY

AKA: RIVERSIDE

DATE: 1897

COLORS: clear, $60.00; clear with gold decor, $65.00; canary, $95.00; canary with gold decor, $105.00.

SIZE: 2¾" tall x 2⅛" wide

NOTES: *The Derby is made to represent a cut line and is a good imitation. It is finely polished flint, with a very strong incut figure and narrow plain flute, showing off the prismatic colors to a good advantage. –April 1897.* Note the two different styles of toothpicks.

Canary

Footed

OMN: EMPRESS, No. 492

DATE: 1899

COLORS: clear, $65.00; clear with gold decor, $70.00; clear with engraving, $80.00; emerald green, $200.00; emerald green with gold, $285.00.

SIZE: 2¾" tall x 2⅛" wide

Clear with gold decoration

Emerald green with gold decoration

OMN: ESTHER

DATE: 1896

COLORS: clear, $60.00; clear with enamel, $70.00; clear with gold decor, $70.00; clear with amber stain, $235.00; clear with ruby stain, $185.00; emerald green, $135.00; emerald green with gold decor, $145.00; clear with etching, $75.00.

SIZE: 2½" tall x 2¼" wide

NOTES: There are a variety of unusual decorations known on pieces of Esther. Whether or not the toothpicks were also decorated in these various manners is unknown. Beaumont applied the gold decoration and others to Esther, including "enameled decoration with wild roses and lilies of the valley."

Clear with enamel decoration

Emerald green with gold decoration

OMN: KANAWHA, No. 593

DATE: ca. 1905

COLORS: clear, $38.00; amber, $38.00; light green, $48.00.

SIZE: 2⅛" tall x 2½" wide at top

NOTES: There is also a cupped-in version of this toothpick that is smaller in top diameter. This pattern was continued by Tygart Valley Glass Co., probably only in clear glass. Eventually McKee acquired the molds for this pattern as it is also found in McKee catalogs. Probably other colors were made. The toothpick has been reproduced. Photos are of new toothpicks.

Light green

Amber

171

OMN: NATIONAL

AKA: PETTICOAT

DATE: 1899

COLORS: clear, $70.00; clear with gold decor, $85.00; canary, $120.00; canary with gold decor, $135.00.

SIZE: 2⅝" tall x 2" wide

*Canary with
gold decoration*

Clear with stained decoration

OMN: ONEATA, No. 592

AKA: CHIMO

DATE: 1907

COLORS: clear, $38.00; clear with gold decor, $48.00; clear with colored stain, $55.00.

SIZE: 2" tall x 2⅛" wide

NOTES: After the closing of Riverside, some molds for this pattern went to Tygart Valley in Grafton, West Virginia. This pattern appears in its catalog also. This is a spoon to a child's table set. Has been reproduced in poor quaility glass in a shorter version.

Clear

Canary

OMN: RANSON, No. 500

AKA: GOLD BAND

DATE: 1899

COLORS: clear, $32.00; clear with gold decor, $42.00; canary, $110.00; canary with gold decor, $125.00.

SIZE: 2⅜" tall x 2" wide

Clear with ruby stain and clear with amber stain

OMN: VICTORIA, No. 434

DATE: 1895

COLORS: clear, $140.00; clear with ruby stain, $380.00; clear with amber stain, $450.00.

SIZE: 2¾" tall x 2⅛" wide

NOTES: Victoria was decorated in ruby and amber stain by the Mueller Glass Staining Co. of Pittsburgh in January 1895. Trade journals also state it was made in "35 pieces, all nicely finished." Two variations exist, one with "eyelashes" and one without.

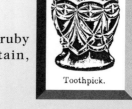

Toothpick.

Clear with enamel decoration

OMN: X-RAY, No. 462

DATE: 1896

COLORS: clear, $40.00; clear with enamel decor, $45.00; clear with gold decor, $45.00; emerald green, $68.00; emerald green with gold, $75.00; royal purple, $100.00; royal purple with gold decor, $115.00.

SIZE: 2¾" tall x 2½" wide

NOTES: *The Beaumont Glass Co... The X-Ray made in enameled and ornate colors is decorated with chrysanthemums. The berry set, pickle jar, and sugar for silver platers are decorated in chaste gold, bright, and matt.* –June 1896, *CGL.* Emerald was called a new color for this pattern in April 1897.

Emerald green
with gold decoration

Royal purple
with gold decoration

ROBINSON GLASS CO.
ZANESVILLE, OHIO
1893 – 1897 & 1899 – 1900

The Robinson Glass Co. of this place [Zanesville, Ohio] will have their new works completed and ready to begin active operations on or about September 1. They are in Fairbanks, South Zanesville, a very nice and desirable location. The factory proper is 80 x 80 feet, with one 15 pot furnace, 5 lears and the usual appurtenances; main building 80 x 120 feet, two stories; stock house, 50 x 100, and mixing room, 40 x 75 feet. The office building, which also contains the sample room, is separate from the works, and has five nice, airy commodious rooms. The electric street cars run within one block of the works. The product will be tableware, bar goods, and novelties and especial attention will be given to private molds. The factory is located on the Muskingum River, which is navigable to the Ohio, and is reached by the Baltimore & Ohio, Pennsylvania lines, Shawnee and Hocking, Bellaire, Zanesville & Cincinnati, Cleveland, Akron & Columbus, and Zanesville & Ohio River railroads. In fact it is a great railroad center and the shipping facilities are unsurpassed. –August 1893, *CGL.*

John and Edwin Robinson organized the Robinson Glass Co. in 1893 at Zanesville, Ohio. The company went into bankruptcy in 1897. In 1899 it became a member of the National Glass Co., designated Factory No. 16, Robinson Glass Works, but the factory never operated during this period. Some of its molds were transferred to the new National factory at Cambridge, Ohio.

Its wares consisted of novelties, tableware, and barware. Patterns include No. 1, No. 43, Puritan, Romola, No. 125 Zanesville, No. 123 Weston, and No. 129 Josephine's Fan.

Clear

OMN: No. 129

AKA: JOSEPHINE'S FAN

DATE: 1896

COLORS: clear, $48.00.

SIZE: 2½" tall x 2⅞" wide

NOTES: *Their No. 129 is an imitation cut pattern, finely executed.* –January 1896, *CGL*. This toothpick holder has at least three makers, but Robinson created the pattern. Through the failure of some companies and the movement of molds, the following also made No. 129: National Glass Co. at the Ohio Flint Glass Works, and the Cambridge Glass Co., as pattern No. 2504.

Clear

OMN: No. 123

AKA: WESTON

DATE: 1896

COLORS: clear, $52.00.

SIZE: 2⅜" tall x 2" wide

NOTES: *Their [Robinson] new No. 123 is a full line of tableware, with plain surface enough between their cut figures to show off both figure and the quality of the metal to excellent advantage.* –January 1896, *CGL*. This toothpick was still illustrated in the National Glass Co. catalog of 1902 as a product of the Ohio Flint Glass Works.

Clear with ruby stain

OMN: No. 122

AKA: ZANESVILLE

DATE: 1895

COLORS: clear, $38.00; clear with satin finish, $48.00; clear with ruby stain, $85.00.

SIZE: 2⅜" tall x 2" wide

NOTES: This pattern was continued by National at the McKee works after Robinson ceased doing business. Apparently, the top of the toothpick was changed when it was made by McKee, as it is shown with a flat top in a National catalog.

STEIMER GLASS CO.
BUCKHANNON, WEST VIRGINIA
1903 – 1906

F. C. Steimer, who was formerly with Macbeth-Evans Glass Co. has plans prepared for a large glass plant to be erected at Buckhannon, W. Va. The company of which Mr. Steimer is the head has a site of 40 acres located on the West Virginia and Pittsburg division of the B. & O. R. R.

A modern factory employing 150 men is to be built. The company will manufacture tableware of all kinds. The plant is to be completed by Sept. 1 and will be put into operation at once.

The rich natural resources of this part of West Virginia are gaining prominence. They have an inexhaustible supply of sand. This is in the midst of the great West Virginia gas field. All the land adjoining the site of the plant is laid out in lots, and a new town will be built. –May 1903, *CGL*.

The Steimer Glass Company originated as the Valley Glass Company in 1903. After several reorganizations, the company became the Steimer Glass Co. in 1904 when T. C. Steimer became president. The plant closed in 1906 after many difficulties.

The company produced high quality tablewares and novelties. Its most notable patterns are Spiral, known as Texas Star, and Diamond, known as Sawtooth Honeycomb. That pattern was also made by the Union Stopper Co. about 1913.

OMN: DIAMOND

AKA: SAWTOOTH HONEYCOMB

DATE: 1906

COLORS: clear, $55.00; clear with ruby stain, $90.00.

SIZE: 2⅜" tall x 2⅜" wide

NOTES: Also made later by the Union Stopper Co. of Morgantown, West Virginia, and then called Radiant (ca. 1913).

Clear with ruby stain

Clear

OMN: SPIRAL

AKA: TEXAS STAR, STAR BASE SWIRL

DATE: 1905

COLORS: clear, $115.00.

SIZE: 2½" tall x 2¼" wide

NOTES: *The glass, which is of beautiful color, has a satin finish which is indescribable. But the effect which is responsible for its great success is the reflection through each piece of the cut star on the bottom... When I say the "Spiral" line with "satin finish" of this West Virginia concern is new and novel, and for this statement I have the word of several highly skilled glass men... –January 1905, CGL.* The bottoms of this large tableware line are satin finish with indented stars, leading to the popular names assigned to the pattern. Has been reproduced in red and possibly other colors.

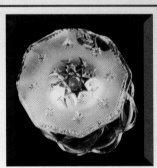

Base

STEUBEN GLASS WORKS
CORNING, NEW YORK
1903 – 1918

CORNING GLASS WORKS
CORNING, NEW YORK
1918 – PRESENT

The Steuben Glass Works was founded in 1903 by T. G. Hawkes and Frederick Carder, who ran the operation of the glass plant. Carder was the art director of the famous English firm Stevens & Williams before his affiliation with the Steuben factory. Carder remained with the Corning Glass Works in a working capacity until his retirement from glassmaking in the 1950s. Steuben may be marked with an acid-etched fleur de lis mark; sometimes Carder's creations are marked "F. Carder," engraved with a stylus.

Steuben glass is still made today, mostly in excellent crystal, often with wonderful engraved designs. It is the premier American glass still being made.

Carder produced many unusual colors and treatments for glass. Included in these are Aurene (iridescent finish), Intarsia, Calcite, Jade, and others.

OMN: unknown
AKA: HEAVY STEUBEN RIB (a)
DATE: 1910
COLORS: Aurene, $480.00+.
SIZE: 2" tall x 2½" wide

Aurene (a-shaped)

OMN: unknown
AKA: HEAVY STEUBEN RIB (b)
DATE: 1910
COLORS: Aurene, $450.00+.
SIZE: 2" tall x 2⅜" wide

Aurene (b-shaped)

OMN: unknown
AKA: PINCHED
DATE: 1896
COLORS: Aurene, $280.00.
SIZE: 1¾" tall x 1½" wide
NOTES: Signed "R-7853."

Aurene

OMN: unknown
AKA: THIN STEUBEN RIB
DATE: 1910
COLORS: Aurene, $525.00+.
SIZE: 3" tall x 2⅜" wide

Aurene

TARENTUM GLASS CO.
TARENTUM, PENNSYLVANIA
1894 – 1918

The Tarentum Glass Co. was organized and started operation in 1894 when the old Richards & Hartley works was purchased from the United States Glass Co. Tarentum was managed by Henry M. Brackenridge, John W. Hemphill, Lambert R. Hartley, and James D. Wilson. Production continued until a fire consumed the factory in 1918.

Products include tableware, novelties, lamps, and shades. Some patterns were Albany, Atlanta, Manhattan, Chicago, Harvard, Princess, Cornell, Hartford, Columbia, Oregon, Georgia, Victoria, Regent, Ladders, Lena, The Brackenridge, and Peerless.

Clear with ruby stain

OMN: ATLANTA
AKA: ROYAL CRYSTAL
DATE: 1894
COLORS: clear, $90.00; clear with ruby stain, $250.00+.
SIZE: 2½" tall x 2⅝" wide
NOTES: This was made in a full line of tableware. The ruby stain was done by the L. J. Rodgers Co. of Pittsburgh. Amber stain was also listed as being done by this company on Atlanta.

Clear with ruby stain

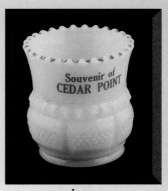

Ivory

OMN: COLUMBIA

AKA: HARVARD, QUIHOTE

DATE: 1899

COLORS: clear, $35.00; clear with ruby stain, $95.00; green opaque, $85.00; ivory, $80.00.

SIZE: 2¼" tall x 2" wide

NOTES: The name is one of a series of patterns named by the company for universities. Today this is widely known as Harvard, but original ads show the true name as Columbia.

Green

Clear with gold decoration

OMN: CORNELL

DATE: 1898

COLORS: clear, $48.00; clear with gold decor, $55.00; green, $68.00.

SIZE: 2½" tall x 2" wide

NOTES: *The Tarentum Glass Co. have another new pattern to add to the galaxy of attractions named after the leading American universities by them. This last is called the "Cornell" and it is a meet companion to the rest, if not the best of the whole of them. The line contains about 150 pieces, the largest number of any got out this season.* –December 1897, *CGL*. Other university patterns are Harvard, Princeton, Oxford, Yale, and possibly others, including Columbia. The green in this pattern varies widely from piece to piece.

Clear with ruby stain

OMN: unknown

AKA: DALTON

DATE: 1904

COLORS: clear, $40.00; clear with ruby stain, $250.00.

SIZE: 2½" tall x 2¼" wide

Pea green opaque

OMN: GEORGIA

AKA: GEORGIA GEM

DATE: 1900

COLORS: clear, $30.00; emerald green, $52.00; pea green opaque, $60.00; ivory, $55.00.

SIZE: 2¾" tall x 2¼" wide

NOTES: *Tarentum Glass Co… The new Georgia pattern is a great thing and they have it in lemon yellow, crystal, emerald, and pea green, each kind in plain color or ornamented besides with gold and floral decorations.* –January 1900.

Tarentum Glass Co.

Rose pink

Harvard Sugar.

OMN: HARVARD

AKA: HARVARD YARD

DATE: 1897

COLORS: clear, $38.00; rose pink, $75.00.

SIZE: 2¾" tall x 2⅝" wide

NOTES: This pattern is widely known as Harvard Yard, the explanation being that there was another Tarentum pattern named Harvard. However, original ads from the company indicate that this is the pattern named Harvard, while the other pattern was named Columbia. There are two shades of pink. The larger size is a breakfast sugar.

Clear

OMN: No. 292

AKA: LADDERS

DATE: 1901

COLORS: clear, $28.00; clear with gold decor, $38.00; light green, $65.00; green with gold, $70.00.

SIZE: 2½" tall x 2⅜" wide

NOTES: *No. 292... All are to be had in plain crystal or in crystal and gold, as required. –January 1901.*

Clear with ruby stain and gold decoration

OMN: unknown

AKA: LADDERS & DIAMONDS

DATE: 1903

COLORS: clear, $42.00; clear with gold decor, $65.00; clear with ruby stain, $185.00.

SIZE: 2½" tall x 2¼" wide

NOTES: Ladders & Diamonds is a poor name for this pattern as there is a Duncan & Miller pattern also using diamonds within a diamond as a motif. The Tarentum pattern has hobnails in the large diamonds.

Clear with gold decoration

OMN: No. 240

DATE: 1908

COLORS: clear, $42.00.

SIZE: 2¼" tall x 2¼" wide

OMN: No. 902

AKA: SERRATED PRISM

DATE: 1902

COLORS: clear, $32.00; clear with ruby stain, $95.00.

SIZE: 2⅛" tall x 1¾" wide

NOTES: Do not confuse this with National Prism, which is similar.

OMN: unknown

AKA: THUMBPRINT, TARENTUM'S

DATE: 1904

COLORS: clear, $38.00; clear with enamel decor, $48.00; clear w/marigold iridescence, $65.00; clear with blue stippling, $85.00; clear with ruby stain, $135.00; ivory, $85.00; pea green opaque, $110.00.

SIZE: 2¼" tall x 2" wide

Clear with enamel decoration

Clear with blue enamel decoration

Clear with ruby stain

Clear

OMN: VERONA

AKA: WAFFLE & STAR BAND

DATE: 1910 – 1915

COLORS: clear, $68.00; clear with ruby stain, $165.00.

SIZE: 2⅜" tall x 2" wide

Tooth-pick.

THOMPSON GLASS CO.
UNIONTOWN, PENNSYLVANIA
1889 – 1896

The Thompson Glass Co., Ltd. began operations in 1889. After many difficulties including shortages of gas and financial problems, the factory was sold at sheriff's sale in 1896. In 1892 a charter was registered for the Thompson Glass Co., the name used after the reorganization. *We will make Glass September 1, 1892. Owing to the shortage of gas we were compelled to close the factory until we could make other arrangements for fuel.*

–September 1892, *CGL*. However, it is likely that little glass was made at the factory after 1890, although most of the factory was destroyed by fire and was rebuilt in 1893.

Two of the more notable patterns made by this company are Summit and Bowtie.

Clear with ruby stain

OMN: SUMMIT

DATE: 1894

COLORS: clear, $85.00; clear with ruby stain, $180.00; clear with leaf engraving, $95.00.

SIZE: 2½" tall x 2¼" wide

NOTES: A December 1894 announcement stated that this pattern was decorated by Oriental Glass. When introduced, this pattern had 70 pieces. The company also advised customers that the line was decorated with a fern leaf engraving. The same report indicated that amber staining was also done on this line. In January of 1895, L. J. Rodgers was also decorating this pattern. It was reissued by the Cambridge Glass Co. in 1901.

Thompson Glass Co.

OMN: No. 77

AKA: TRUNCATED CUBE

DATE: 1894

COLORS: clear, $65.00; clear with ruby stain, $135.00.

SIZE: 2⅝" tall x 2¼" wide

NOTES: *No. 77 is a brand new pattern, of which they have a large line. This is a handsomely modeled pattern and the ware is well finished. –January 1894, CGL. [Oriental Glass]...They have had a good run on their No. 77 in both ruby and amber. –December 1894.* No. 77 was made in at least 35 pieces. At this time, several Thompson patterns were being decorated by the Oriental Glass Co. of Pittsburgh. Be aware that the toothpick might also have been made with amber stain as listed in the quote.

Clear with ruby stain

L. C. Tiffany Glass Co.

The Tiffany Glass & Decorating Co. has been incorporated in Jersey City, with a capital of $400,000. Louis C. Tiffany, president of the Tiffany Glass Co., will be president of the new company. All of the directors of the old company will be directors of the new company... –March 1892.

The L. C. Tiffany Glass Co. was owned and operated by Louis Comfort Tiffany and made much art glass that is well known today. In addition to art glass wares which Tiffany developed, the company also made very intricate and beautiful stained glass windows for churches and exclusive homes.

Iridescent

OMN: FAVRILE

DATE: prior to 1905

COLORS: iridescent, $250.00+.

SIZE: 2" tall x 1⅝" wide

NOTES: Signed "L. C. T." and "# T 6743"

Tiffin Glass Co.
Early 1880s – 1892 – Tiffin, Ohio

Sneath Glass Co.
1892 – 1894 – Tiffin, Ohio

The Sneath Glass Co., of Tiffin, Ohio, formerly known as the Tiffin Glass Co., was purchased on January 22 by S. B. Sneath... They are now running 8 shops and are making lantern globes, jellies, and tumblers principally, and are just starting on some tableware. One set, known as No. 90, is particularly handsome. They intend soon to add the manufacture of green fruit jars to their products. –March 1892, CGL.

The Sneath Glass Co., whose factory at Tiffin, Ohio, was burned last March, will start up a new factory at Hartford City, Ind., this week, to run on their specialty, lantern globes. –September 1894, CGL.

The Tiffin Glass Co. was a small factory located in Tiffin, Ohio, in the 1890s. Do not confuse this with the later Tiffin Glass Co. that was the successor to the giant U.S. Glass Co. This small company made some pressed tableware, although not much is known about its designs.

The most well-known items made are the animals and carts with the monkey lids shown in an early ad. These are eagerly sought by toothpick and individual salt collectors. Prices of these items listed should be increased by at least half if the original lid is present.

OMN: DOG CART

DATE: 1886

COLORS: clear, $250.00.

SIZE: 3¼" tall x 2¼" wide x 5" long at base

NOTES: The original ad showing these three pieces reads "Donkey, Dog, and Goat Carts, either can be used for mustard, spices, matches, Tooth Picks, Ink Stands, Perfumery, Ornaments, or Toys."

OMN: DONKEY CART

DATE: 1886

COLORS: clear, $250.00.

SIZE: unknown

OMN: GOAT CART

DATE: 1886

COLORS: clear, $250.00.

SIZE: 3⅛" tall x 2⅛" wide x 5½" long

UNITED STATES GLASS CO.
PITTSBURGH, PENNSYLVANIA
1891 – 1938
TIFFIN, OHIO — 1938 – 1984

The United States Glass Company was chartered in early 1891 and elected a board of directors consisting, in part, of Daniel C. Ripley, James Lyon, William C. King, Andrew Bryce, A. A. Adams, A. H. Heisey, H. E. Waddell, D. C. Jenkins, A. J. Smith, and William Shinn. Following the organization, member factories became known by letter designations, as follows:

Factory A — Adams & Co., Pittsburgh, Pennsylvania
Factory B — Bryce Brothers, Pittsburgh, Pennsylvania
Factory C — Challinor, Taylor & Co., Tarentum, Pennsylvania
Factory D — George Duncan & Sons, Pittsburgh, Pennsylvania
Factory E — Richards & Hartley, Tarentum, Pennsylvania
Factory F — Ripley & Co., Pittsburgh, Pennsylvania
Factory G — Gillinder & Sons, Greensburg, Pennsylvania
Factory H — Hobbs Glass Co., Wheeling, West Virginia
Factory J — Columbia Glass Co., Findlay, Ohio

Factory K — King, Son & Co., Pittsburgh, Pennsylvania
Factory L — O'Hara Glass Co., Pittsburgh, Pennsylvania
Factory M — Bellaire Goblet Co., Findlay, Ohio
Factory N — Nickel Plate Glass Co., Fostoria, Ohio
Factory O — Central Glass Co., Wheeling, West Virginia
Factory P — Doyle & Co., Pittsburgh, Pennsylvania
Factory R — A. J. Beatty & Sons, Tiffin, Ohio
Factory S — A. J. Beatty & Sons, Steubenville, Ohio
   (never in operation)
Factory T — Novelty Glass Co., Fostoria, Ohio

In addition to the above factories, the company also built two new factories:
Factory G — Glassport, Pennsylvania
   (designated Factory G after Gillinder had been closed)
Factory U — Gas City, Indiana

United States Glass Co.

These factories were supplied with automatic machinery for making glass. Because of this and other factors, the glassworkers went on strike for many months. U.S. Glass proved to be too powerful, and eventually the union stopped the strike.

Shortly after the organization, several factories burned and others were closed due to problems of the strike and lack of sales. In 1892, Factory D burned and was not rebuilt. In 1893 Factories M, N, and J were closed, and Factories C and T were destroyed by fire and never reopened. In 1894, Factory E was sold. In 1895, Factory N was destroyed by fire. By 1898 Factories G and K had been closed. Other factories were operating or closed, depending on specific dates. The two new factories were successful for the most part.

In 1938, the headquarters of U.S. Glass was moved from Pittsburgh to Tiffin, Ohio. The firm filed for bankruptcy in 1963.

Dewey Blue is sometimes called cobalt blue today, but Dewey Blue is the original company name. *They are showing specialties in light green decorations that are pleasing. The effect is a delicate one that is not likely to offend the taste. There are also decorations in ruby, amber, claret and in gold.* –March 1905.

Catalogs of U.S. Glass member companies (ca. 1891) have caused many misinterpretations by glass researchers. U.S. Glass first assembled current catalogs of individual member companies and used them as its own catalogs, labeling them by stamping them "U.S. Glass Co. — Factory __." Since these catalogs were printed and used by the original member companies before joining U.S. Glass, anything contained in those catalogs was originated by those companies, not by U.S. Glass, regardless of the ink stamp identification. To further complicate these member catalogs, often in the past they were found bound together, which sometimes gave the false impression that they were one catalog rather than many gathered together. Researchers have sometimes indicated that U.S. Glass "reproduced" patterns contained in these catalogs. In reality, the member companies continued to produce any pattern that was a good seller. As factories quickly closed over the next months, molds may have been moved to other factories under U.S. Glass Co.'s control to continue production of popular patterns. However, for well over a year, many of the U.S. Glass member companies were closed or suffered disastrous fires. As far as our research indicates, the U.S. Glass Co. did not begin to print its own catalogs until 1892 or 1893, when it planned a series of at least five catalogs to cover all aspects of its production. It is doubtful that all of these were printed, but at least the lamps, the stemware, and the tumblers catalogs were printed. Plans were made for a tableware catalog, but if it has survived (or was ever produced), we have not been able to find a copy of it.

During the heyday of toothpick making, many patterns were made by the member companies. Space prevents listing all, but some were Nail, Broken Column, Double Arch, Victor, Superior, Electric, Waverly, and the States series.

Factory A — Formerly Adams & Co.

OMN: BLOSSOM, No. 15,045

AKA: WARD'S REGAL

DATE: 1895

COLORS: clear, $28.00; clear with gold decor, $38.00; clear with engraving, $38.00; emerald green, $48.00; emerald green with gold decor, $58.00.

SIZE: 2½" tall x 2½" wide

NOTES: This toothpick was decorated with Wreath and Star engravings. The violet bowl in this pattern may have been made from the toothpick mold.

Emerald green with gold decoration

OMN: No. 15,041

AKA: PINEAPPLE & FAN, CUBE & FAN

DATE: 1895

COLORS: clear, $48.00; clear with gold edges, $55.00.

SIZE: unknown

NOTES: Decorated by Oriental Glass Co. in 1895. Made at Factories A and G, Adams and Glassport.

OMN: No. 15,042

AKA: ZIPPERED SWIRL & DIAMOND

DATE: 1895

COLORS: clear, $38.00; clear with gold decor, $45.00.

SIZE: 2⅜" tall x 2½" wide

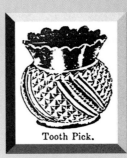

Clear with gold decor

Factory B — Bryce Bros.

OMN: No. 15,090

AKA: BULL'S-EYE & FAN

DATE: 1905

COLORS: clear, $42.00; clear with oriole decor, $72.00; blue, $90.00; emerald green, $90.00.

SIZE: 2⅞" tall x 2¼" wide

NOTES: Oriole decoration was listed in an original catalog but not illustrated or described.

Emerald green

Clear

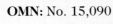

OMN: No. 15,025

AKA: DIAMOND WAFFLE

DATE: 1891

COLORS: clear, $60.00; clear with gold decor, $68.00.

SIZE: 2⅝" tall x 2¼" wide

NOTES: Made at Factory B and, following that, at Factory G (Glassport).

Clear with gold decoration

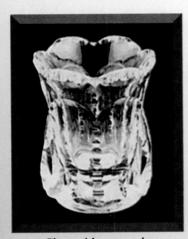

OMN: FORT PITT, No. 15,123

DATE: 1910

COLORS: clear, $38.00; clear with cutting, $52.00.

SIZE: 2⅜" tall x 2" wide

Clear with cut notches

OMN: No. 15,003

AKA: PLEATING

DATE: 1892

COLORS: clear, $52.00; clear with ruby stain, $165.00.

SIZE: 2½" tall x 2" wide

NOTES: Reportedly made by Factory B. This has also been reported as being made prior to the merger by Bryce Brothers and Gillinder and Sons, but we have found no evidence to support either of these attributions.

Clear with ruby stain

United States Glass Co.

Clear

OMN: SPIRAL, No. 15,085

AKA: BEADED SWIRL & DISC, BEADED SWIRL & LENS

DATE: 1904

COLORS: clear, $48.00; blue, $95.00; emerald green, $95.00.

SIZE: 2½" tall x 1⅞" wide

NOTES: Although widely known by its assigned names, the pattern was originally called Spiral, and catalogs indicate it was decorated "T. Rose." This would imply some sort of rose stain, but this is uncertain. Known in crystal with pink and yellow stain; value, $95.00.

Toothpick.

Blue

Factory C — Challinor, Taylor & Co.

Clear

OMN: No. 16,008

AKA: FLEUR DE LIS

DATE: ca. 1900

COLORS: clear, $50.00; clear with ruby stain, $140.00.

SIZE: 4" tall x 3" wide at base; top is 2" x 1¾".

16008. Tooth Pick.
Half Size.

Factory F — Ripley & Co.

Clear

OMN: No. 15,091

AKA: ARCHED OVALS, CONCAVE ALMOND

DATE: 1905

COLORS: clear, $28.00; clear with gold band, $38.00; clear with ruby stain, $90.00; clear with amber stain, $90.00; clear with roseblush, $90.00; clear with Cupids, $48.00; clear with wildflowers, $48.00; clear with yellow decor, $48.00; emerald green, $80.00.

SIZE: 2⅛" tall x 2" wide

Toothpick.

Clear with yellow decoration

NOTES: Original catalogs indicate this pattern was made at the Ripley & Co. factory. Decorations listed in the catalog were "roseblush, cupids, gold band, and wildflowers." *One of the new patterns is No. 15,091, which has been designed expressly for the English trade. The shallow round and oval dishes are quite after the English taste. This is a line that seems well suited to the catering trades and to hotels. –March 1905.*

Clear with Claret decoration

OMN: NEW HAMPSHIRE, No. 15,084

AKA: BENT BUCKLE

DATE: 1903

COLORS: clear, $48.00; clear with gold decor, $52.00; clear with rose stain, $70.00; clear with rose stain and gold decor, $75.00; clear with ruby stain, $180.00.

SIZE: 3⅜" tall x 2½" wide

NOTES: In this case, the U.S. Glass Co. named the ruby stain Claret, as shown in an original catalog. This piece was also shown as a toothpick or a match safe.

Clear with rose stain

Toothpick or Match Safe.

Clear with etched advertising

OMN: WASHINGTON, No. 15,074

DATE: 1901

COLORS: clear, $28.00; clear with amber stain, $170.00; clear with ruby stain, $95.00; clear with enamel decor, $48.00; clear with etching, $48.00; ivory, $70.00.

SIZE: 2⅝" tall x 2¼" wide

NOTES: Original catalogs indicate that Washington was "enameled and Wild Rose decorated."

Ivory

Clear with ruby stain

Clear with amber stain

Factory G (GP) — Glassport

Clear with ruby stain

OMN: ALABAMA, No. 15,062

DATE: 1899

COLORS: clear, $70.00; clear with ruby stain, $275.00+; emerald green, $275.00+.

SIZE: 2½" tall x 2" wide

NOTES: Decorated by Oriental Glass Co. in January 1900.

Toothpick.

OMN: BUCKINGHAM, No. 15,106

DATE: 1907

COLORS: clear, $65.00; clear with stain, $155.00; clear with gold decoration, $85.00.

SIZE: 2⅛" tall x 2" wide

Clear with rose stain

OMN: COLUMBIA, No. 15,082

AKA: CHURCH WINDOWS

DATE: 1903

COLORS: Toothpick: clear, $28.00; clear with gold decor, $35.00; clear with magenta stain, $50.00; clear with tulip stain, $50.00. Match safe: clear, $28.00; clear with gold decor, $32.00; clear with magenta stain, $45.00; clear with tulip stain, $45.00.

SIZE: Toothpick: 2½" tall x 2¾" wide

Clear

Match Safe.

Tulip stain

NOTES: Original catalogs use the terms in the Colors section above for decorations and indicate the Glassport factory as the place of manufacture. Tulip stain is multicolored yellow/green stain and magenta stain on alternating petals.

OMN: No. 15,141

AKA: FLOWER WITH CANE

DATE: 1912

COLORS: clear, $48.00; clear with any stain, $72.00.

SIZE: 3⅝" tall x 2" wide

Clear with amethyst stain and gold decoration

OMN: ILLINOIS, No. 15,052

DATE: 1897

COLORS: clear, $68.00; clear with advertising, $68.00; clear with gold decor, $70.00.

SIZE: 2½" tall x 2⅛" wide

Clear with gold decoration

TOOTHPICK HOLDER.

NOTES: *The Illinois is square shaped, imitation cut pattern of excellent design, rosetted, with deep incuts and splendid figure... January 1897. The Illinois pattern...was the best imitation cut glass pattern put on the market last spring... Remains in favor among that large class of American buyers who desire something better than ordinary pressed glassware, and yet are not inclined to pay the price of cut glass. –June 1897. There may be advertising in the bottom of the Illinois toothpick.*

Clear with ruby stain

Clear with yellow enamel decoration

OMN: MICHIGAN, No. 15,077

DATE: 1902

COLORS: clear, $62.00; clear with rose stain and gold decor, $185.00; clear with ruby stain, $260.00+; clear with enamels, $120.00.

SIZE: 2⅜" tall x 2¼" wide

NOTES: Widely reproduced by Degenhart and subsequently Boyd of Cambridge, OH, in many colors and with straight (not flared) top rim.

Toothpick.

Clear with blue enamel decoration

OMN: MIRROR PLATE, No. 15,086

AKA: GALLOWAY

DATE: 1904

COLORS: clear, $28.00; clear with gold decor, $35.00; clear with enamel, $50.00; clear with creme de menthe stain, $70.00; clear with golden rod stain, $70.00; clear with magenta stain, $70.00.

SIZE: 2⅝" tall x 1⅞" wide

NOTES: Catalogs indicate the following decorations: "also made decorated gold, magenta, golden rod, and creme-de-menthe." Reproduced by Degenhart and subsequently Boyd of Cambridge, OH, in many colors and with straight sides.

Clear with gold decoration

Toothpick.

Clear with enamel decoration   *Clear with magenta stain*

Toothpick.

OMN: PANAMA, No. 15,088

AKA: VIKING

DATE: 1904

COLORS: clear, $70.00; clear with rose stain, $135.00.

SIZE: unknown

NOTES: Original catalog pictures show the toothpick with a notched cover to be a horseradish and cover.

OMN: ST. REGIS, No. 15,107

AKA: BEVELED WINDOWS

DATE: 1909

COLORS: clear, $48.00.

SIZE: 2⅜" tall x 2⅛" wide

Clear

Toothpick.

OMN: No. 15,092

AKA: STAR IN BULL'S-EYE

DATE: 1905

COLORS: Toothpick: clear, $32.00; clear with gold decor, $42.00; clear with rose and gold decor, $62.00. Match holder: clear, $32.00; clear with gold decor, $38.00; clear with rose and gold decor, $60.00.

Clear

Match-holder.

SIZE: Toothpick: 2½" tall x 2½" wide. Match holder: 3⅛" tall x 2½" wide

NOTES: *There are other new patterns (one No. 15,092 on show, which, like those already named, are shown in flint, flint and gold, rose and gold, etc.)* –March 1905. The match holder is sometimes found with advertising inscriptions.

OMN: TRILBY

AKA: DIAMOND POINT HEART

DATE: 1895

COLORS: clear, $75.00.

SIZE: unknown

NOTES: *Of course the glass business could not wholly escape the Trilby craze, and among the novelties shown are toothpicks, match safes, a half gallon pitcher and goblet in which the "Trilby heart" idea is worked out most effectively.* –October 1895. Reproduced in many colors, none of which were originally made.

Clear with ruby stain

OMN: VICTOR, NO. 15,046

AKA: SHOSHONE

DATE: 1896

COLORS: clear, $45.00; clear with amber stain, $185.00; clear with gold decor, $55.00; clear with ruby stain, $145.00; emerald green, $185.00.

SIZE: 2⅝" tall x 2" wide

Toothpick.

Factory J — Columbia Glass Co.

Toy spoon

OMN: No. 15,006

AKA: POINTED JEWEL, LONG DIAMOND

DATE: 1892

COLORS: clear, $68.00.

SIZE: 2½" tall

NOTES: This is not a true toothpick holder but is a spooner to a child's table set. It bears little resemblance to the remainder of the pattern. Pointed Jewel was made in a wide variety of shapes as an extended tableware line.

Factory N — Nickel Plate Glass Co.

Clear with gold coins

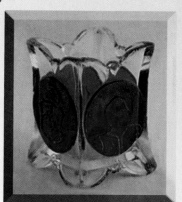
Clear with ruby stain

OMN: WORLD'S FAIR, No. 15,005½

AKA: COLUMBIAN COIN

DATE: 1892

COLORS: clear, $85.00; clear with satin coins, $98.00; clear with gold coins, $115.00; clear with silver coins, $115.00; clear with ruby stain, $350.00+.

SIZE: 2⅞" tall x 2" wide

NOTES: *Plant N of the United States Glass Co. has been assigned pattern No. 15005½, which will be turned out in silver and gold decoration, and sold to jobbers only. It will be known as the World's Fair pattern. –1892.* After the Treasury Department had the molds of the Silver Age (U.S. Coin) pattern defaced at Central Glass, apparently U.S. Glass had the molds moved to Nickel Plate, where they were redesigned as Columbian Coin. The faces on the coins are likenesses of Christopher Columbus and Amerigo Vespucci.

Factory U — Gas City, Indiana

OMN: JUNGLE, No. 15,142

AKA: FLAMING THISTLE, FIELD THISTLE

DATE: ca. 1912

COLORS: clear, $38.00.

SIZE: 3¼" tall x 2⅝" wide at base

Factory Unspecified

Amber

OMN: ANVIL, DAISY & BUTTON

DATE: ca. 1886

COLORS: clear, $45.00; amber, $68.00; blue, $78.00.

SIZE: 2" tall x 1⅝" wide x 2½" long

Clear

OMN: ATHENIA, No. 15,140

AKA: REVERSE 44, PANELED 44

DATE: 1912

COLORS: clear, $48.00; clear with gold decor, $58.00; clear with platinum decor, $58.00; clear with amber stain, $90.00; clear with light marigold luster finish, $90.00.

SIZE: 2⅜" tall, 1⅞" wide

Floradora decoration

Clear with allover rose stain and gold, clear with rose stain and gold on design, emerald green with gold decoration

OMN: BOHEMIAN, No. 15,063

AKA: FLORADORA

DATE: 1899

COLORS: clear, $68.00; clear with satin finish, $85.00; clear with Floradora decor, $195.00; clear with allover rose stain and gold decor, $235.00; clear with rose stain and gold decor on design, $235.00; emerald green, $240.00; emerald green with gold decor, $250.00.

SIZE: 2⅝" tall x 1¼" tall

NOTES: The clear with enamel and satin finish was advertised as Floradora decoration.

OMN: BRILLIANT, No. 15,095

AKA: PANELED PALM

DATE: 1906

COLORS: clear, $45.00; clear with gold decor, $48.00; clear with rose stain and gold decor, $115.00.

SIZE: 2⅜" tall x 2" wide

NOTES: *The 15095 line will catch your eye immediately... It is now completed, is of light finish, panel pattern, plain, crystal, and gold, and gold and rose decorations. –December 1905.*

Clear with rose stain and gold decoration

Clear

OMN: No. 15,101

AKA: BUZZ STAR, WHIRLIGIG

DATE: 1907

COLORS: clear, $38.00; clear with enamel decoration, $42.00; green, $48.00.

SIZE: 2¼" tall x 2" wide

Emerald green

OMN: CALIFORNIA, No. 15,059

AKA: BEADED GRAPE

DATE: 1899

COLORS: clear, $45.00; emerald green, $75.00.

SIZE: 2⅜" tall x 1⅞" wide

NOTES: Reproductions of this pattern were made by Westmoreland in colors and opal (milk glass).

AKA: COAL BUCKET, TOY

DATE: unknown

COLORS: clear, $28.00; clear with ruby stain, $55.00.

SIZE: 2" tall x 2" wide x 4" long

Clear with ruby stain

OMN: unknown

AKA: COLONIAL

DATE: unknown

COLORS: clear, $55.00; clear with cutting, $68.00.

SIZE: 2⅝" tall x 2¼" wide

NOTES: Not identified as to pattern number or name, but has U.S. Glass Co. logo molded in bottom.

Clear with cutting

OMN: COLONIAL, No. 15,047

AKA: PLAIN SCALLOPED PANEL

DATE: 1896

COLORS: clear, $40.00; clear in "solid gold" decoration, $55.00; Dewey Blue, $78.00; emerald green, $72.00; light green, $72.00; clear with enamel decoration, $65.00.

SIZE: 2⅝" tall x 2⅛" wide at top

NOTES: Introduced in January 1896 with a notation that it was available in "a novelty in decoration in 'solid gold.'" *It is made to follow closely the lines of the silverware in use in this country in Colonial times, and, while almost severely plain, the general effect is certainly very pleasing.* –January 1896. The clear and colors may be decorated with a gold top rim.

Emerald green

Clear in solid gold decoration

Dewey Blue

Clear with enamel decoration

United States Glass Co.

OMN: COLORADO, No. 15,057 (first name); JEWEL (later name)

AKA: LACY MEDALLION

DATE: 1898

COLORS: Colorado: clear, $40.00; clear with gold decor, $45.00; clear with ruby stain, $80.00; Dewey blue, $75.00; emerald, $60.00; emerald with gold decor, $68.00; clambroth, $75.00; clambroth with gold decor, $85.00. Jewel: clear, $40.00; clear with gold decor, $48.00; clear with ruby stain and gold decor, $75.00; emerald green, $60.00; emerald green with gold, $68.00; clambroth with gold, $85.00.

SIZE: 2⅜" tall x 2½" wide

NOTES: *Oriental Glass Co... No. 15057 of this company, in emerald, is a decidedly pretty thing.* –March 1900. The small violet vase is also sometimes found in toothpick collections. It was made in a pale white opaque (clambroth) and Dewey blue. The early Colorado toothpicks have the three small feet, while Jewel is not footed. Jewel is the original name of pieces of Colorado continued by U.S. Glass into the first of the twentieth century. It is often called Lacy Medallion today. Pieces of Jewel all have bottom rings of glass on the bases. Contrary to reports made by other authors, the original catalog of this pattern shows some non-footed pieces as Colorado. Previously these were thought to be only in Jewel.

Clear with ruby stain

Opal, rose bowl

Clambroth with gold decoration

Clear with ruby stain and gold decoration

Emerald with gold decoration

OMN: CONNECTICUT, No. 15,068

DATE: 1900

COLORS: clear, $78.00; clear with enamel, $90.00; clear with engraving, $90.00; clear with ruby stain, $240.00.

SIZE: 2" tall x 2⅛" wide

NOTES: *The Connecticut, No. 15068, is a full line, of plain contour, and they have it engraved and enameled both.* –January 1900. Heacock attributes this pattern to Factory K. Made as shown and also with top flared.

Clear with silk screen enamel

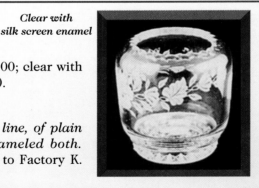

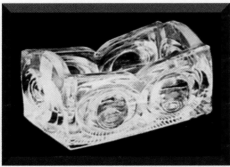

Stained bull's-eyes

OMN: CROMWELL, No. 15,155

AKA: KNOBBY BULL'S-EYE

DATE: 1915

COLORS: clear, $45.00; clear with various stains, $70.00.

SIZE: 1¾ tall x 2⅛" wide x 3½" long

TOOTHPICK.

*Emerald with gold decoration,
clear with rose stain and gold on design,
clear with allover rose stain and gold decoration*

OMN: DELAWARE, No. 15,065

AKA: FOUR PETAL FLOWER, NEW CENTURY

DATE: 1899

COLORS: clear, $45.00; clear with rose stain and gold on design, $95.00; clear with allover rose stain and gold, $95.00; emerald green, $70.00; emerald green with gold, $95.00; clear with amethyst stain and gold, $95.00.

SIZE: 2⅜" tall x 2" wide

NOTES: *The Delaware, got out last fall, they are now reproducing in rose pink and with gold decoration or alone this has a most attractive effect.* –January 1900. *This is made in crystal with rose and gold decoration and in emerald with gold decoration.* –March 1900.

Allover stain with enamel decoration

OMN: No. 15,087

AKA: DIAMOND MAT BAND

DATE: 1904

COLORS: clear, $45.00; clear with stain, $62.00; clear with enamels, $65.00.

SIZE: 2⅜" tall x 2¼" wide

NOTES: Erroneously identified as Frazier in the past. However, the pattern Metz named Frazier is not this U.S. Glass pattern.

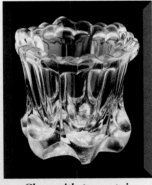

Clear with green stain

OMN: No. 15,134

AKA: ELEPHANT TOES

DATE: ca. 1912

COLORS: clear, $45.00; clear with amethyst stain, $88.00; clear with green stain, $88.00; clear with rose stain, $90.00; clear with gold decor, $60.00; clear with yellow stain, $88.00.

SIZE: 2½" tall x 2⅜" wide

NOTES: The stains are on the thumbprints around the bottom of the toothpick.

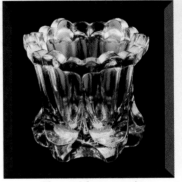

Clear with rose stain

Blue

OMN: FAN

DATE: 1898, possibly earlier

COLORS: clear, $55.00; amber, $72.00; blue, $90.00; opal, gold decor, $70.00.

SIZE: 3⅞" tall x 3¼" wide x 2" deep

NOTES: Catalog illustration states "assorted," meaning these came in several colors.

Opal with gold decoration

Clear with engraving

OMN: FLORICUT MARJORIE, No. 15,167

DATE: ca. 1916

COLORS: clear with engraving, $38.00.

SIZE: unknown

NOTES: U.S. Glass stated that this was a cut-over pressed pattern.

OMN: GEORGIAN, No. 15,152

DATE: ca. 1919

COLORS: clear, $48.00; clear with cutting, $55.00.

SIZE: 2" tall x 1¾" wide

NOTES: Shown in U. S. Glass Co.'s 1919 export catalog.

Clear

Green Pepper Toothpick
Illustration ½ size
Price per dozen 50 cents

OMN: GREEN PEPPER

DATE: ca. 1909

COLORS: emerald green, $68.00.

SIZE: unknown

NOTES: Any of these in any color would be quite hard to find.

OMN: No. 15,125

AKA: INTAGLIO SUNFLOWER

DATE: 1910 or 1912

COLORS: clear, $60.00; clear with gold decor, $85.00; clear with rose stain and gold decor, $130.00.

SIZE: 2⅜" tall x 1⅞" wide

NOTES: No. 15,133, Intaglio Daisy, has the same shape and design except that the flower has rounded petals. Values and colors are the same.

Clear with rose stain and gold decoration

Clear

OMN: No. 15,024

AKA: INTERLOCKING CRESCENTS, DOUBLE ARCH

DATE: 1891

COLORS: clear, $50.00; clear with ruby stain, $135.00; clear with amber stain, $175.00.

SIZE: 2¾" tall x 2¼" wide

NOTES: Attributed to King & Son by Revi.

Clear with ruby stain

Clear with rose stain

Footed Iowa

OMN: IOWA, No. 15,069

AKA: PANELED ZIPPER

DATE: 1900

COLORS: clear, $45.00; clear with gold decor, $55.00; clear with rose stain, $110.00; clear with ruby stain, $275.00; clear footed, $85.00.

SIZE: 2⅜" tall x 2¼" wide

NOTES: *The Iowa, No. 15069, may be regarded as the leader among the new patterns of the present season. They have this in plain crystal as well as in gold, rose, and other decorations, and it is one of the most elaborate lines in the market today. –January 1900, CGL.*

Clear

Toothpick.

OMN: KANSAS, No. 15,072

AKA: JEWEL & DEWDROPS

DATE: 1903

COLORS: clear, $55.00; clear with rose stain, $115.00.

SIZE: 2½" tall x 2" wide

OMN: KENTUCKY, No. 15,051

DATE: 1897

COLORS: clear, $60.00; clear with gold decor, $65.00; clear with ruby stain, $210.00; emerald green, $70.00; emerald green with gold decor, $80.00.

SIZE: 2⅝" tall x 2⅛" wide

Emerald green
with gold decoration

Small blue and larger size amber with wire bail

OMN: KETTLE, CANE

DATE: 1891, but probably made earlier also

COLORS: clear, $24.00; amber, $42.00; blue, $45.00; canary, $48.00.

SIZE: unknown

NOTES: There are two sizes. The larger is most likely a mustard, but the smaller one might very well be a toothpick.

Saucer, Mustard and Cover.

Match Safe.

OMN: LOUISIANA, No. 15,053

DATE: 1898

COLORS: clear, $58.00.

SIZE: unknown

NOTES: Made in a full line of tableware. Note that the item most commonly collected as a toothpick is a match safe. With a lid, this piece becomes a covered mustard with saucer.

Emerald

OMN: LOVING CUP, TOY

DATE: ca. 1909

COLORS: clear, $30.00; clear with gold decor, $35.00; clear with ruby stain, $70.00; green, $48.00; green with gold decor, $55.00; clear with silver decor, $35.00; opaline (clambroth), $40.00; opaline, decorated, $45.00; clear with allover gold decor, $35.00.

SIZE: 2¼" tall x 1⅞" tall

NOTES: A ca. 1909 catalog refers to this as a toy loving cup and shows only two handles. See Trophy (p. 201) for the three-handled version.

9528 Toy Loving Cup
38 dozen in barrel, ⅓ size
Price per dozen 80 cents

Clear

OMN: MAINE, No. 15,066

AKA: STIPPLED PANELED FLOWER

DATE: 1899

COLORS: clear, $350.00+; clear with colored stain areas, $600.00+; emerald green, $500.00+.

SIZE: 2½" tall x 2+" wide at top

NOTES: *The Maine, No. 15066, is a jobbing line, figured, and they have it also decorated. –January 1900, CGL.* This toothpick is quite rare and is difficult to find.

Clear with colored stain decoration

Clear

OMN: MANHATTAN, No. 15,078

DATE: 1898

COLORS: clear, $40.00; clear with gold decor, $45.00; clear with blue stain, $58.00; clear with rose stain, $58.00.

SIZE: 2¼" tall x 2⅛" wide

NOTES: *...the highly ornate Manhattan pattern of the United States Glass Co... This is only one of a half a dozen distinctive patterns the company have now ready... –January 1898, CGL.*

Toothpick.

Clear

OMN: MARYLAND, No. 15,049

DATE: 1897

COLORS: clear, $185.00; clear with ruby stain, $400.00+.

SIZE: 2¾" tall x 2¼" wide at top

NOTES: *...a figured and plain pattern, having a rounded link in relief... –January 1897.* Interestingly, this pattern was also introduced as "new" in January 1898 in *CGL.*

TOOTHPICK.

TOOTHPICK.

OMN: MASSACHUSETTS, No. 15,054

DATE: 1898

COLORS: Toothpick: clear, $50.00; clear with gold decor, $58.00; clear with light marigold luster, $58.00; green, $125.00; green with gold decoration, $145.00. Match safe: clear, $50.00; clear with gold decor, $58.00; clear with light marigold luster, $58.00.

SIZE: 2⅜" tall x 2⅛" wide

Clear with gold decoration

Clear with gold decoration

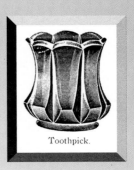

Toothpick.

OMN: MAYFLOWER, No. 15,121

AKA: PORTLAND

DATE: 1898

COLORS: clear, $45.00; clear with gold decor, $50.00; light green, $65.00.

SIZE: unknown

Clear with ruby stain

OMN: No. 15,016

AKA: MILLARD

DATE: 1893

COLORS: clear, $65.00; clear with amber stain, $210.00; clear with ruby stain, $210.00.

SIZE: 2⅝" tall x 2⅛" wide

Emerald green

TOOTHPICK HOLDER.

OMN: MINNESOTA, No. 15,055

DATE: 1898

COLORS: clear, $40.00; clear with gold decor, $45.00; clear with ruby stain, $230.00; emerald green, $200.00; emerald green with gold decor, $230.00. Match safe: clear, $40.00; clear with gold decor, $48.00.

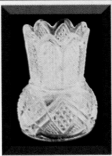

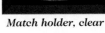

MATCH SAFE.

Match holder, clear

SIZE: Toothpick: 2½" tall x 2⅛" wide. Match Safe: 3⅜" tall x 2½" wide

NOTES: Decorated by Oriental Glass in ruby and crystal with gold. Heacock named the match holder USA, but it is a part of the Minnesota pattern as shown in an original U.S. Glass Co. catalog. Both styles also have a marigold luster finish. Match holder is known embossed with "The Geo. Anderson Dry Goods Co."

Blue

OMN: MONKEY

AKA: MONKEY ON A STUMP

DATE: late 1880s

COLORS: clear, $50.00; amber, $58.00; blue, $68.00.

SIZE: 2½" tall x 2" wide

NOTES: Included in 1904 U.S. Glass catalog. Judging from the colors produced, this was most likely made by one of the member companies prior to the merger. Reproduced with poor detail of hair and toes. Sold by A. A. Importing in clear, amber, blue, and milk glass.

Amber

United States Glass Co.

Clear with engraving

OMN: NEVADA, No. 15,075

DATE: 1902

COLORS: clear, $65.00; clear with gold decor, $75.00; clear with enamel, $75.00; clear with engraving, $78.00; clear with royal flush, $98.00; clear with allover ruby stain, $185.00.

SIZE: 2¼" tall x 2¼" wide

NOTES: Original catalogs indicate the following decorations: "Royal Flush, enameled or gold decorated."

Clear with enamel decoration

Clear with ruby stain

OMN: NEW JERSEY, No. 15,070

DATE: 1900

COLORS: clear, $58.00; clear with gold decor, $68.00; clear with ruby stain, $350.00.

SIZE: 2½" tall x 2⅛" wide

OMN: No. 15,152

AKA: PARTHENON

DATE: ca. 1914

COLORS: clear, $55.00

SIZE: 3¼" tall x 3½" wide across handles

NOTES: Same shape as the Athenia toothpick holder and may be from the retooled Athenia mold.

Clear satin, enameled decoration

Emerald green with gold decoration

OMN: PENNSYLVANIA, No. 15,048

DATE: 1898

COLORS: clear, $45.00; clear with gold decor, $55.00; clear with blue decor, $68.00; clear with ruby stain, $245.00; emerald green, $85.00; emerald green with gold decor, $110.00. Toy spoon: clear, $45.00; emerald green, $95.00.

SIZE: Toothpick: 2⅜" tall x 2¼" wide. Toy spoon: 2¼" tall x 2¼" wide

NOTES: Made in a full tableware line. Trade journal reports indicate that Oriental Glass decorated Pennsylvania "in blue and ruby, also clear with gold." A Butler Brothers catalog also lists the bar glass as a tumbler toothpick.

OMN: RAMBLER, No. 15,136
DATE: 1912
COLORS: clear, $38.00.
SIZE: unknown

OMN: REGAL, No. 15,098
DATE: 1906
COLORS: clear, $32.00.

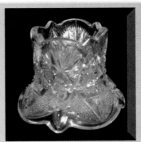

Clear

OMN: unknown
AKA: ROOSTER WITH RINGS
DATE: 1898
COLORS: clear, $145.00.
SIZE: unknown
NOTES: The holder portion is actually meant to look like a stack of coins, not rings.

OMN: ROYAL, No. 15,099
AKA: SPINNING STAR
DATE: ca. 1906
COLORS: clear, $38.00.

Clear

Clear with ruby stain

OMN: No. 15,026
AKA: SCALLOPED SWIRL, YORK HERRINGBONE
DATE: 1893
COLORS: clear, $50.00; clear with ruby stain, $155.00.
SIZE: 2⅜" tall x 2⅝" wide

Tooth Pick.

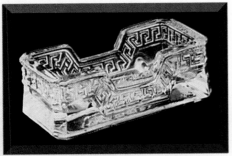

Clear

OMN: SHERATON, No. 15,144
DATE: 1910
COLORS: clear, $38.00; clear with gold decor, $50.00.
SIZE: 1¼" tall x 1⅝" wide x 3¼" long
NOTES: This toothpick is of the flat, sanitary type.

Emerald green

OMN: STATE OF NEW YORK, No. 15,061
AKA: U.S. RIB
DATE: 1899
COLORS: clear, $32.00; clear with gold decor, $45.00; emerald green, $70.00; emerald green with gold decor, $90.00.
SIZE: 2⅜" tall x 2⅛" wide
NOTES: The original catalog of this pattern lists it as The State of New York.

Toothpick

OMN: STATE OF OREGON, No. 15,073

AKA: OREGON, BEADED LOOPS

DATE: 1901

COLORS: clear, $110.00.

SIZE: 2⅜" tall x 2¼" tall

NOTES: The original catalog of this pattern calls it State of Oregon, not simply Oregon.

Clear

Clear

OMN: THE STATES, No. 15,093

DATE: 1905

COLORS: clear, $52.00.

SIZE: 2" tall x 2" wide x 2⅜" long

NOTES: *Another pattern is designated as "The States." The works number of this is 15,093; but, as it was got out specially for this year's trade, the company are calling it "States 1905" pattern… The pattern is a good one, on the lines of a heavy cut design. –March 1905.* A few pieces of this pattern are found in emerald green, so that is a possible color for this sanitary toothpick.

OMN: SUNBEAM, No. 15,139

AKA: TWIN SNOWSHOES

DATE: 1912

COLORS: clear, $52.00.

SIZE: 2⅛" tall x 1⅝" wide

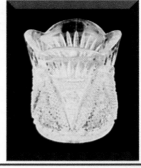

Clear

OMN: SUNRISE, No. 15,110

AKA: RISING SUN

DATE: 1908

COLORS: clear, $38.00; clear with gold decor, $45.00; clear with rose stain, $70.00; clear with amethyst stain, $70.00; clear with green stain, $70.00.

SIZE: 2⅜" tall x 2⅛" wide

NOTES: Notice how closely the collector's name for this pattern matches the original name! The various colored stains are applied to the suns of the pattern.

Clear with rose stain and gold decoration

Clear

OMN: TENNESSEE, No. 15,064

DATE: 1900

COLORS: clear, $100.00.

SIZE: 2⅝" tall x 1⅞" wide

NOTES: *The Tennessee, No. 15064, is a similar line [as Maine, listed as a jobbing line] but different in shapes and pattern. –January 1900.*

Toothpick.

OMN: TEXAS, No. 15,067

DATE: 1900

COLORS: clear, $45.00; clear with gold decor, $58.00; clear with rose stain, $135.00; clear with ruby stain, $235.00+.

SIZE: 2¾" tall x 2¼" wide

NOTES: *The Texas, No. 15067, is a figured pattern with rose decorations. There is also a full line of this. –January 1900.* The toothpick holder included in most collections does not have the same top as that of the toothpick shown in the original catalog; it has a straight top.

Clear with rose stain

Clear

OMN: No. 15,019

AKA: TREGO

DATE: 1891

COLORS: clear, $45.00; clear decorated, $55.00; opal, $150.00; opal decorated, $225.00.

SIZE: 2⅝" tall x 2¼" wide

NOTES: Included in the 1891 catalog along with other Challinor pieces, so Challinor is a likely maker.

15019. Toothpick.

Clear with ruby stain and gold

OMN: unknown

AKA: TROPHY

DATE: ca. 1900

COLORS: clear, $28.00; clear with ruby stain, $48.00; blue, $48.00; light pink, $38.00; clear with allover gold decor, $32.00; amethyst, $48.00; clear with silver overlay, $42.00.

SIZE: 2¼" tall x 1⅞" wide

NOTES: Probably made in the early twentieth century. This item is often seen with souvenir inscriptions. Attribution is based on the similarity to the Loving Cup pattern that is shown in U.S. Glass catalogs.

OMN: VENETIAN

DATE: ca. 1904

COLORS: clear, $55.00.

SIZE: unknown

9521 Venetian Match Holder

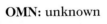

Emerald green with gold

OMN: VERMONT, No. 15,060

DATE: 1899

COLORS: clear, $38.00; clear with gold decor, $42.00; emerald green, $65.00; emerald green with gold decor, $75.00; ivory, $72.00; ivory with enamel decor, $90.00; amber, $75.00; blue, $90.00.

SIZE: 2⅝" tall x 2¼" wide

NOTES: This toothpick has been highly reproduced by Degenhart in many colors.

Ivory with enamel decoration

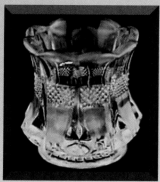

Clear

Clear with rose stain

OMN: VIRGINIA, No. 15,071

AKA: BANDED PORTLAND

DATE: 1901

COLORS: clear, $38.00; clear with Maiden Blush stain, $72.00; clear with green stain, $70.00.

SIZE: 2⅜" tall x 2¼" wide

NOTES: Original catalogs indicate that Maiden Blush is the correct name for the rose decoration.

Opaque blue

OMN: WASTE BASKET

DATE: 1898

COLORS: clear, $32.00; blue, opaque, $52.00; opal, $40.00.

SIZE: 1¾" tall x 2¼" wide without handles

NOTES: The Canton Glass Co. also made a wastebasket very similar to this. Reproductions of a basket similar to this were done by Degenhart Glass Co. and may bear its trademark of a *D* in a heart.

Clear

Toothpick.

OMN: WISCONSIN, No. 15,079

DATE: 1898

COLORS: clear, $45.00.

SIZE: 2⅛" tall x 2⅛" wide

NOTES: Highly reproduced in many colors.

Clear with ruby stain

OMN: unknown

AKA: WITCH'S KETTLE

DATE: 1909

COLORS: clear with ruby stain, $52.00.

SIZE: 2" tall x 2⅜" wide

NOTES: May have originally been a candy container.

WEST VIRGINIA GLASS CO.
ELSON GLASS CO.
1882 – 1899

The Elson Glass Co. was organized in 1882 by William K. Elson, M. Sheets, William H. Robinson, and Ed Muhlman. In 1893 the company went through a reorganization with William Robinson as president, H. E. Waddell as secretary, and Percy Beaumont as chemist; the name of the company was changed to the West Virginia Glass Co. In 1896, with reorganization under the supervision of Charles Muhlman, the company's name was changed to West Virginia Glass & Manufacturing Co. In 1899 this company became Factory #19 of the National Glass Co. and was known as the West Virginia Glass Works. The plant was closed in 1903 by National. In May of 1905 a part of the factory was leased to Fenton Decorating Co. The factory was sold in 1906 to the Haskins Glass Co., and Fenton Decorating remained to buy the glassware and decorate without the expense of freight costs.

Some of the company's better known patterns were #213 Scroll with Cane Band, #204 West Virginia Optic, #205 Polka Dot, #219 IOU, Dew Drop, Hero, Hobnail, Pandora, Octagon, Dew Drop, and Gem.

OMN: No. 209

AKA: MEDALLION SPRIG

DATE: 1894

COLORS: clear, $185.00; violet, $360.00+; blue, $360.00+; green, $360.00+; ruby, $360.00+; opal, $245.00; opal with enamel decor, $265.00.

SIZE: 2½" tall x 2¼" wide

NOTES: *No. 209 blown crystal in an entirely new shape is a flash in four different colors, violet, ruby, blue, and green. The blending of colors makes it singularly and unusually attractive. The colors are as delicate as it is possible to get, the color beginning at the top of each piece of ware and disappearing towards the center, making each from violet down to plain crystal, green down to crystal and ruby to crystal. –July 1894.*

Opal with enamel decoration

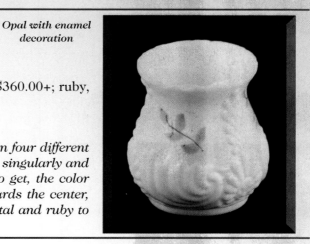

Blue opalescent

OMN: No. 205

AKA: POLKA DOT

DATE: 1894

COLORS: blue with opal outer layer, $675.00+; ruby with opal outer layer, $675.00+.

SIZE: 2¼" tall x 2⅛" wide

NOTES: *The No. 205 line is an entirely new effect in polkadot made in blown crystal ruby opalescent. This, like the No. 209, is quite different from anything heretofore attempted in glass, and is not only made in a full line of tableware, but in water sets as well. The No. 205 water sets in polkadot are made in solid colors, in ruby, green, amber, blue and crystal, also the opalescent. –July 1894.* Original trade journal accounts state that No. 205 was decorated with No. 12 decoration, but the type of decoration was not mentioned. This toothpick is from the same mold as West Virginia Optic.

OMN: No. 204

AKA: RIBBED FERN

DATE: 1894

COLORS: clear opalescent, $280.00; blue opalescent, $390.00+; ruby opalescent, $390.00+.

SIZE: 2¼" tall x 2⅛" wide

NOTES: Made in the same mold as West Virginia Optic (see next page). Note that the ad states that a patent was applied for.

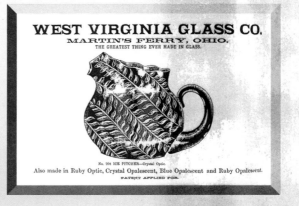

203

Clear with amber stain

Clear with ruby stain

OMN: No. 213

AKA: SCROLL WITH CANE BAND

DATE: 1894

COLORS: clear, $45.00; clear with amber stain, $95.00; clear with rose stain, $110.00; clear with dark ruby stain, $90.00; clear with light ruby stain, $85.00.

SIZE: 2⅜" tall x 2¼" wide

NOTES: *No. 213, one of the new lines, is shown in crystal, amber stained and ruby stained... It is a heavy pressed pattern. It is as near an approach to cut glass patterns as is possible to get it, and even more brilliant. The decorations in ruby and amber are dainty and delicate...have not been over done.* –January 1895.

Green

Blue

OMN: No. 203

AKA: WEST VIRGINIA OPTIC

DATE: 1894

COLORS: clear, $95.00; blue, $150.00; green, $120.00; ruby, $155.00; opal, $120.00.

SIZE: 2¼" tall x 2⅛" wide

NOTES: This toothpick uses the same mold as Polka Dot. Still shown in wholesale catalogs in 1901.

WESTMORELAND SPECIALTY CO.
GRAPEVILLE, PENNSYLVANIA
1889 – 1924

WESTMORELAND GLASS CO.
1924 – 1985

The Westmoreland Specialty Co. was organized in 1889 by George and Charles West. The company name was changed to Westmoreland Glass Co. in 1924.

The company was best known for pattern glass and novelties. Many of the Shrine souvenir items were manufactured at this factory. Some of the better known patterns made by Westmoreland are Sterling, Victor, Elite, Waverly, and Daisy.

OMN: BARREL-SHRINE SOUVENIR

DATE: 1905

COLORS: clear with ruby stain, $225.00; cobalt with carnival finish, $225.00.

SIZE: 2½" tall x 1½" wide

NOTES: Shriner's Convention of 1905 at Niagara Falls, New York.

Clear with red and gold enamel, clear with red and gold enamel, blue iridized with white enamel

Opal with gold decoration

OMN: unknown

AKA: BASKETWEAVE, ROPE EDGE BASKETWEAVE

DATE: ca. 1904

COLORS: amethyst, $32.00; blue, $32.00; opal, $32.00; opal with gold decor, $42.00.

SIZE: 1⅞" tall x 1⅞" wide

NOTES: While this has formerly been credited to the Bellaire Goblet Co., it is a Westmoreland product.

OMN: No. 180

AKA: BIG WHEEL

DATE: 1899

COLORS: clear, $48.00.

SIZE: unknown

NOTES: Made in a full tableware line.

Match Holder

OMN: COLONIAL, No. 1700

DATE: 1912

COLORS: clear, $38.00; clear with ruby stain, $68.00; blue, $68.00; cobalt with enamel decoration, $75.00.

SIZE: unknown

NOTES: This is shown in an original Westmoreland catalog as a match holder. It may be found with the Westmoreland trademark, a *W* in a keystone.

OMN: No. 185

AKA: COLUMNED THUMBPRINTS

DATE: 1902

COLORS: clear, $58.00; clear with magenta stain, $70.00; clear with green stain, $70.00; clear with blue stain, $72.00; clear with yellow stain, $70.00.

SIZE: 2⅜" tall x 2⅛" wide

NOTES: Made as part of a moderately sized line of basic tableware service.

Clear

OMN: DOG HOUSE

DATE: ca. 1960s

COLORS: any color, $35.00.

SIZE: 2⅝" tall x 1⅞" wide at base

NOTES: The company made this in later years in many colors, including slags. Pieces are sometimes marked with "WG," Westmoreland's trademark. A similar candy container, from the early 1900s, was made in opal, clear, and possibly other colors.

OMN: ELITE

AKA: PILLOWS AND SUNBURST

DATE: 1895

COLORS: clear, $38.00; clear with gold decor, $45.00.

SIZE: 2¾" tall x 2" wide

NOTES: According to old trade journal reports, this line consisted of 103 pieces. Over 50 pieces were still in production in 1904.

Clear with gold decoration

Clear with silver decoration

OMN: FILIGREE

AKA: CAPITOL

DATE: 1909

COLORS: clear, $32.00; clear with silver decor, $45.00; clear with gold decor, $45.00.

SIZE: 2⅜" tall x 2" wide

OMN: FLUTE & CROWN, QUADRAPOD

DATE: late 1890s or early 1900s

COLORS: opal, $42.00.

SIZE: 2⅝" tall x 2¼" wide

Opal

No. 81 Hi-Hat

OMN: HI-HAT

DATE: ca. 1920s

COLORS: clear, $38.00; Depression green, $48.00.

SIZE: unknown

NOTES: We have found little information about this toothpick or match holder. Westmoreland also made a Hi-Hat in its No. 555 English Hobnail pattern in the 1930s and 1940s.

OMN: No. 228

AKA: MILLARD'S ATLANTA

DATE: 1902

COLORS: clear, $48.00.

SIZE: 2½" tall x 2" wide at top

NOTES: Made in a full tableware line.

OMN: No. 301

DATE: ca. 1913

COLORS: clear, $42.00.

SIZE: unknown

NOTES: This is a toy spoon from a child's set, not a true toothpick. Westmoreland made another child's set with the same pattern in which the spoon, orginially numbered 299, is handled. Hazel Marie Wetherman named this second set Thumbelina.

No. 301 Pattern.
TOY SET
CUTS FULL SIZE: 1 Set in paper box

Butter

Spoon

Cream

Sugar

OMN: No. 575

AKA: PADDLE WHEEL

DATE: 1912

COLORS: clear, $42.00; clear with gold decor, $48.00.

SIZE: 2¾" tall x 2⅛" wide

Clear with gold decoration

Bud Vase or Toothpick

OMN: PAUL REVERE

DATE: 1912

COLORS: clear, $125.00; clear with ruby stain, $165.00.

SIZE: 3⅜" tall x 4¼" wide at handles

NOTES: The original catalog states that this was a bud vase or toothpick.

Clear with ruby stain

OMN: SHRINE SOUVENIR

DATE: 1903

COLORS: clear with purple decor $225.00

SIZE: 2½" tall x 1⅞" wide

NOTES: Made for the Shriners Convention in Los Angeles. The pattern is grapes decorated in purple. The names on the toothpick are those of the officers of the Shriners.

Clear with purple decoration

Paperweight base, clear with red stain

OMN: SHRINE SOUVENIR

DATE: 1907

COLORS: clear with light red stain, $225.00.

SIZE: 2⅛" tall x 1¼" wide

NOTES: This is a shot glass souvenir of the Shriners Convention in Los Angeles. The base is of paperweight style.

Clear with green stain and gold decoration

OMN: unknown

AKA: SHRINE SOUVENIR, SHEAF OF WHEAT

DATE: 1908

COLORS: clear with green stain, $225.00; clear with rose stain, $225.00; clear with gold decor, $225.00.

SIZE: 2⅛" tall x 1⅝" wide

NOTES: Made for the Shriners Convention in 1908.

Clear with rose stain and gold decoration

Clear with gold decoration

Opal with gold decoration

AKA: SWANS IN RUSHES

DATE: unknown

COLORS: opal, $50.00; opal with gold decor, $60.00.

SIZE: 2¼" tall x 2" wide

NOTES: Some examples are marked "WG," for Westmoreland Glass. These may be later reissues by the company.

OMN: No. 400

AKA: WELLINGTON

DATE: 1903

COLORS: clear, $65.00; clear with gold decor, $75.00.

SIZE: 2⅛" tall x 2⅛" wide

NOTES: Made in an extensive tableware line.

Clear with gold decoration

Clear

OMN: WESTMORELAND, No. 98

AKA: LATE WESTMORELAND

DATE: ca. 1897

COLORS: clear, $45.00; teal green, $68.00; semi-opaque dark aqua, $75.00.

SIZE: 2⅝" tall x 2¼" wide

NOTES: Made in an extensive tableware line with almost 50 pieces still available in 1904.

Teal

WINDSOR GLASS CO.
PITTSBURGH, PENNSYLVANIA
1886 – 1890

Windsor Glass Co. was organized in 1886 by A. M. Bacon and others in Pittsburgh. The plant was located in the Homestead division of Pittsburgh. Problems plagued the factory from the beginning, resulting in its being closed about half the time of its existence. It was completely destroyed by fire in May of 1887 and was rebuilt.

Eventually the factory closed for good in 1890, due to problems with fuel availability.

Products included tableware and novelties in colors popular at the time.

OMN: unknown

AKA: ANVIL, FINECUT

DATE: Patented May 17, 1887

COLORS: clear, $45.00; amber, $60.00; blue, $68.00.

SIZE: 2⅛" tall x 1¼" wide

NOTES: For other types of anvils, see Co-operative Flint Glass Co. and U.S. Glass Co. Reproductions exist in modern colors.

Blue

Clear with ruby stain

OMN: unknown

AKA: JERSEY SWIRL

DATE: 1887

COLORS: clear, $48.00; clear with ruby stain, $85.00.

SIZE: 1⅝" tall x 2⅜" wide

NOTES: This has the shape of a miniature spittoon. Most likely it was intended to be a miniature vase.

UNATTRIBUTED AND UNKNOWN MAKERS

Little information is known about any of the following toothpicks other than they exist in colors and decorations listed. Dates can rarely be given due to lack of data. Occasionally we have estimated the date because of colors or decorations.

A few toothpicks in patterns which are attributed to more than one factory with no primary reference information (catalogs and price lists or period advertisements) are also listed here. Also if we could not determine which factory originated a pattern, it is listed here.

AKA: ACORN, DIAMOND POINT BASE

DATE: unknown

COLORS: pink, $58.00.

SIZE: 2⅛" tall x 2" wide

Clear

Opal

AKA: ALLIGATOR, CROCODILE

DATE: 1890

COLORS: clear, $185.00; amber, $255.00; opal, $375.00+; blue, $375.00+.

SIZE: 3" tall x 3⅝" wide

NOTES: Butler Brothers in 1890 listed this as a toothpick or candle holder, calling it Alligator.

AKA: BABY OWL

DATE: unknown

COLORS: opal, $48.00; opal with enamel decor, $65.00; blue opaque, $70.00.

SIZE: 2½" tall x 2" wide

NOTES: This has been reproduced in modern colors, including satin finishes. Later items have been seen with Westmoreland sticker. Possibly Westmoreland was the original maker.

Opal

AKA: BARRED HOBNAIL, TWISTED HOBNAIL

DATE: unknown

COLORS: clear, $42.00.

SIZE: 2¼" tall x 2⅛" wide

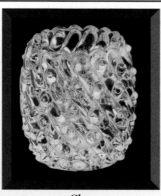

Clear

Clear

AKA: BARRED HOBNAIL VARIANT

DATE: unknown

COLORS: clear, $38.00.

SIZE: 2⅜" tall x 1¾" tall

Amber

AKA: BARREL, DAISY & BUTTON WITH METAL BANDS

DATE: unknown

COLORS: clear, $38.00; amber, $60.00; blue, $60.00; canary, $65.00.

SIZE: 2⅝" tall x 2" wide

Blue

Unattributed and Unknown Makers

Opaline

AKA: BARREL, FLARED TOP

DATE: unknown

COLORS: opaline, $65.00.

SIZE: 2⅛" tall x 2" wide at body

AKA: BARREL, THUMBPRINT OPTIC

DATE: unknown, but Victorian

COLORS: ruby, $85.00.

SIZE: 2½" tall x 1⅞" wide at body

Ruby

Clear with etching

OMN: BEAD & SCROLL

DATE: unknown

COLORS: clear, $48.00; clear with etching, $55.00; clear with satin finish, $50.00; clear with ruby stain, $135.00; green, $115.00; cobalt blue, $135.00.

SIZE: 2⅜" tall x 2¼" tall

NOTES: Other authors have attributed this to U.S. Glass. We have been unable to document this.

Clear with ruby stain

Opal with gold decoration

AKA: BEADED BELT

DATE: unknown

COLORS: opal, $55.00; opal with gold decor, $62.00; clear, $42.00.

SIZE: 2⅛" tall x 1¾" wide

AKA: BEADED MATCH

DATE: ca. 1903

COLORS: clear, $38.00; clear with satin finish, $45.00; opal, $60.00; opaque blue, $68.00.

SIZE: 2½" tall x 2" wide

Opal

Clear

AKA: BEAR IN A LOG

DATE: unknown

COLORS: clear, $70.00.

SIZE: 2⅛" tall x 2¼" wide

Clear

AKA: BETHLEHEM STAR

DATE: unknown

COLORS: clear, $42.00.

SIZE: 2¼" tall x 2" wide

NOTES: Also is found without cut star.

AKA: BETTY

DATE: unknown

COLORS: clear, $32.00.

SIZE: 2¼" tall x 2" wide

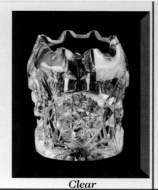

Clear

AKA: BEVELED HEXAGONS

DATE: unknown

COLORS: clear, $38.00; clear with gold interior, $45.00.

SIZE: 2" tall x 2⅛" wide across flats

Clear with gold interior

AKA: BIRD BASKET

DATE: possibly ca. 1885

COLORS: clear, $28.00; amber, $38.00; blue, $42.00.

SIZE: 2½" tall with handle x 2½" wide including bird.

NOTES: Ruth Webb Lee attributed this to Bryce Bros., ca. 1885, but we have been unable to confirm this.

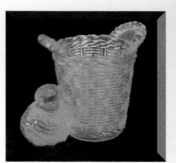

Blue

Clear

AKA: BIRD IN EGGSHELL

DATE: unknown

COLORS: clear, $38.00.

SIZE: 2" tall x 1¾" wide

NOTES: Reproductions have leaves on the holder portions.

Clear

AKA: BLAZING HEART

DATE: unknown

COLORS: clear, $45.00; clear with stain, $65.00.

SIZE: 2½" tall x 2¼" wide

NOTES: Heacock attributes to U.S. Glass, ca. 1913, but we have not found original material to verify this. (See also Paisley, Blazing Cornucopia on page 228.)

Blue and amber

No. 23. Bon Ton Toothpick Stand, optic pattern, cut base, four colors. *Illustrated* 45 5 25

OMN: BON TON

DATE: mid-1880s based on color availability

COLORS: clear, $45.00; amber, $85.00; blue, $90.00; canary, $90.00.

SIZE: 2⅛" tall x 2" wide

NOTES: This name is taken from the wholesaler's catalog. These jobbers often changed the official company names to their own. Since no original company or name is known, we endorse the use of Bon Ton.

Unattributed and Unknown Makers

AKA: B P O E

DATE: unknown

COLORS: clear, $72.00; opal, $140.00.

SIZE: 2⅜" tall x 2" wide

Clear

AKA: BUBBLE LATTICE

DATE: unknown

COLORS: clear opalescent, $225.00; blue opalescent, $500.00+; ruby opalescent, $500.00+.

SIZE: 2¼" tall x 2⅛" wide

NOTES: Found with glossy or satin finish.

Ruby opalescent, satin finish

AKA: BULGE BASE IVT

DATE: unknown

COLORS: amberina, $190.00; amberina plated with opal, $265.00; bluina, $195.00; rubina, $190.00; rubina with enamel decor, $215.00.

SIZE: 2¼" tall x 1⅞" wide

NOTES: This shape was made in several color combinations, and it is possible more exist than those listed above.

Amberina

Rubina with enamel decoration

AKA: BUTTERFLY MATCH

DATE: unknown

COLORS: opal, $85.00; opal, decorated, $110.00.

SIZE: 1¾" tall x 2½" wide x 1½" deep

NOTES: Refer to Challinor, Taylor to see another wall-hanging butterfly match; it is very similar to this one. Note the differences.

Decorated opal

AKA: BUTTON & BULGE

DATE: ca. 1895

COLORS: opal, decorated, $285.00.

SIZE: 2½" tall x 2⁷⁄₁₆" wide

NOTES: Date established due to type of decoration. May be Mt. Washington, but proof is elusive.

Opal, decorated, floral

Opal, decorated, scenic

214

Opal

AKA: CANE BASKET

DATE: unknown

COLORS: clear, $32.00; amber, $50.00; opal, $52.00.

SIZE: 2¼" tall x 2⅛" wide

NOTES: Note that this basket has no handles.

Clear

AKA: CHARLIE CHAPLIN

DATE: Patented in 1915, assigned to Geo. Borgfeldt.

COLORS: clear, $58.00; clear with enamel decoration, $85.00.

SIZE: 2⅛" tall x 1⅝" wide

NOTES: Originally a candy container, but also collected as a toothpick. Example shown is the type covered in the patent and may have "Charlie Chaplin" on base below Charlie. Underside of base may have "Geo. Borgfeldt & Co. New York, sole Licensees" and possibly "Patent Applied For." A later version with a straight-sided holder with a screw top rather than the barrel has "L. E. Smith and Co. Net Wt. 1½ oz." on underside of base. Known in at least four sizes. Reproductions are known but lack the details of the originals and are found in several colors.

Blue opaque

AKA: CHESTNUT LEAF

DATE: unknown

COLORS: All opaques: blue to opal, $190.00; pink to opal, $190.00; blue, $190.00; green, $160.00; ivory, $225.00; opal, $180.00.

SIZE: 2" tall x 2½" wide

OMN: CLEMATIS

AKA: FLOWER & PLEAT

DATE: ca. 1892

COLORS: clear, $85.00; clear with ruby stain, $370.00+; clear with stained flowers and satin leaves, $120.00.

SIZE: 2⅛" tall x 2⅛" wide

NOTES: Has been attributed to U.S. Glass, but we've found no confirmation that this is true.

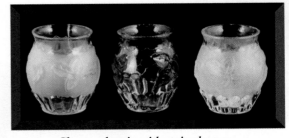

*Clear and satin with stained areas,
clear with ruby stain, clear with satin finish*

AKA: COAL HOD

DATE: unknown

COLORS: blue, $148.00; clear, $65.00, amber, $145.00.

SIZE: 2½" tall x 2" wide

NOTES: This may match a Bryce Bros. mug originally called Daisy.

Blue

Opal with enamel decoration

AKA: COILING SERPENT

DATE: unknown

COLORS: opal, $48.00; opal with enamel decor, $58.00.

SIZE: 2¼" tall x 2" wide

AKA: COLONIAL BELLE

DATE: unknown

COLORS: opal, $48.00.

SIZE: 2⅛" tall x 2½" wide at top

Clear

Light aqua opalescent

AKA: COLONIAL STAIRSTEPS

DATE: ca. 1900

COLORS: clear, $50.00; clear opalescent, $68.00; light aqua, $115.00; light aqua opalescent, $195.00; light blue, $118.00; light blue opalescent, $195.00.

SIZE: 2¾" tall x 1⅞" wide

Apple green

AKA: CONDIMENT SET

DATE: ca. 1886

COLORS: apple green, $265.00; canary, $285.00; light blue, $285.00.

SIZE: 2¼" tall x 2" wide (for toothpick only)

Apple green

NOTES: Dating is approximately the mid-1880s based on the colors. This is definitely a toothpick holder, as it has no plain ridge for a friction top of a mustard nor does it have any threads for a top.

AKA: CORN WITH HUSKS

DATE: unknown

COLORS: opal decorated, $90.00.

SIZE: 2" tall x 2¼" wide

Opal with painted decoration

AKA: CROCODILE TEARS

DATE: unknown

COLORS: All opaques: blue, $230.00; blue green, $230.00; pink, $230.00; opal, $225.00; yellow, $235.00.

SIZE: 2⅜" tall x 2⅜" wide

NOTES: Based on the matching night lamp, this was most likely a product of National/Northwood, or later from Dugan, which is known to have made the night lamp.

Blue opaque

AKA: CYLINDER

DATE: ca. 1895

COLORS: opal, decorated as shown, $95.00

SIZE: 2¼" tall x 1¾" wide

NOTES: The decoration is very similar to those done by Boston & Sandwich, but we have not been able to verify that this decoration was done by that company.

Opal with
hand-painted decoration

Amber

Blue

AKA: DAISY & BUTTON

DATE: unknown

COLORS: clear, $45.00; amber, $65.00; amethyst, $90.00; blue, $90.00.

SIZE: 2⅜" tall x 2" wide

Amber

AKA: DAISY & BUTTON, FOOTED

DATE: unknown

COLORS: clear, $38.00; amber, $60.00; blue, $70.00.

SIZE: 2⅞" tall x 2⅛" wide

NOTES: This has the form of an egg cup.

AKA: DAISY & BUTTON, SQUARE

DATE: unknown

COLORS: clear, $45.00; blue, $88.00; canary, $95.00; amber, $68.00.

SIZE: 2" tall x 2" wide

NOTES: This may be a mustard base.

Canary

Clear

AKA: DAISY DELITE

DATE: unknown

COLORS: clear, $42.00; clear with gold decor, $45.00.

SIZE: 2¼" tall x 2" wide

Blue

Light blue

AKA: DAISY ROSETTE

DATE: unknown

COLORS: clear, $35.00; amber, $52.00; blue, $60.00; canary, $65.00; light blue, $60.00.

SIZE: 2⅛" tall x 2⅛" wide

Amber

AKA: DIAMOND DANDY

DATE: unknown

COLORS: clear, $48.00.

SIZE: 2⅝" tall x 2" wide at top x 2¾" wide at base

Clear

Clear

AKA: DIAMOND POINT SKIRT

DATE: unknown

COLORS: clear, $75.00; clear with amber stain, $245.00; clear with cranberry stain, $250.00; clear with blue stain, $250.00.

SIZE: 2¾" tall x 2⅛" wide

Clear with amber stained base

Clear

AKA: DIVIDED DROPLETS

DATE: unknown

COLORS: clear, $68.00.

SIZE: unknown

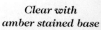

Clear

AKA: DOLPHIN MATCH, THREE DOLPHINS

DATE: unknown

COLORS: clear, $42.00; amber, $78.00; blue, $82.00; canary, $85.00.

SIZE: 4½" tall x 2" wide

NOTES: This match holder uses the motif of the Stars and Bars pattern made by Bellaire Goblet Co., but it is not known if it was made by Bellaire. It has also been ascribed to Bryce Bros., but we have not seen it in a catalog.

Clear

AKA: DOMINO

DATE: unknown

COLORS: clear, $90.00.

SIZE: 2⅝" tall x 1½" wide

Clear

AKA: DOUBLE BARS & FANS

DATE: unknown

COLORS: clear, $58.00.

SIZE: 2" tall x 1⅞" wide

AKA: DOUBLE DAHLIA WITH LENS

DATE: unknown

COLORS: clear, $65.00; clear with rose stain, $235.00; clear with stained flowers and leaves, $148.00; green, $225.00; green with gold decor, $240.00.

SIZE: 2½" tall x 2" wide

NOTES: Attributed to U.S. Glass because of colors and decorations, but unverified.

Clear with stain

Green with gold decoration

AKA: DOUBLE RING PANEL

DATE: unknown

COLORS: apple green, $45.00; black, $45.00; pink, $45.00; transparent blue, $45.00.

SIZE: 2¼" tall x 1⅞" wide

Apple green

AKA: DRUMMER BOY

DATE: unknown

COLORS: opal, $65.00; opal, decorated, $78.00.

SIZE: 1¾" tall x 2" wide

Opal decorated

AKA: FERN BURST

DATE: 1890s or 1900s

COLORS: clear, $38.00.

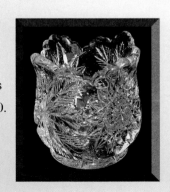

AKA: FERN HEART

COLORS: opal, $42.00.

SIZE: 2½" tall x 1⅞" wide

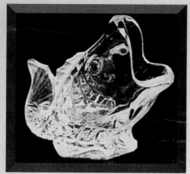

Clear

AKA: FISH

DATE: unknown

COLORS: clear, $48.00; blue, $60.00; clear with satin finish, $55.00; amber, $58.00.

SIZE: 3" tall x 1¾" wide

NOTES: Possibly a foreign toothpick.

AKA: FISH BOWL

DATE: unknown

COLORS: clear, $85.00; clear with enamel decoration, $35.00.

SIZE: 2¼" tall x 2¼" wide

NOTES: This toothpick might be found in other colors.

Emerald green

AKA: FOOTED COLUMN

DATE: unknown

COLORS: opal with blue interior, cut back, $450.00.

SIZE: unknown

NOTES: This may have been made by Boston & Sandwich, as it made similar wares.

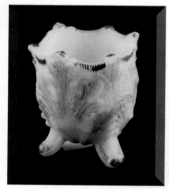

Opal with decoration

AKA: FOOTED PALM LEAF

DATE: unknown

COLORS: opal with green decor and gold, $50.00.

SIZE: 2⅝" tall x 2" wide

AKA: FOUR RABBITS

DATE: ca. 1900

COLORS: opal, $65.00.

SIZE: 2" tall

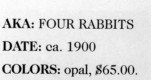

Canary

AKA: GARLAND OF ROSES

DATE: unknown

COLORS: clear, $65.00; canary, $110.00; chocolate, $250.00+.

SIZE: 3" tall x 2¼" wide

NOTES: Undocumented, but probably made by a member company of National Glass.

AKA: GRECIAN COLUMNS

DATE: late 1890s or early 1900s

COLORS: light blue opaque, $90.00; pink opaque, $90.00; light green opaque, $75.00.

SIZE: 2¼" tall x 2" wide

Pink opaque

Clear with ruby stain and gold

AKA: HALL OF MIRRORS

DATE: unknown

COLORS: clear, $48.00; clear with gold decor, $58.00; clear with ruby stain, $145.00.

SIZE: 2¼" tall x 1⅞" wide

NOTES: Has three handles.

AKA: HAND WITH FLOWER

DATE: 1886

COLORS: clear, $55.00.

SIZE: unknown

NOTES: "Fancy glass hand-shaped holder, assorted colors, which can be used as a toothpick holder when emptied," according to the wholesale catalog in which this appears. Assorted colors probably means the standards of amber, blue, and possibly canary.

AKA: HANDY DANDY

DATE: unknown

COLORS: clear, $38.00.

SIZE: 2⅜" tall x 2" wide

AKA: HANGING FLOWERS

DATE: unknown

COLORS: clear, $42.00; opal, $68.00; opal, decorated, $75.00.

SIZE: 2⅛" tall x 1½" wide

Opal decorated

Canary

AKA: HAT, DAISY & STAR

DATE: ca. 1886

COLORS: clear, $45.00; amber, $55.00; blue, $70.00; canary, $75.00.

SIZE: 2⅜" tall x 3⅜" across brim

NOTES: The pattern differs from Daisy & Button because, instead of having a hobnail between daisies, it has a four-pointed star. This is much harder to find than the standard Daisy & Button hats. Also made in a tub shape.

AKA: HAT, FAN BRIM

DATE: ca. 1886

COLORS: clear, $20.00; canary, $30.00.

SIZE: 2⅛" tall x 2" wide across bottom

NOTES: Also comes as an ashtray with a cigarette rest on the brim.

Canary

AKA: HAT, FINECUT

DATE: ca. 1886

COLORS: clear, $32.00; amber, $42.00; blue, $58.00; canary, $60.00.

SIZE: 2⅜" tall x 3⅛" across brim

NOTES: It is tempting to credit this hat to Windsor Glass because of the similarity of the known Finecut Anvil that it made. However, with no proof, it remains a mystery.

Blue

Blue

AKA: HAT, WHIMSY

DATE: unknown

COLORS: blue, $90.00.

SIZE: unknown

NOTES: A blown whimsy hat. Attribution of manufacturer and date of production unknown.

AKA: HEFTY

DATE: unknown

COLORS: clear, $48.00.

SIZE: 3⅛" tall x 2¼" wide

Clear

AKA: HIGH HANDLED HEXAGON

DATE: 1898

COLORS: clear, $38.00.

SIZE: 2¼" tall x 1⅝" wide across flats

Clear

AKA: HORSESHOE WITH CLOVER

DATE: 1898

COLORS: clear, $45.00; opal, $95.00; opal with gold decor, $105.00.

SIZE: 2¼" tall x 1¾" wide

Opal with gold decoration

AKA: HUB

DATE: unknown

COLORS: amber satin, $42.00; blue satin, $42.00; canary satin, $42.00.

SIZE: 2⁹⁄₁₆" tall x 2" at widest point

NOTES: Found with metal bands around top and bottom.

Canary satin

Clear with ruby stain

AKA: INSIDE RIBBING

DATE: unknown

COLORS: clear, $38.00; clear with ruby stain, $72.00.

SIZE: 2¼" tall x 2¼" wide

223

Clear with silver overlay

AKA: INTAGLIO VINE & FLOWER, CUT COSMOS

DATE: 1910s

COLORS: clear with silver overlay, $38.00.

SIZE: 2⅛" tall x 2⁵⁄₁₆" wide across flats.

Blue with gold decoration

AKA: IVY SCROLL

DATE: unknown

COLORS: clear, $65.00; apple green, $145.00; blue, $160.00; blue with gold decor, $175.00.

SIZE: 2½" tall x 2⅜" wide

Clear

AKA: KEWPIE

DATE: Patented in 1915, assigned to Geo. Borgfeldt & Co.

COLORS: clear, $48.00.

SIZE: 1¾" tall x 1¾" wide

NOTES: This originally was distributed by Geo. Borgfeldt & Co., of New York. Containers are marked Geo. Borgfeldt & Co. N. Y., Kewpie, Reg. U. S. Pat. Off., Des. Pat 3650. Jefferson Glass Works made some items for Borgfeldt, but there is no documentation for this piece. Reproductions exist marked "Taiwan." Originally a candy container. Some or all were originally decorated in enamel colors.

AKA: KNOTTY PINE

DATE: 1900s

COLORS: opal, $45.00.

SIZE: 2¼" tall x 2⁹⁄₁₆" across feet

AKA: LADY ANNE

DATE: ca. 1890s

COLORS: ruby, $85.00.

SIZE: 2¼" tall x 2¼" wide

Opaque pink shaded to opal

AKA: LITTLE SCROLLER

DATE: ca. 1900

COLORS: All opaque: green, $75.00; opal, $75.00; pink, $75.00; pink shaded to opal, $80.00.

SIZE: 1⅝" tall x 2" wide

AKA: LOWER MANHATTAN

DATE: unknown

COLORS: clear, $45.00; clear with stain, $68.00; clear with gold decor, $55.00.

SIZE: 2½" tall x 2¼" wide

Clear

AKA: MAE WEST

DATE: probably early 1900s

COLORS: clear, $32.00; amber, $48.00; blue, $52.00; green, $48.00; ruby, $50.00.

SIZE: 2⅛" tall x 2" wide

NOTES: All colors are known with enamel decorations.

Ivory with decoration

AKA: MAPLE LEAF

DATE: unknown

COLORS: ivory, decorated, $1,100.00+.

SIZE: 2¼" tall x 1¾" wide

NOTES: L. G. Wright reproduced a version without handles in clear, cobalt, amberina, carnival finish, green opalescent, and possibly other colors. This was made in a new mold ordered by the company in 1972. There is debate whether this pattern originally was made by Northwood, National, or Dugan.

AKA: MARGARITA

DATE: unknown

COLORS: clear, $38.00.

SIZE: 2½" tall x 2" wide

NOTES: Not really a toothpick, as it has a lid.

Clear

Clear with ruby stain

AKA: MARIE

DATE: unknown

COLORS: clear, $48.00; clear with ruby stain, $130.00.

SIZE: 2¾" tall x 2" wide

NOTES: This toothpick has three handles and three feet. Some have a luster finish. Another version exists with the "toes" pointing out instead of in.

AKA: MARY GREGORY

DATE: 1893

COLORS: blue with hand-painted enamel, $235.00.

SIZE: 2½" tall x 1⅝" wide

NOTES: This toothpick is marked as a souvenir of the 1893 World's Fair. Many Mary Gregory decorated pieces were imported.

Blue with white enamel

AKA: METAL TOP WITH FLOWERS

DATE: 1900s

COLORS: clear, $28.00; opal, $32.00.

SIZE: 2⅛" tall x 2½" wide across widest portion

AKA: MONKEY WITH HAT

DATE: unknown

COLORS: clear, $55.00; amber, $110.00; blue, $110.00; green, $110.00; opal, $110.00.

SIZE: 2½" tall x 1¾" wide x 3" long. Hat only: 1⅜" tall x 1⅝" wide

Blue

Opal

AKA: MONTANA

DATE: 1890s

COLORS: clear with red stain, $65.00.

SIZE: 2⅛" tall x 2¾" wide

NOTES: This is similar to the Montana pattern made by Ripley & Co., Pittsburgh, but it is not certain this is part of that pattern.

AKA: MYRTLE

DATE: 1920s

COLORS: pink, $20.00; pink with cutting, $28.00.

SIZE: 2¼" tall x 2" wide across widest portion

Pink with cutting

AKA: NEPTUNE'S NET

DATE: 1900s

COLORS: opal with hand-painted decoration, $38.00.

SIZE: 2½" tall x 2⅛" wide at top

AKA: NURSERY RHYME

DATE: unknown

COLORS: clear, $52.00.

SIZE: 1⅞" tall x 1½" wide

NOTES: Spoon holder from toy table set. This child's set may be shown in a U.S. Glass catalog, but the quality of the drawing is so poor we cannot be certain.

Clear

AKA: PAIRPOINT POINTER

DATE: unknown

COLORS: opal with any hand-painted decoration, $235.00.

SIZE: 2¼" tall x 2⅛" wide

NOTES: No documentation has been found for this toothpick, neither for the decoration nor for the maker of the glass blank. Other similar decorations are found on this shape, sometimes attributed to Handel.

Opal with enameled portrait

Pony

Buffalo

Unattributed and Unknown Makers

Clear with rose stain

AKA: PAISLEY, BLAZING CORNUCOPIA

DATE: unknown

COLORS: clear, $55.00; clear with stain, $90.00.

SIZE: 2½" tall x 2¼" wide

NOTES: Welker attributes this to U. S. Glass and dates it to approximately 1913. However, we have found no specific catalog reference or ads showing this pattern. (See also Blazing Heart, page 213.)

AKA: PANELED MIRROR

DATE: 1900s

COLORS: clear, $35.00.

SIZE: 2¼" tall x 1⅞" wide across base

NOTES: The panels are separated by large miters.

Clear

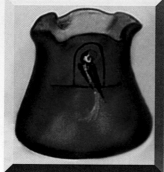

Green enameled decoration

OMN: PARAKEET TWINS

DATE: 1926

COLORS: yellow, blue, orange, and green enamel finishes, $45.00.

SIZE: 2⅛" tall x 2¼" wide

NOTES: Also found without the parakeet decoration. This was formerly attributed to U.S. Glass because of the Parakeet decoration. However, the parakeets do not exactly match, and this decoration is found on pieces of glass that were not made by U.S. Glass.

Opal

AKA: PARLOR ALBUM

DATE: unknown

COLORS: opal, $130.00.

SIZE: 3" tall x 1¼" wide x 2" long

NOTES: Also found decorated.

AKA: PARROT WITH TOP HAT

DATE: unknown

COLORS: opal, $52.00; opal with gold decor, $70.00.

SIZE: 2⅛" tall x 2¼" wide

Opal with gold decoration

Clear

AKA: PATRIOTIC SHIELD

DATE: unknown

COLORS: clear, $70.00; dark green, $85.00, amber, $85.00; allover ruby stain, $225.00; cobalt, $85.00; light green, $80.00.

SIZE: 2⅜" tall x 2¼" wide

NOTES: Base is inscribed "Safety Night Light Co. Brooklyn NY." This was probably a match holder given away by that company.

AKA: PEARLS AND SHELLS

DATE: early 1900s

COLORS: opal, with hand-painted decoration with gold, $38.00.

SIZE: 1⅞" tall x 2⅛" wide at widest portion

NOTES: Note that there are two versions, one with two rows of beads around the top and one with only one row.

Clear with enamel

AKA: PETITE PANEL

DATE: unknown

COLORS: clear with enamel, $52.00.

SIZE: 2⅞" tall x 1⅝" wide

AKA: PLEAT & BOW

DATE: unknown

COLORS: clear, $65.00; clear with satin finish, $88.00; opal, $130.00; amber, $130.00; blue, $130.00.

SIZE: 2⅛" tall x 2⅛" wide

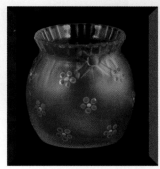

Clear with satin finish and enamel decoration

Clear

AKA: PRETTY MAIDEN

DATE: unknown

COLORS: clear, $75.00.

SIZE: 5¼" tall; base is 3⅛" x 3⅛".

NOTES: Recently reproduced in colors. Reproduced with poor detail of hair and texture of shawl.

AKA: PURSE, FINECUT

DATE: unknown

COLORS: clear, $65.00; amber, $105.00; blue, $110.00; canary, $125.00.

SIZE: 2" tall x 1¾" wide x 2½" long

Blue, canary, and amber

AKA: RABBIT & TREE STUMP

DATE: unknown

COLORS: clear, $65.00; amber, $95.00.

SIZE: 2⅜" tall x 2" wide

Clear

Clear opalescent

Blue opalescent

Ruby opalescent

Blue with opal frit

AKA: REVERSE SWIRL

DATE: unknown

COLORS: clear opalescent, $135.00; blue opalescent, $245.00; blue with opal frit, $235.00; ruby opalescent, $245.00; canary opalescent, glossy or satin finish, $245.00; opal, $85.00.

SIZE: 2" tall x 2" wide

NOTES: This has been attributed to both Buckeye Glass and Model Flint in Albany, Indiana, but we have not found any documentation for either attribution.

Clear opalescent

AKA: REVERSE SWIRL, COLLARED

DATE: 1880s or 1890s

COLORS: clear opalescent, $65.00; blue opalescent, $110.00; canary opalescent, $125.00; ruby opalescent, $125.00.

SIZE: 2⅛" tall x 2" wide

NOTES: Very similar to Reverse Swirl, but with a taller collar at the top. May have been made by Buckeye Glass or Model Flint.

Ivory

Green opaque

AKA: RIB BASE

DATE: unknown

COLORS: ivory, $45.00; ivory decorated, $30.00; green opaque, $55.00.

SIZE: 2½" tall x 2" wide

NOTES: Appears to be a bar glass rather than a toothpick. Often decorated with a simple gold band.

Blue

AKA: RIB BASE HOBNAIL

DATE: ca. 1890s

COLORS: clear, $28.00; amber, $45.00; blue, $60.00.

NOTES: We previously listed this in error as Doyle's No. 150. Doyle's 150 has only the child's spoon and has a thumbprint base, while this toothpick has ribs around the base instead of thumbprints.

AKA: RIBBED BASE

DATE: unknown

COLORS: opal, $48.00; opal decorated, $60.00.

SIZE: 2¼" tall x 2" wide

Opal with enamel decoration

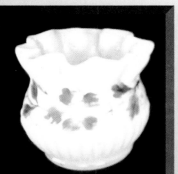

Clear opalescent

AKA: RIBBED OPAL LATTICE

DATE: unknown

COLORS: clear opalescent, $185.00; blue opalescent, $255.00; ruby opalescent, $255.00.

SIZE: 2⅛" tall x 1⅞" wide

Blue opalescent   *Ruby opalescent*

AKA: FLUTED URN, RIBBON OVERLAY

DATE: 1900s

COLORS: opal with pink interior, hand-painted flowers, $125.00.

SIZE: 2⅛" tall x 2" wide

AKA: RUBY DIAMOND

DATE: 1890s

COLORS: clear, $35.00; clear with ruby stain, $115.00.

SIZE: 2¼" tall x 2" wide

Clear

Clear

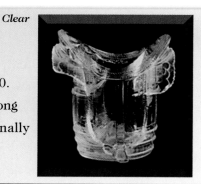

AKA: SADDLE

DATE: unknown

COLORS: clear, $38.00; amber, $52.00; blue, $52.00.

SIZE: Old: 3" x 3". New: 2⅜" tall x 1¾" wide x 2⅝" long

NOTES: Many reproductions in colors not originally made. Copies are slightly smaller than originals.

AKA: SERRATED SPEARPOINT

DATE: unknown

COLORS: clear, $45.00.

SIZE: 2⅜" tall x 1⅞" wide

Clear

AKA: SHAMROCK

DATE: unknown

COLORS: clear, $42.00; clear with ruby stain, $140.00; green, $95.00; green with gold decor, $115.00.

SIZE: 2¼" tall x 1⅞" wide

Clear with ruby stain

Green

AKA: SHELL & SCALE

DATE: 1890s

COLORS: ivory, $110.00; opal, $70.00.

SIZE: 2½" tall x 2¼" wide at top

AKA: SHORT & DUMPY

DATE: 1900s

COLORS: clear with hand-painted flowers, $48.00.

SIZE: 2" tall x 2⅛" wide

NOTES: This toothpick holder is mold blown, not pressed.

AKA: SIMPLICITY SCROLL

DATE: 1890s

COLORS: clear, $18.00; clear with gold, $22.00; amethyst with gold, $32.00; opal, $28.00; opal with hand-painted decoration, $32.00.

SIZE: unknown

Canary and blue

AKA: SPITTOON

DATE: unknown

COLORS: clear, $65.00; blue, $90.00; canary, $95.00.

SIZE: 1½" tall x 3" wide

Amber

AKA: STACKED HEXAGONS

DATE: unknown

COLORS: clear, $42.00; amber, $65.00.

SIZE: 2" tall x 1⅞" wide

NOTES: Named by authors. We formerly called this Stacked Diamonds, but Stacked Hexagons is more accurate.

AKA: STIPPLED DEWDROP & RAINDROP

DATE: 1880s

COLORS: clear, $28.00; amber, $38.00; blue, $42.00; cobalt blue, $48.00.

SIZE: 2⅛" tall x 1¾" wide at top

NOTES: This is a toy spoon to a child's table set.

AKA: STIPPLED FANS

DATE: unknown

COLORS: clear, $42.00; clear with allover gold, $50.00.

SIZE: 2¼" tall x 2" wide at top

NOTES: Has been attributed to Lancaster Glass Co., but we have not seen positive proof.

Clear with allover gold

AKA: STIPPLED VINES & BEADS

DATE: unknown

COLORS: clear, $42.00; blue, $68.00.

SIZE: 2" tall x 2" wide

Clear

AKA: STREAMERS

DATE: ca. 1900

COLORS: clear, $28.00.

SIZE: 2⅝" tall x 2¾" wide

AKA: STRIPE, OPALESCENT

DATE: 1880s

COLORS: clear opalescent, $65.00; blue opalescent, $110.00.

SIZE: unknown

AKA: SWIRL & DEWDROP, BEADED SWIRL

DATE: unknown

COLORS: clear, $42.00.

SIZE: 2⅜" tall x 2⅛" wide

Clear

AKA: SWIRL & LEAF

DATE: unknown

COLORS: All opaques: opal, $85.00; blue, $115.00; green, $115.00; pink, $115.00.

SIZE: 2¼" tall x 2" wide

NOTES: Colors may be found with a clear exterior plating. This may have been made by National at the Northwood Works.

Blue opaque and green opaque

Clear

AKA: THREE FRUITS

DATE: unknown

COLORS: clear, $55.00.

SIZE: 2⅜" tall x 1¾" wide

NOTES: Cherries, pears, and grapes are the three fruits depicted on this toothpick. This toothpick closely resembles others made by Kokomo Glass.

AKA: THUMBPRINT ON THUMBPRINT

DATE: unknown

COLORS: clear, $38.00; clear with ruby stain, $68.00.

SIZE: 2⅛" tall x 1⅞" wide

NOTES: Named by authors.

Clear with ruby stain

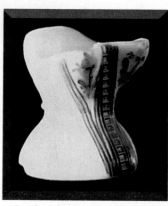

Opal with enamel decoration

AKA: TIGHT CORSET

DATE: 1889 (in a wholesaler's catalog)

COLORS: opal, $135.00; opal with enamel decor, $140.00.

SIZE: 3" tall x 2½" wide

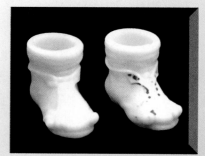

Opal

AKA: TRAMP SHOES

DATE: uncertain, but probably 1890s or 1900s

COLORS: opal, $38.00 each.

SIZE: 2⅛" tall x 2⅞" long

NOTES: Made in both right and left feet. Sometimes found with cold paint decoration.

Light green

AKA: TREE OF LIFE

DATE: unknown

COLORS: clear, $65.00; blue, $150.00; canary, $155.00; green, $150.00.

SIZE: 3" tall x 2" wide

NOTES: Many companies made this standard Tree of Life design. At this point, we cannot document which of these made this toothpick.

AKA: TRIPLETS

DATE: 1900s

COLORS: clear, $28.00; clear with hand-painted decoration, $30.00.

SIZE: 2½" tall x 2⅛" wide

Milk glass with enamel decoration

AKA: TROUGH

DATE: unknown

COLORS: opal, decorated, $295.00.

SIZE: 1⅝" tall x 1⅞" wide x 3⅛" long

AKA: TWO BAND

DATE: unknown

COLORS: clear, $58.00.

SIZE: 2⅞" tall x 1⅝" wide

NOTES: This is a spoon to a child's tableset.

Clear

AKA: TWO ROOSTERS

DATE: unknown

COLORS: clear, $65.00; amber, $90.00; blue, $95.00.

SIZE: 3" tall x 1⅝" wide x 5⅛" long

NOTES: Reproduced in many colors with poor detail and a difference in the basketweave.

Clear

Amber

AKA: U.S. COIN, AMERICAN LEGION

DATE: 1976

COLORS: clear, $55.00.

SIZE: 2⅞" tall x 2" wide

NOTES: Made in the style of Silver Age (U.S. Coin), but much later.

Clear

Blue

AKA: VALISE

DATE: unknown

COLORS: clear, $90.00; amber, $120.00; blue, $120.00.

SIZE: 2⅛" tall x 2⅞" wide

Amberina

AKA: VENETIAN DIAMOND

DATE: unknown

COLORS: reverse amberina, $285.00; amber, $250.00; blue, $350.00.

SIZE: 2" tall x 1⅞" wide

NOTES: Hexagonal in shape. Recently attributed to Phoenix Glass Co. in the new book *Phoenix Art Glass* by Leland Marple.

AKA: VIRGO

DATE: unknown

COLORS: clear, $65.00; clear with cutting, $75.00.

SIZE: 2¾" tall x 2" wide

Clear with cutting

AKA: WASHINGTON, DC

DATE: 1890s

COLORS: opal, $42.00.

SIZE: 2½" tall x 2½" wide

NOTES: The name is derived from the similarity to the US Glass pattern Washington, but this toothpick holder lacks the beads on Washington. This is a blown toothpick, not a pressed one. This has been attributed to U. S. Glass, but we can find no documentation.

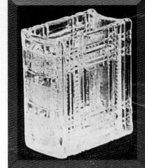

AKA: WEBSTER DICTIONARY

DATE: unknown

COLORS: clear, $170.00; amber, $180.00.

SIZE: 2½" tall x 1¼" wide x 2¼" long

NOTES: "Webster" is printed on the spine of the book.

Clear

AKA: WHEAT & BURR

DATE: unknown

COLORS: clear, $65.00; clear with gold decor, $75.00.

SIZE: 2⅜" tall x 2" wide

Clear with gold decoration

AKA: WHEAT BUNDLE

DATE: 1893

COLORS: clear, $95.00; canary, $125.00.

SIZE: 4⅞" tall x 2 1/16" wide at top

NOTES: Marked on underneath side "World's Fair 1893 Souvenir." Above the base ring are two tiny rabbits. It is most likely that this is a small vase.

Canary

Clear opalescent

AKA: WILD BOUQUET

DATE: ca. 1900

COLORS: clear opalescent, $235.00; blue opalescent, $550.00+; green opalescent, $500.00+; ivory, $1,100.00+.

SIZE: 2½" tall x 2⅜" wide

NOTES: Other authors have speculated that this may be National/Northwood. We can find no documentation. Sometimes decorated with enamels on features of the pattern.

Ivory with enamel decoration

Opal with enamel decoration

AKA: WINDERMERE'S FAN

DATE: 1890s

COLORS: black, $48.00; opal, $48.00.

SIZE: 2⅛" tall x 2⅛" at widest portion

NOTES: Both black and opal are also available with decoration. Also made without the divider.

Opal

AKA: WISHING WELL BUCKET

DATE: unknown

COLORS: opal, $235.00.

SIZE: 2" tall x 2⅝" wide

NOTES: This item has a divider down the center, possibly indicating it is a container for used and unused matches. Also made without a divider.

AKA: X BULL'S-EYE

DATE: unknown

COLORS: clear, $70.00.

SIZE: 2¼" tall x 2" wide

Clear

FOREIGN TOOTHPICK HOLDERS

The following are only some of the foreign-made toothpick holders that are available to collectors. This small sampling should give the collector some idea of what styles and types were made.

AKA: ALEXANDRA

DATE: Unknown, but of Victorian era

COLORS: opal with blue interior, $160.00; opal with pink interior, $160.00.

SIZE: 3½" tall x 2" wide at bottom

NOTES: These were probably made by an English firm.

AKA: BALL SHAPE, HEXAGONAL TOP

DATE: 1890s

COLORS: Burmese, $550.00.

SIZE: 2¼" tall

NOTES: Finely decorated. Made by Webb, Stourbridge, England.

AKA: BARREL

DATE: unknown

COLORS: as shown, $180.00.

SIZE: 1¾" tall x 1½" wide at middle

NOTES: Definitely art glass, possibly Monot-Stumpf.

AKA: BARREL, LATE

DATE: probably 1920s

COLORS: clear with ruby overlay, cut back, $45.00.

SIZE: 2⅜" tall x 1⅞" wide

NOTES: Probably a bar glass.

AKA: BASKET

DATE: ca. 1890s

COLORS: canary, $85.00.

SIZE: unknown

NOTES: Attributed to Sowerby, Gateshead-On-Tyne, England.

AKA: BASKET, BEADED RIM

DATE: unknown

COLORS: green semi-opaque, $30.00.

SIZE: 2¼" tall x 2⅝" wide

AKA: BEADED FLOWER BAND
DATE: 1890s
COLORS: clear, $35.00.
SIZE: unknown
NOTES: Probably a French piece.

AKA: BEES ON BASKET

DATE: ca. 1887

COLORS: opal decorated, $55.00.

SIZE: unknown

NOTES: There are several versions of this toothpick holder. Some have no handles, some one handle, some two handles. The known Sowerby version is No. 1213 and shown in its catalogs with two kinds of handles, one opposite the bees and one on the same side as the bees. Whether or not Sowerby made all the variations is not known. Some may be of U.S. manufacture, but this is undocumented. With this uncertainty, it seemed best to list these as of foreign manufacture. Many colors also exist, including clear, transparent sapphire blue, purple mosaic (slag), cream opaque, opal, gray opaque (in varying depth of color), and black. The bees may also be found with gold or other colored decoration.

Opal

Blue

OMN: No. 3994

AKA: BEGGAR'S HAND

DATE: ca. 1904

COLORS: opal, $75.00; blue, $95.00; canary, $125.00; dark green, $95.00.

SIZE: 3½" tall x 2" wide

NOTES: Some are marked "Portieux" (France).

AKA: BERRY & MITER
DATE: unknown
COLORS: clear, $35.00.
SIZE: 3⅛" tall x 1¾" wide
NOTES: Probably French. Has a sharp pontil.

AKA: BOULTINGHOUSE NO. 161

DATE: unknown

COLORS: opal, $95.00; opal with enamel decor, $130.00.

SIZE: 2½" tall x 1⅞" wide

Opal with enamel decoration

AKA: BRITISH BARREL

DATE: probably 1890s

COLORS: yellow opaline with green feet, $90.00; ruby with amber feet, $175.00; amber with blue feet and enamel, $150.00.

SIZE: 2¾" tall x 2 wide; amber 3" tall

NOTES: These two toothpicks may not be exactly alike, but are very similar, with blown bodies and applied wishbone feet.

AKA: CHILDREN WITH BASKET

DATE: 1900s

COLORS: clear with satin figures, $400.00.

SIZE: 3½" tall x 4⅞" long

NOTES: Attributed to Baccarat, France. May be a match holder.

AKA: DECO DIAMOND

DATE: ca. 1920s

COLORS: as shown with silver deposit, $50.00.

SIZE: 2³⁄₁₆" tall x 1½" across bottom

NOTES: This may be a bar glass. European in style.

AKA: FINE RIBS

DATE: 1890s

COLORS: nugget, $150.00.

SIZE: 1⅞" tall x 2¼" at widest point

NOTES: Marked with Sowerby (England) trademark of a peacock head. The original name for the blue color with mica inclusions is Nugget.

AKA: FOOTED CYLINDER

DATE: unknown

COLORS: clear with ruby stain and silver overlay, $48.00; amber with hunting scene decoration, $48.00.

SIZE: 2½" tall x 2¼" across bottom

AKA: FOOTED CYLINDER

DATE: unknown

COLORS: clear with green trim, engraved, $125.00.

SIZE: 2⅝" tall x 2⅜" across base

NOTES: Toothpick holder with cover. Probably Moser of Karlsbad, Austria/Bohemia.

AKA: FOREST, SPRING SCENE

DATE: unknown

COLORS: as shown, $1,400.00.

SIZE: 2" tall

NOTES: Signed "Daum Nancy." The Daum factory is located in Nancy, France.

AKA: FRAMED OVALS

DATE: unknown

Opal

COLORS: clear, $28.00; clear, decorated, $40.00; blue, opaque, $48.00; cobalt blue gold decorated, $45.00; opal, $48.00.

SIZE: 2¾" tall x 2" wide

NOTES: A slightly shorter version with very similar design is known in opal.

Cobalt blue, gold decorated

Clear with decoration

AKA: FRENCH PANELS

DATE: unknown

COLORS: amber, $55.00; opaline, $55.00.

SIZE: 3" tall x 2⅛" wide

NOTES: In Baccarat style.

AKA: GERMAN WINDOWS

DATE: unknown

COLORS: opaline with silver-plated, windowed frame, $60.00.

SIZE: 1⅞" tall x 1¾" wide

NOTES: The metal frame is marked "Germany."

AKA: HEXAGONAL PANELS

DATE: unknown

COLORS: blue or pink, with enamel decoration, $80.00.

SIZE: 2" tall x 1¾" wide

NOTES: Definitely European, possibly Moser, Karlsbad, Austria/Bohemia.

AKA: LAYDOWN

DATE: ca. 1890s

COLORS: multicolor, $110.00.

SIZE: unknown

AKA: MADAME BOVARY

DATE: ca. 1890s

COLORS: amber with blue base, $65.00.

SIZE: unknown

NOTES: Base is marked "France."

AKA: MAN WITH HAT

DATE: unknown

COLORS: amber, $75.00; blue, $85.00.

SIZE: 3⅜" tall

NOTES: Most likely made in a variety of colors.

AKA: NANCY

DATE: unknown

COLORS: clear with iridescent finish, $125.00.

SIZE: 2¼" tall x 1¾" wide

NOTES: Has cut flutes on lower portion and cut base. In Moser style.

AKA: PEACH OPAL DIAMONDS

DATE: unknown

COLORS: peach opalescent, $150.00.

SIZE: 2⅜" tall x 1¾" wide

NOTES: Similar to Monot-Stumpf glass.

*Peach Opal
Diamonds*

AKA: PILLARS & PLEATS

DATE: after 1918

VALUE: $40.00.

SIZE: 2¼" tall x 2¼" wide

NOTES: This is a Czechoslovakian piece.

AKA: POINTED PANELS WITH OVALS

DATE: unknown, probably 1890s or 1900s

COLORS: amber, $55.00.

SIZE: 3" tall x 2¼" wide

NOTES: Appears to be of French origin.

AKA: RAINBOW, DIAMOND QUILTED
MOTHER OF PEARL

DATE: unknown

COLORS: as shown, $2,500.00.

SIZE: unknown

AKA: RAINBOW RIBBON

DATE: unknown

COLORS: smooth exterior, $450.00; ribbed
exterior, $475.00.

SIZE: 2⅛" tall

NOTES: Attributed to Stevens & Williams,
Stourbridge, England. Note that the toothpick
holder was made with a smooth exterior and with
a ribbed exterior. Hand tooling produces
differences in shapes.

Smooth exterior

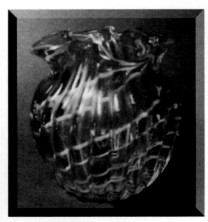

Ribbed exterior

AKA: RAZZMATAZZ

DATE: probably 1890s

COLORS: green semi-opaque, $55.00.

SIZE: 3" tall x 2⅞" at base

NOTES: Typical of French designs.

AKA: RIBBED KETTLE

DATE: unknown

COLORS: purple mosaic (slag), $60.00.

SIZE: 2½" tall x 2½" wide

NOTES: Possibly Sowerby or another English firm. Purple mosaic is very difficult to identify properly, as both English and U.S. companies made this color.

AKA: RIBBON EDGE

DATE: unknown

COLORS: canary opalescent, $300.00; opal with turquoise lining, $350.00.

SIZE: 2" tall x 1¾" wide at top

NOTES: Probably English. Polished pontil.

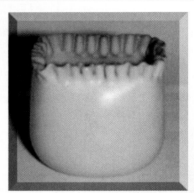

Canary opalescent

Opal with turquoise lining

AKA: RING BASE, EXTERNAL SWIRL

DATE: probably 1890s

COLORS: blue, $85.00.

SIZE: 2⅛" tall x 1⅝" wide

NOTES: Has mica inclusions.

AKA: SHELL FORM

DATE: unknown, but Victorian era

COLORS: pink opaline with amber, $55.00.

SIZE: 2½" tall

NOTES: Definitely European art glass.

AKA: SNAKE

DATE: unknown

COLORS: silver iridescent with blue striations and green snake, $350.00 – 400.00.

SIZE: 2½" tall x 1¼" wide

NOTES: Made by Loetz of Klostermuhle, Austria/Bohemia.

AKA: SPITTOON

DATE: unknown

COLORS: canary opalescent, $125.00.

SIZE: unknown

NOTES: Probably English.

AKA: SQUARE TOP

DATE: unknown

COLORS: cased rubina satin with coralene decoration, $1,250.00.

SIZE: unknown

NOTES: Probably Webb, Stourbridge, England.

AKA: SQUARE TOP, RUFFLED

DATE: unknown

COLORS: peachblow, decorated, $650.00.

SIZE: 2½" tall

NOTES: Made by Webb, Stourbridge, England.

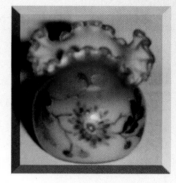

AKA: SWIRL, CRIMPED TOP

DATE: unknown

COLORS: green to clear, $350.00.

SIZE: 2" tall

NOTES: Cut design. Made by Moser, Karlsbad, Austria/Bohemia.

AKA: THIMBLE

DATE: unknown, but Victorian era

COLORS: purple mosaic, $60.00.

SIZE: 2½" tall x 2⅜" wide

NOTES: Probably an English piece made by Sowerby or another English firm.

AKA: TWIN DIAMOND BLOCK

DATE: probably 1920s

COLORS: clear, decorated as shown, $50.00.

SIZE: 2⅞" tall x 2" wide

AKA: VASE, EXPANDED DIAMOND

DATE: unknown

COLORS: reverse amberina, $310.00.

SIZE: 2" tall x 1¾" wide

Reverse amberina with expanded diamond optic

AKA: VASE, IRIDESCENT

DATE: ca. 1880s – 1890s

COLORS: black with subtle iridescence, $100.00.

SIZE: 2½" tall x 2" wide

NOTES: Made by Kralik of Lenora, Austria/Bohemia.

AKA: VASE, SCALLOPED TOP

DATE: ca. 1900s

COLORS: ruby with applied clear base enamel flowers, $325.00.

SIZE: 3⅛" tall

NOTES: Made by Moser, Karlsbad, Austria/Bohemia.

AKA: WICKER BASKET

DATE: unknown

COLORS: clear, $65.00; blue, $115.00; canary, $115.00; opal, $95.00; blue opaque, $95.00.

SIZE: 2⅞" tall x 2⅛" wide at top

NOTES: Typical of a foreign-made, possibly French, toothpick holder.

TOOTHPICKS IN METAL MOUNTINGS

The metal mountings, or frames, holding toothpick holders add greatly to the value of the piece, depending on the quality and maker of the frames. Several toothpick holders are also known in metal cages. These cages also add to the value of the toothpick holder, but less so than the more elaborate mountings.

AKA: DAISY & BUTTON CANOE

DATE: 1890s

COLORS: apple green, $395.00; blue in Tufts silver-plated frame, $400.00.

SIZE: green, 4" tall x 1¾" wide; blue, 4⅜" long x 1⅜" wide

Green

Blue

AKA: DIAMOND QUILTED

DATE: 1890s

COLORS: apricot die away, $950.00.

SIZE: unknown

NOTES: In an Aurora Quadruple silver-plated frame. Probably Webb, Stourbridge, England.

AKA: DIAMOND QUILTED, RUFFLED RIM

DATE: 1890s

COLORS: apricot die away, $875.00.

SIZE: unknown

NOTES: In Barbour silver-plated frame. Probably Webb, Stourbridge, England.

AKA: LAYDOWN, METAL FRAME

DATE: ca. 1890s

COLORS: green, $85.00; ruby, $85.00.

SIZE: unknown

Reverse amberina with expanded diamond optic

AKA: LAYDOWN, WIRE HOLDER

DATE: ca. 1890s

COLORS: blue, $85.00; green opaque, $85.00; lavender opaque, $85.00.

SIZE: unknown

AKA: QUEEN MARY

DATE: ca. 1900

COLORS: yellow with opal interior, $800.00.

SIZE: 2⅝" tall

NOTES: In Roger Smith Quadruple silver-plated frame. Probably Webb, Stourbridge, England.

AKA: RUBY FLOWER

DATE: unknown

COLORS: ruby in metal frame, $225.00.

SIZE: unknown

CONTEMPORARY TOOTHPICK HOLDERS

This chapter contains some examples of the more modern toothpick holders produced after the heyday of the Victorian and Edwardian eras, primarily from the 1950s and later. Many of these are handmade by studio artisans, so colors, decorations, sizes, and values can vary considerably.

This is only an introduction to this area of toothpick holder collecting as many, many more toothpicks are available. Values for most toothpicks are from $25.00 to $35.00, but values for the studio art glass creations are much higher.

BOYD GLASS COMPANY — CAMBRIDGE, OHIO

Boyd is located on the site of the old Crystal Art Glass (Degenhart) factory. In 1973 Mr. Boyd purchased the site and many of the Degenhart molds, which he continues to use today. Most pieces were marked with a *B* in a diamond from 1978 to 1983. From 1983 to 1988, a line was added under the diamond. Lines below and above the diamond indicate pieces made from 1988 to the present.

BASKET

DATE: unknown

COLORS: blue, $25.00.

SIZE: unknown

NOTES: Made from 1983 to 1988.

MICHIGAN

DATE: unknown

COLORS: red carnival, made 1983-1988 $25.00.

SIZE: 2¾" tall, 2" wide

NOTES: Made in many colors and still being made.

TERRY CRIDER

Most of the following are signed Crider or Terry Crider and most are dated. All the following are valued at $65.00+ each. Crider and his wife Donna began making glass in their home in Wapakoneta, OH, and began selling items in 1977.

BOWL SHAPE

DATE: 1986

COLORS: green iridescent.

SIZE: unknown

CUSPIDOR SHAPE

DATE: undated

COLORS: amethyst with opal pulled feather and threading.

NOTES: 1¾" tall x 2¼" wide

FREE FORM SHAPE

DATE: undated

COLORS: amethyst iridescent.

SIZE: 2⅜" tall x 1½" wide

JACK IN THE PULPIT

DATE: 1985

COLORS: royal blue iridescent.

SIZE: 2¾" tall at back, 1¾" x 2½" wide

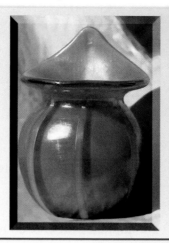

JACK IN THE PULPIT

DATE: 1978

COLORS: yellow with opal iridescent interior, exterior opal lines.

NOTES: 2¾" tall, 2" x 1⅞" wide

JACK IN THE PULPIT

DATE: 1985

COLORS: pink with black rim.

NOTES: 2¾" tall x 2¼" wide

PULLED FEATHER

DATE: 1987

COLORS: blue iridescent.

NOTES: 2½" tall x 2½" wide

SNAKE

DATE: 1984

COLORS: butterscotch with opal rim.

NOTES: 2¼" tall x 2½" wide

THREADED

DATE: 1984

COLORS: teal blue iridescent with threading.

NOTES: 2¼" tall x 2" wide

VASE SHAPE

DATE: 1980

COLORS: ruby red with white rim, clover-shaped top.

SIZE: 2½" tall x 2" wide

DANIEL DAGGETT
DAGGETT GLASS STUDIOS, LOVELAND, CO

DATE: unknown

COLORS: clear with multi-colored flecks, iridized $45.00.

SIZE: 2¼" tall x 2¼" wide

NOTES: Limited edition of 2000.

FENTON ART GLASS CO.
WILLIAMSTOWN, WV — 1907 TO PRESENT

AZTEC

DATE: 1995

COLORS: Dusty Rose and Cobalt Carnival.

SIZE: 2¼" tall x 1¼" wide

NOTES: Sold on QVC as a pair in 1995 for $30.00.

CACTUS

DATE: 1995

COLORS: aqua opalescent carnival, $45.00.

SIZE: 2¾" tall x 1¾" wide

NOTES: Made for Levay, mold No. 3495.

NO. 9592

DATE: 1970s – 1980s

COLORS: riverboat design, $55.00; blue roses on custard, $35.00; burmese with pink roses, $55.00.

SIZE: 2½" tall x 2" wide

NOTES: Made with various decorations, including a commemorative of Bill Heacock. Made in various colors. The Burmese shown was part of Mary Walrath's Love Bouquet in 1982.

Riverbooat design

Burmese with pink roses

Blue roses on custard

FAN VASE

DATE: 1942 – 1944

COLORS: blue opalescent, $65.00 – 85.00+.

SIZE: 2½" tall x 2" wide

HAT, HOBNAIL

DATE: 1941 – 1943, 1959 – 1962

COLORS: topaz opalescent, $45.00.

SIZE: 2½" tall x 3" wide

HEART TOP

DATE: 1997

COLORS: red with gold rim, $50.00 – $60.00.

SIZE: 2" tall x 1¼" wide

NOTES: Made for JFGS building fund.

HOBNAIL, FOOTED

DATE: 1963 – 1985

COLORS: Colonial Blue, $20.00 – 25.00.

SIZE: unknown

NOTES: Made in many colors.

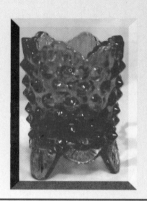

JACK IN THE PULPIT

DATE: 1998

COLORS: plum opalescent, $70.00 – 80.00.

SIZE: 2¼" tall, 1½" x 2" wide

NOTES: Made as a souvenir for the Fenton Art Glass Society.

JACK IN THE PULPIT

DATE: unknown

COLORS: velva rose iridescent stretch, $25.00.

SIZE: unknown

RUFFLED TOP

DATE: 1942 –1944

COLORS: pink opalescent, snow crest, $100.00+.

SIZE: 2¼" tall x 2" wide

THISTLE

DATE: 2001

COLORS: amethyst carnival, $17.50.

SIZE: 2¼" tall x 2¼" wide

URN

DATE: 1980s

COLORS: black amethyst stretch, $110.00.

SIZE: unknown

NOTES: Made for Levay, mold no. 1590.

GIBSON GLASS CO. — MILTON, WV

Charles Gibson established his glass house in 1982 and continues to make glass today. He formerly worked for St. Clair, and many of his designs are similar to St. Clair designs. Pieces are stamped with "Gibson" and the date.

HAT

DATE: 2001

COLORS: blue iridescent, $30.00.

SIZE: 2¼" tall x 2¼" wide

NOTES: Stamped "Gibson 2001."

JACK IN THE PULPIT

DATE: 1988

COLORS: vaseline opalescent, $45.00+.

SIZE: 4" tall at back, 2" x 2½" wide

NOTES: Stamped "Gibson 1998."

JACK IN THE PULPIT

DATE: unknown

COLORS: blue iridescent, $40.00.

SIZE: unknown

GUERNSEY GLASS CO.
CAMBRIDGE, OHIO

Founded by Harold Bennett. Guernsey Glass made many reproduction toothpick holders. Some items are marked with a *B* in a triangle.

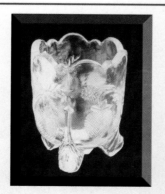

STRAWBERRY

DATE: 1970s or 1980s

COLORS: clear, $48.00.

SIZE: 2½" tall x 2" wide

NOTES: Not an early toothpick. Made by Guernsey Glass, Cambridge, Ohio, but sometimes marked "Near Cut," which causes confusion with old pieces.

KEMPLE GLASS CO.
EAST PALESTINE, OH — 1945 – 1970
This company primarily made reproductions, often using old molds acquired from defunct glass companies.

DOUBLE DOT SCROLL

DATE: 1963

COLORS: West Virginia Red, $25.00.

SIZE: 2" tall x 1⅞" across bottom

NOTES: Made in 1963 for the West Virginia Centennial. The color was developed especially for this occasion.

HEX SCROLL

DATE: 1963

COLORS: West Virginia Red, $25.00.

SIZE: 2" tall x 1⅝" across flats

NOTES: Also made in 1963 for the West Virginia Centennial.

LEVAY DISTRIBUTING CO.
ALTON, ILLINOIS

All Levay toothpicks are valued at $50.00 each. Gary Levi opened his giftware business, Levay Distributing Co./Intaglio Studios, in Alton, Illinois. Levay toothpicks were often made by the Fenton Art Glass Co. and by Westmoreland Glass Co.

JACK IN THE PULPIT

DATE: 1995

COLORS: Burmese.

SIZE: 3½" tall at back, 2¼" at beginning of flare, 1¼" across

NOTES: Signed "Levay" and dated " '95."

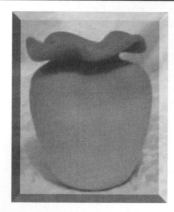

RUFFLED TOP

DATE: 1994 – 1995

COLORS: Burmese.

SIZE: 2¼" tall x 2" wide

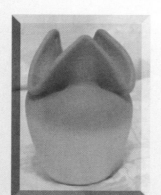

TRI-FOLD TOP

DATE: unknown

COLORS: Burmese.

SIZE: 2½" tall x 1¾" wide

NOTES: Signed "Levay."

VASE SHAPES

DATE: unknown

COLORS: amethyst iridescent.

SIZE: A: 2¾" tall x 2" wide;
B: 2½" tall x 2¾" wide;
C: 2¼" tall x 2" wide

NOTES: All are signed "Levay" and "177."

LUNDBERG STUDIOS

James and Steven Lundberg established their glass studio, Nouevo Glass, in 1970 in San Jose, California. In 1973, they moved the company to Davenport, California, and named it Lundberg Studios.

Steven Lundberg left 1997 to establish his own studio. The toothpicks in the follwing list signed "SL" were made by Steven Lundberg.

A

DATE: 1975

COLORS: amethyst with iridescence and white and brown ribbon decoration, $150.00+.

SIZE: 2½" tall x 1" wide

NOTES: Signed "Lundberg Studios 1975 SL."

B

DATE: 1975

COLORS: amethyst with brick and yellow design, $150.00+.

SIZE: 2½" tall x 1" wide

NOTES: Signed "Lundberg Studios 1975 SL."

C

DATE: 2002

COLORS: blue iridescent, $60.00.

SIZE: 2¾" tall x 2" wide

NOTES: Signed "S Lundberg Glass Art 2002." Also had gold foil label that read "Steven Lundberg Glass Art."

D

DATE: 2000

COLORS: clear with iridescent finish, $60.00.

SIZE: 2" tall x 1¼" wide

NOTES: Signed "Lundberg Studios" and dated 2000.

PILGRIM GLASS CO. — CEREDO, WV

The Pilgrim Glass Co. began an association with Kelsey Murphy, glass artisan, in the 1980s. Ms. Murphy, along with Bob Bomkamp, developed a process of making true hand-carved cameo glass of many different layers. Most pieces are marked "Kelsey-Pilgrim." Those also marked "Made In Heaven" or "MIH" were executed by the artist herself. These cameo pieces were always expensive and are eagerly sought — both by collectors and museums.

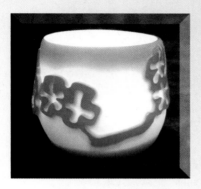

CAMEO

DATE: late 1980s

COLORS: opal with ruby exterior, $125.00+.

SIZE: 1¾" tall x 1⅞" wide at top

POSCHINGER

Poschinger is a contemporary Czechoslovakian art glass company.

VASE, THREADED

DATE: contemporary

COLORS: blue with white, lightly iridescent, $30.00.

SIZE: 2¼" tall x 1¾" wide

NOTES: Made by Poschinger, but unmarked.

GRANT RANDOLN

THREADED

DATE: 1986

COLORS: amethyst iridescent, $125.00.

SIZE: 2⁹⁄₁₆" tall x 1" wide

NOTES: Signed "Grant Randoln 1986 R1364." Also had gold sticker with a fancy *R* embossed.

JOE ST. CLAIR — ELWOOD, IN

Joe St. Clair founded his glass studio in 1938 and continued to run it into the 1960s. His sons and relatives continue to make glass today in Elwood, Indiana.

PATRIOTIC

DATE: unknown

COLORS: iridescent cobalt blue, $40.00.

SIZE: 2¾" tall x 2" wide

NOTES: Each side has a different motif: the flag of the United States, the Liberty Bell, George Washington, and an American Indian.

SQUARE TWIST

DATE: 1971

COLORS: black amethyst carnival, $40.00.

SIZE: unknown

NOTES: Cartouche on front reads "Grand Opening 6-26-27-1971."

DAVID SALAZAR

Salazar worked at the Lundberg Studies, but has since worked on his own and is well known, especially for high-end art glass paperweights.

RIBBED

DATE: unknown

COLORS: cobalt iridescent, $45.00.

SIZE: 1¾" tall x 1⅝" wide

NOTES: Made to order.

ZEPHYR ART GLASS

Located in southern California. Some artisans, such as David Salazar and Mark Cantor, worked at Zephyr and also at Lundberg Studios.

URN

DATE: 1980s

COLORS: gold iridescent, $65.00.

SIZE: 2" tall x 1¼" wide

NOTES: Signed "Zephyr" and dated.

LOW BOWL SHAPE

DATE: probably 1980s

COLORS: gold iridescent, $65.00.

SIZE: 1¾" tall x 2¼" wide

NOTES: Signed "Zephyr."

VENETIAN

FOOTED URN

DATE: probably the 1970s

COLORS: multicolored, $30.00.

SIZE: 3" tall x 2¼" wide

NOTES: Millefiore type widely made in Murano, Italy.

Bond, Marcella. *The Beauty of Albany Glass (1893 – 1902)*. Publishers Printing House, 1972.

Boultinghouse, Mark. *Art and Colored Glass Toothpick Holders*. Privately published, 1966.

Bredehoft, Neila & Tom. *Duncan Toothpick Holders*. St. Louisville, Ohio: Cherry Hill Publications, 1995.

_____. *Findlay Toothpick Holders*. St. Louisville, Ohio: Cherry Hill Publications, 1994.

_____. *Heisey Toothpicks*. St. Louisville, Ohio: Cherry Hill Publications, 1993.

_____. *Victorian Novelties & Figurals, Geo. Duncan & Sons*. St. Louisville, Ohio: Cherry Hill Publications, 1989.

Bredehoft, Neila M., George A. Fogg, and Francis C. Maloney. *Early Duncan Glassware, Geo. Duncan & Sons, 1874 – 1892*. Boston, Massachusetts: Privately published, 1987.

Bredehoft & Sanford. *Findlay Flint Glass Co.* St. Louisville, Ohio: Cherry Hill Publications, 1994.

_____. *Columbia Glass Co.* Researched glass facts, 2000.

Fauster, Carl. *Libbey Glass Since 1918*. Len Beach Press, 1979.

Ferson, Regis F. & Mary F. *Yesterday's Milk Glass Today*. Chas. H. Henry Printing Co., 1981.

Gorham, C. W. *Riverside Glass Works*. Privately published, 1995.

Heacock, William. *Collecting Glass*, vols. 1 – 3. Marietta, Ohio: Antique Publications, 1984 – 1986.

_____. *Encyclopedia of Victorian Colored Pattern Glass*, books 1 – 7. Marietta, Ohio: Antique Publications, 1974 – 1981.

_____. *1000 Toothpick Holders*. Marietta, Ohio: Antique Publications, 1977.

_____. *Fenton Glass — The First Twenty-five Years*. O-Val Advertising Corp., 1978.

_____. *Old Pattern Glass According to Heacock*. Marietta, Ohio: Antique Publications, 1981.

_____. *Rare and Unlisted Toothpick Holders*. Marietta, Ohio: Antique Publications, 1984.

Heacock, William, James Measell, and Berry Wiggins. *Dugan/Diamond*. Marietta, Ohio: Antique Publications, 1993.

Innes, Lowell. *Pittsburgh Glass 1797 – 1891*. Houghton Mifflin Co., 1976.

Jones, Nancy and David. *Heisey Toothpick Holders*. Newark, Ohio: Heisey Collectors of America, Inc., 1982.

Kamm, Minnie Watson. *Two Hundred Pattern Glass Pitchers*, vols. 1 – 8. Privately published, 1939 – 1954.

Lechler, Doris and Virginia O'Neill. *Children's Glass Dishes*. Nelson Publishers, 1976.

Lee, Ruth Webb. *Early American Pressed Glass*. Privately published. 1931.

_____. *Victorian Glass Specialties of the Nineteenth Century*. Lee Publications, 1944.

Lindsey, Bessie M. *American Historical Glass*. Charles E. Tuttle Co., 1967.

Lucas, Robert I. *Tarentum Pattern Glass*. Privately published, 1981.

Measell, Brenda & James. *A Guide to Reproductions of Greentown Glass*. Privately published, 1974.

Measell, James. *Greentown Glass: The Indiana Tumbler & Goblet Co.* Grand Rapids, Michigan: Grand Rapids Public Museum, 1979.

Measell, James and Don Smith. *Findlay Glass Tableware Manufacturers, 1886 – 1902*. Marietta, Ohio: Antique Publications, 1986.

Mighell, Florence. *A Collector's Book on Toothpick Holders*. Wallace-Homestead, 1973.

Millard, S. T. *Opaque Glass*. Central Press, 1953.

Murray, Melvin L. *Fostoria, Ohio Glass II*. Fostoria, Ohio: Privately published, 1992.

Pyne Press. *Pennsylvania Glassware 1870 – 1904*. Charles Scribner's Sons, 1972.

Revi, Albert Christian. *American Pressed Glass and Figure Bottles*. Thomas Nelson & Sons, 1964.

Sanford, Jo & Bob. *The Canton Glass Co.* Researched glass facts, 1998.

Sanford, Jo & Bob. *Victorian Glass Novelties*. Atglen, Pennsylvania: Schiffer Publishing, Ltd., 2003.

Smith, Don. *Findlay Pattern Glass*. Findlay, Ohio: Privately published, 1970.

Stout, Sandra McPhee. *The Complete Book of McKee Glass*. Trojan Press, Inc., 1972.

Teal, Ron, Sr. *Albany Glass*. Marietta, Ohio: The Glass Press, Inc., 1997.

Toothpick Holders, China, Glass & Metal. Antique Publications, 1992.

Warman, Edwin G. *Milk Glass Addenda*. E. G. Warman Publishing Co., 1959.

Weatherman, Hazel Marie. *Fostoria, Its First Fifty Years*. Privately published, 1972.

Welker, John W. and Elizabeth F. *Pressed Glass in America. Encyclopedia of the First Hundred Years, 1825 – 1925*. Antique Acres Press, 1985.

FACTORY CATALOGS

Adams & Co.

A. J. Beatty & Co.

Beaumont Glass Co.

Bellaire Goblet Co.

Bryce Bros. Glass Co.

Cambridge Glass Co.

Canton Glass Co.

Central Glass Co.

Columbia Glass Co.

Co-operative Flint Glass Co.

Dugan Glass Co.

Duncan & Miller Glass Co.

Fostoria Glass Co.

Geo. Duncan & Sons Glass Co.

A. H. Heisey & Co.

Hobbs, Brockunier & Co.

Imperial Glass Corporation

King, Son & Co.

Libbey Glass Co.

McKee & Bros.

National Glass Co.

Nickel Plate Glass Co.

H. Northwood Co.

O'Hara Glass Co.

Tygart Valley Glass Co.

U.S. Glass Co., various dates

Westmoreland Glass Specialty Co.

TRADE JOURNALS

China, Glass & Lamps, various issues, 1890 – 1906

Commoner, various issues, 1885 – 1887

Crockery & Glass Journal, various issues, 1880 – 1902

JOBBERS' CATALOGS

Baltimore Bargain House

Butler Brothers

Ogden, Merrill & Greer

Spelman Bros.

Wallace & Co.

Index

Index

Index

Index

COLLECTOR BOOKS
informing today's collector

www.collectorbooks.com

For over two decades we have been keeping collectors informed on trends and values in all fields of antiques and collectibles.

DOLLS, FIGURES & TEDDY BEARS

6315	**American Character Dolls**, Izen	$24.95
6317	**Arranbee Dolls**, The Dolls that Sell on Sight, DeMillar/Brevik	$24.95
2079	**Barbie Doll** Fashion, Volume I, Eames	$24.95
4846	**Barbie Doll** Fashion, Volume II, Eames	$24.95
6319	**Barbie Doll** Fashion, Volume III, Eames	$29.95
6022	The **Barbie Doll** Years, 5th Ed., Olds	$19.95
5352	Collector's Ency. of **Barbie** Doll Exclusives & More, 2nd Ed., Augustyniak	$24.95
5904	Collector's Guide to **Celebrity Dolls**, Spurgeon	$24.95
5599	Collector's Guide to **Dolls of the 1960s and 1970s**, Sabulis	$24.95
6030	Collector's Guide to **Horsman Dolls**, Jensen	$29.95
6224	**Doll Values**, Antique to Modern, 7th Ed., Moyer	$12.95
6033	**Modern Collectible Dolls**, Volume VI, Moyer	$24.95
5689	**Nippon Dolls** & Playthings, Van Patten/Lau	$29.95
5365	**Peanuts Collectibles**, Podley/Bang	$24.95
6336	Official **Precious Moments** Collector's Guide to Company **Dolls**, Bomm	$19.95
6026	**Small Dolls of the 40s & 50s**, Stover	$29.95
5253	Story of **Barbie**, 2nd Ed., Westenhouser	$24.95
5277	**Talking Toys** of the 20th Century, Lewis	$15.95
2084	**Teddy Bears, Annalee's & Steiff** Animals, 3rd Series, Mandel	$19.95
4880	World of **Raggedy Ann** Collectibles, Avery	$24.95

TOYS & MARBLES

2333	Antique & Collectible **Marbles**, 3rd Ed., Grist	$9.95
5900	Collector's Guide to **Battery Toys**, 2nd Edition, Hultzman	$24.95
4566	Collector's Guide to **Tootsietoys**, 2nd Ed., Richter	$19.95
5169	Collector's Guide to **TV Toys** & Memorabilia, 2nd Ed., Davis/Morgan	$24.95
5593	Grist's Big Book of **Marbles**, 2nd Ed.	$24.95
3970	Grist's Machine-Made & Contemporary **Marbles**, 2nd Ed.	$9.95
6128	**Hot Wheels**, The Ultimate Redline Guide, 1968 – 1977, Clark/Wicker	$24.95
5830	**McDonald's** Collectibles, 2nd Edition, Henriques/DuVall	$24.95
1540	Modern **Toys**, 1930–1980, Baker	$19.95
6237	**Rubber Toy Vehicles**, Leopard	$19.95
6340	**Schroeder's Collectible Toys**, Antique to Modern Price Guide, 9th Ed.	$17.95
5908	**Toy Car** Collector's Guide, Johnson	$19.95

FURNITURE

3716	American **Oak** Furniture, Book II, McNerney	$12.95
1118	Antique **Oak** Furniture, Hill	$7.95
3720	Collector's Encyclopedia of **American** Furniture, Vol. III, Swedberg	$24.95
5359	Early **American** Furniture, Obbard	$12.95
3906	**Heywood-Wakefield** Modern Furniture, Rouland	$18.95
6338	**Roycroft** Furniture & Collectibles, Koon	$24.95
6343	**Stickley Brothers** Furniture, Koon	$24.95
1885	**Victorian** Furniture, Our American Heritage, McNerney	$9.95
3829	**Victorian** Furniture, Our American Heritage, Book II, McNerney	$9.95

JEWELRY, HATPINS, WATCHES & PURSES

4704	Antique & Collectible **Buttons**, Wisniewski	$19.95
6323	**Christmas Pins**, Past & Present, 2nd Edition, Gallina	$19.95
4850	Collectible **Costume Jewelry**, Simonds	$24.95
5675	Collectible **Silver Jewelry**, Rezazadeh	$24.95
3722	Collector's Ency. of **Compacts**, Carryalls & Face Powder Boxes, Mueller	$24.95
4940	**Costume Jewelry**, A Practical Handbook & Value Guide, Rezazadeh	$24.95
5812	Fifty Years of Collectible **Fashion Jewelry**, 1925 – 1975, Baker	$24.95
6330	**Handkerchiefs**: A Collector's Guide, Guarnaccia/Guggenheim	$24.95
1424	**Hatpins** & Hatpin Holders, Baker	$9.95

5695	**Ladies' Vintage Accessories**, Bruton	$24.95
1181	100 Years of Collectible **Jewelry**, 1850 – 1950, Baker	$9.95
6337	**Purse Masterpieces**, Schwartz	$29.95
4729	**Sewing Tools** & Trinkets, Thompson	$24.95
6038	**Sewing Tools** & Trinkets, Volume 2, Thompson	$24.95
6039	Signed Beauties of **Costume Jewelry**, Brown	$24.95
6341	Signed Beauties of **Costume Jewelry**, Volume II, Brown	$24.95
5620	Unsigned Beauties of **Costume Jewelry**, Brown	$24.95
4878	Vintage & Contemporary **Purse Accessories**, Gerson	$24.95
5696	Vintage & Vogue Ladies' **Compacts**, 2nd Edition, Gerson	$29.95
5923	**Vintage Jewelry** for Investment & Casual Wear, Edeen	$24.95

ARTIFACTS, GUNS, KNIVES, TOOLS, PRIMITIVES

6021	**Arrowheads** of the Central Great Plains, Fox	$19.95
1868	Antique **Tools**, Our American Heritage, McNerney	$9.95
6469	Big Book of **Pocket Knives**, 2nd Edition, Stewart/Ritchie	$19.95
4943	Field Gde. to Flint **Arrowheads & Knives** of the N. American Indian, Tully	$9.95
3885	**Indian Artifacts** of the Midwest, Book II, Hothem	$16.95
4870	**Indian Artifacts** of the Midwest, Book III, Hothem	$18.95
5685	**Indian Artifacts** of the Midwest, Book IV, Hothem	$19.95
6132	**Modern Guns**, Identification & Values, 14th Ed., Quertermous	$14.95
2164	**Primitives**, Our American Heritage, McNerney	$9.95
1759	**Primitives**, Our American Heritage, 2nd Series, McNerney	$14.95
6031	Standard **Knife** Collector's Guide, 4th Ed., Ritchie & Stewart	$14.95
5999	**Wilderness Survivor's Guide**, Hamper	$12.95

PAPER COLLECTIBLES & BOOKS

5902	**Boys' & Girls' Book** Series, Jones	$19.95
5153	Collector's Guide to **Children's Books**, 1850 to 1950, Volume II, Jones	$19.95
1441	Collector's Guide to **Post Cards**, Wood	$9.95
5926	**Duck Stamps**, Chappell	$9.95
2081	Guide to Collecting **Cookbooks**, Allen	$14.95
2080	Price Guide to **Cookbooks & Recipe Leaflets**, Dickinson	$9.95
3973	**Sheet Music** Reference & Price Guide, 2nd Ed., Pafik & Guiheen	$19.95
6041	Vintage **Postcards for the Holidays**, Reed	$24.95

GLASSWARE

5602	Anchor Hocking's **Fire-King** & More, 2nd Ed.	$24.95
6321	**Carnival Glass**, The Best of the Best, Edwards/Carwile	$29.95
5823	Collectible **Glass Shoes**, 2nd Edition, Wheatley	$24.95
6325	Coll. **Glassware from the 40s, 50s & 60s**, 7th Ed., Florence	$19.95
1810	Collector's Encyclopedia of **American Art Glass**, Shuman	$29.95
6327	Collector's Encyclopedia of **Depression Glass**, 16th Ed., Florence	$19.95
1961	Collector's Encyclopedia of **Fry Glassware**, Fry Glass Society	$24.95
1664	Collector's Encyclopedia of **Heisey Glass**, 1925 – 1938, Bredehoft	$24.95
3905	Collector's Encyclopedia of **Milk Glass**, Newbound	$24.95
5820	Collector's Guide to **Glass Banks**, Reynolds	$24.95
6454	**Crackle Glass** From Around the World, Weitman	$24.95
6559	**Elegant Glassware** of the Depression Era, 11th Ed., Florence	$24.95
6334	Encyclopedia of **Paden City Glass**, Domitz	$24.95
3981	Evers' Standard **Cut Glass** Value Guide	$12.95
6462	Florence's **Glass Kitchen Shakers**, 1930 – 1950s	$19.95
5042	Florence's **Glassware Pattern Identification** Guide, Vol. I	$18.95
5615	Florence's **Glassware Pattern Identification** Guide, Vol. II	$19.95
6142	Florence's **Glassware Pattern Identification** Guide, Vol. III	$19.95
4719	**Fostoria**, Etched, Carved & Cut Designs, Vol. II, Kerr	$24.95
6226	**Fostoria** Value Guide, Long/Seate	$19.95

5899	**Glass & Ceramic Baskets**, White	$19.95
6460	**Glass Animals**, Second Edition, Spencer	$24.95
6127	The **Glass Candlestick** Book, Volume 1, Akro Agate to Fenton, Felt/Stoer	$24.95
6228	The **Glass Candlestick** Book, Volume 2, Fostoria to Jefferson, Felt/Stoer	$24.95
6461	The **Glass Candlestick** Book, Volume 3, Kanawha to Wright, Felt/Stoer	$29.95
6329	**Glass Tumblers**, 1860s to 1920s, Bredehoft	$29.95
5840	**Heisey Glass**, 1896 to 1957, Bredehoft	$24.95
4644	**Imperial Carnival Glass**, Burns	$18.95
5827	**Kitchen Glassware** of the Depression Years, 6th Ed., Florence	$24.95
5600	Much More Early American **Pattern Glass**, Metz	$17.95
6133	**Mt. Washington Art Glass**, Sisk	$49.95
6556	Pocket Guide to **Depression Glass** & More, 14th Ed., Florence	$12.95
6448	Standard Encyclopedia of **Carnival Glass**, 9th Ed., Edwards/Carwile	$29.95
6449	Standard **Carnival Glass** Price Guide, 14th Ed., Edwards/Carwile	$9.95
6035	Standard Encyclopedia of **Opalescent Glass**, 4th Ed., Edwards/Carwile	$24.95
6241	Treasures of **Very Rare Depression Glass**, Florence	$39.95

POTTERY

4929	**American Art Pottery**, Sigafoose	$24.95
1312	**Blue & White Stoneware**, McNerney	$9.95
4851	Collectible **Cups & Saucers**, Harran	$18.95
6326	Collectible **Cups & Saucers**, Book III, Harran	$24.95
6344	Collectible **Vernon Kilns**, 2nd Edition, Nelson	$29.95
6331	Collecting **Head Vases**, Barron	$24.95
1373	Collector's Encyclopedia of **American Dinnerware**, Cunningham	$24.95
4931	Collector's Encyclopedia of **Bauer Pottery**, Chipman	$24.95
5034	Collector's Encyclopedia of **California Pottery**, 2nd Ed., Chipman	$24.95
3723	Collector's Encyclopedia of **Cookie Jars**, Book II, Roerig	$24.95
4939	Collector's Encyclopedia of **Cookie Jars**, Book III, Roerig	$24.95
5748	Collector's Encyclopedia of **Fiesta**, 9th Ed., Huxford	$24.95
3961	Collector's Encyclopedia of **Early Noritake**, Alden	$24.95
3812	Collector's Encyclopedia of **Flow Blue China**, 2nd Ed., Gaston	$24.95
3431	Collector's Encyclopedia of **Homer Laughlin China**, Jasper	$24.95
1276	Collector's Encyclopedia of **Hull Pottery**, Roberts	$19.95
5609	Collector's Encyclopedia of **Limoges Porcelain**, 3rd Ed., Gaston	$29.95
2334	Collector's Encyclopedia of **Majolica Pottery**, Katz-Marks	$19.95
1358	Collector's Encyclopedia of **McCoy Pottery**, Huxford	$19.95
5677	Collector's Encyclopedia of **Niloak**, 2nd Edition, Gifford	$29.95
5564	Collector's Encyclopedia of **Pickard China**, Reed	$29.95
5679	Collector's Encyclopedia of **Red Wing Art Pottery**, Dollen	$24.95
5618	Collector's Encyclopedia of **Rosemeade Pottery**, Dommel	$24.95
5841	Collector's Encyclopedia of **Roseville Pottery**, Revised, Huxford/Nickel	$24.95
5842	Collector's Encyclopedia of **Roseville Pottery**, 2nd Series, Huxford/Nickel	$24.95
5917	Collector's Encyclopedia of **Russel Wright**, 3rd Editon, Kerr	$29.95
5921	Collector's Encyclopedia of **Stangl Artware**, Lamps, and Birds, Runge	$29.95
3314	Collector's Encyclopedia of **Van Briggle Art Pottery**, Sasicki	$24.95
5680	Collector's Guide to **Feather Edge Ware**, McAllister	$19.95
6124	Collector's Guide to **Made in Japan Ceramics**, Book IV, White	$24.95
1425	**Cookie Jars**, Westfall	$9.95
3440	**Cookie Jars**, Book II, Westfall	$19.95
6316	Decorative **American Pottery & Whiteware**, Wilby	$29.95
5909	**Dresden Porcelain** Studios, Harran	$29.95
5918	Florence's Big Book of **Salt & Pepper Shakers**	$24.95
6320	Gaston's **Blue Willow**, 3rd Edition	$19.95
2379	Lehner's Ency. of **U.S. Marks** on Pottery, Porcelain & China	$24.95
4722	**McCoy Pottery**, Collector's Reference & Value Guide, Hanson/Nissen	$19.95
5913	**McCoy Pottery**, Volume III, Hanson & Nissen	$24.95
6333	**McCoy Pottery Wall Pockets** & Decorations, Nissen	$24.95
6135	**North Carolina Art Pottery**, 1900 – 1960, James/Leftwich	$24.95
6335	Pictorial Guide to **Pottery & Porcelain Marks**, Lage	$29.95

5691	**Post86 Fiesta**, Identification & Value Guide, Racheter	$19.95
1670	**Red Wing Collectibles**, DePasquale	$9.95
1440	**Red Wing Stoneware**, DePasquale	$9.95
6037	**Rookwood Pottery**, Nicholson & Thomas	$24.95
6236	**Rookwood Pottery**, 10 Years of Auction Results, 1990 – 2002, Treadway	$39.95
1632	**Salt & Pepper Shakers**, Guarnaccia	$9.95
5091	**Salt & Pepper Shakers** II, Guarnaccia	$18.95
3443	**Salt & Pepper Shakers** IV, Guarnaccia	$18.95
3738	**Shawnee Pottery**, Mangus	$24.95
4629	Turn of the Century **American Dinnerware**, 1880s–1920s, Jasper	$24.95
5924	**Zanesville Stoneware** Company, Rans, Ralston & Russell	$24.95

OTHER COLLECTIBLES

5916	Advertising **Paperweights**, Holiner & Kammerman	$24.95
5838	Advertising **Thermometers**, Merritt	$16.95
5898	Antique & Contemporary **Advertising Memorabilia**, Summers	$24.95
5814	Antique **Brass & Copper** Collectibles, Gaston	$24.95
1880	Antique **Iron**, McNerney	$9.95
3872	Antique **Tins**, Dodge	$24.95
4845	Antique **Typewriters & Office Collectibles**, Rehr	$19.95
5607	Antiquing and Collecting on the **Internet**, Parry	$12.95
1128	**Bottle** Pricing Guide, 3rd Ed., Cleveland	$7.95
6345	**Business & Tax Guide** for Antiques & Collectibles, Kelly	$14.95
6225	Captain John's **Fishing Tackle** Price Guide, Kolbeck/Lewis	$19.95
3718	Collectible **Aluminum**, Grist	$16.95
6342	Collectible **Soda Pop** Memorabilia, Summers	$24.95
5060	Collectible **Souvenir Spoons**, Bednersh	$19.95
5676	Collectible **Souvenir Spoons**, Book II, Bednersh	$29.95
5666	Collector's Encyclopedia of **Granite Ware**, Book 2, Greguire	$29.95
5836	Collector's Guide to **Antique Radios**, 5th Ed., Bunis	$19.95
3966	Collector's Guide to **Inkwells**, Identification & Values, Badders	$18.95
4947	Collector's Guide to **Inkwells**, Book II, Badders	$19.95
5681	Collector's Guide to **Lunchboxes**, White	$19.95
4864	Collector's Guide to **Wallace Nutting Pictures**, Ivankovich	$18.95
5683	**Fishing Lure** Collectibles, Vol. 1, Murphy/Edmisten	$29.95
6328	**Flea Market Trader**, 14th Ed., Huxford	$12.95
6459	**Garage Sale** & Flea Market Annual, 12th Edition, Huxford	$19.95
4945	**G-Men and FBI Toys** and Collectibles, Whitworth	$18.95
3819	**General Store** Collectibles, Wilson	$24.95
5912	The **Heddon** Legacy, A Century of Classic **Lures**, Roberts & Pavey	$29.95
2216	**Kitchen Antiques**, 1790–1940, McNerney	$14.95
5991	**Lighting Devices** & Accessories of the 17th – 19th Centuries, Hamper	$9.95
5686	**Lighting Fixtures** of the Depression Era, Book I, Thomas	$24.95
4950	The **Lone Ranger**, Collector's Reference & Value Guide, Felbinger	$18.95
6028	Modern **Fishing Lure** Collectibles, Vol. 1, Lewis	$24.95
6131	Modern **Fishing Lure** Collectibles, Vol. 2, Lewis	$24.95
6322	Pictorial Guide to **Christmas Ornaments** & Collectibles, Johnson	$29.95
2026	**Railroad** Collectibles, 4th Ed., Baker	$14.95
5619	**Roy Rogers and Dale Evans** Toys & Memorabilia, Coyle	$24.95
6570	**Schroeder's Antiques** Price Guide, 23rd Edition	$14.95
5007	**Silverplated Flatware**, Revised 4th Edition, Hagan	$18.95
6239	**Star Wars** Super Collector's Wish Book, 2nd Ed., Carlton	$29.95
6139	Summers' Guide to **Coca-Cola**, 4th Ed.	$24.95
6324	Summers' Pocket Guide to **Coca-Cola**, 4th Ed.	$12.95
3977	Value Guide to **Gas Station Memorabilia**, Summers & Priddy	$24.95
4877	Vintage **Bar Ware**, Visakay	$24.95
5925	The Vintage Era of **Golf Club Collectibles**, John	$29.95
6010	The Vintage Era of **Golf Club Collectibles** Collector's Log, John	$9.95
6036	Vintage **Quilts**, Aug, Newman & Roy	$24.95
4935	The **W.F. Cody Buffalo Bill** Collector's Guide with Values	$24.95

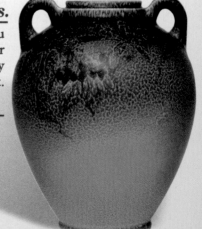